D0266054

# KEN NEWELL

## CAPTURED BY A VISION

### A MEMOIR

**COLOURPOINT**

To my parents, Norman and Evelyn,
and all those who have encouraged me
to live out what lay deepest in my heart.

Published 2016 by Colourpoint Books
an imprint of Colourpoint Creative Ltd
Colourpoint House, Jubilee Business Park
21 Jubilee Road, Newtownards, BT23 4YH
Tel: 028 9182 6339
Fax: 028 9182 1900
E-mail: sales@colourpoint.co.uk
Web: www.colourpoint.co.uk

First Edition
First Impression

Text © Ken Newell, 2016
Illustrations © Ken Newell, unless otherwise acknowledged

All rights reserved. No part of this publication may be reproduced,
stored in a retrieval system or transmitted in any form or by any means, electronic,
mechanical, photocopying, scanning, recording or otherwise, without the prior
written permission of the copyright owners and publisher of this book.

The author has asserted his right under the Copyright,
Designs and Patents Act, 1988, to be identified as author of this work.

A catalogue record for this book is available from the British Library.

Designed by April Sky Design, Newtownards
Tel: 028 9182 7195
Web: www.aprilsky.co.uk

Printed by GPS Colour Graphics, Belfast

ISBN 978-1-78073-103-2

Front cover: Photograph with permission of Bernie Brown (ARPS) photographer,
www.berniebrown.biz

# Contents

# Acknowledgements

Writing this memoir brought to mind an insight the ancient Greek philosopher Epicurus shared with his students: "What you now have was once among the things you only hoped for." Many of my dreams – for love, family, friendship, travel and Christian ministry – have been fulfilled beyond my expectations. As a result, I have entered my retirement years with a deepening sense of gratitude to God and indebtedness to those who instilled in me a vision of what could be and inspired me to travel towards it with faith and determination. In Northern Ireland, where hope is hard to hold on to, I have glimpsed a promised land where estrangement and conflict finally give way to peace and reconciliation. In those moments I have danced with joy, before turning my feet back to that communal trek on which we can always go further.

I would never have had the confidence to venture into writing this book, nor the stamina to stay with the task until its completion, but for the encouragement and patience of Dr Ronald A Wells, Emeritus Professor of History at Calvin College, Grand Rapids, Michigan, USA. For four decades he has written about conflict, Christianity and peacemaking in Northern Ireland – not as a remote academic, but as one who loves this place and has befriended its people with respect and affection.

Delving into my memories has been, as some writers point out, like mining the past in order to shed light on the present and make sense of an individual life. The more I have dug, the more I have realised how I have been shaped by the people around me, especially my parents, Eva and Norman, and my sisters, Margaret and Audrey, who ensured that I had a loving, stable and supportive childhood. Three congregations of the Presbyterian Church in Ireland (PCI) have moulded the form of spirituality which has inspired

7

me. Seaview nurtured my faith in Christ; Hamilton Road trained me to be a Christian pastor and preacher; and Fitzroy gave me the space to express my deepest self as a follower of Christ and accompanied me on an arduous journey of love and bridge-building during some of the most gruesome years of the Troubles. To have been their minister for 32 years has been the greatest honour of my life.

Friendship is one of the hardest things in the world to explain, but its capacity to motivate is unquestionable. I am unable to detail all the long-term friendships I have been blessed to enjoy, but two have been especially significant. Fr Gerry Reynolds of Clonard Monastery has taught me how, like Christ, to act from a calm centre in a busy life and to look for the best in others. His vocation to bring together the divided children of God in all churches has touched the lives of thousands of Protestants as well as those of the Catholics who flock into the oasis of grace that is Clonard Church. Rev Ivan Hull of Ulsterville Presbyterian Church in Belfast has shared with me an enriching friendship for over 30 years. His missional mindset and penetrating insight into the Scriptures have stretched my heart and my understanding again and again.

Finally, I am immensely indebted to my wife, Val, whose faithfulness, cheerfulness and constant encouragement have enabled me to face challenges I would otherwise have been tempted to avoid. It has also been a great relief to escape from the intensity of life and relax in the company of my daughter, Jennie, my son, Tim, his wife, Siobhan, and our three energetic grandchildren, Joseph, Maya and Toby, whose love of the guitar, hockey and Lego, in that order, transport me to another but equally real world.

**KNE Newell**
Belfast
Advent 2015

# Introduction

People like me do not typically write memoirs. That is usually the province of those who have had success in politics, the military or the arts. I had an ordinary, working-class upbringing in Belfast. I am a Protestant minister, like many others. Yet I am writing a memoir because I have had the unexpected and extraordinary opportunity to participate in, or at least to view up close, some of the most important events in the recent history of Northern Ireland. I accept that readers of this book may be more interested in those events than in me. But I must enter into the text too. This is the story of the events as I saw them.

The title of the book comes from St Patrick, Ireland's patron saint. I first read Patrick's *Confessions* – a short memoir he wrote before his death in AD 461 – when I took a course on the Celtic Church at the Presbyterian College, Belfast.

In it Patrick tells how as a 16-year-old he was taken captive by a marauding band of Irish slave-traders and transported to the north-east of Ireland with thousands of others. There he was pressed into the service of a local chieftain, who sent him to look after his sheep on the slopes of Slemish Mountain. The prospect of lifelong enslavement and exile was bitter to Patrick. But during that time he also was led to the joyous experience of being "taken captive" by the love of Christ. After six years of slavery, he escaped and made his way back to Britain.

Back in Britain, in a further twist to this story of remarkable change, Patrick was seized by a vision. He wrote in his *Confession*:

It was there one night I saw the vision of a man called Victor, who appeared to have come from Ireland with an unlimited number of letters. He gave me one of them and I read the opening words which were: "The voice of the Irish." As I read the beginning of the letter I seemed at the same moment to hear the voice of those who were by the wood of Voclut which is near the Western Sea. They shouted with one voice: "We ask you, holy boy, come and walk once more among us." I was cut to the heart and could read no more, and so I learned by experience. Thank God, after very many years the Lord answered their cry.

This vision engendered a lifelong vocation to embrace the people of Ireland and share with them the liberating message of Christ – a calling Patrick had never envisaged as a slave, shivering on the heights of Slemish.

Like Patrick, I too was "captured" by Christ in my late teens, but it took the bombing of the Oxford Street Bus Station in Belfast in 1972 to instil in me a desire to be involved, some time in the future, in working for peace in a country slipping into the abyss of carnage and disintegration.

I was fortunate to discover early on in my life that the dynamic of the Christian faith lies in its creating an internal process of change, which St Paul calls "transformation" (Romans 12:2). In retrospect, I see that most of the changes in me have taken place slowly. Sometimes they have taken years. On other occasions, the extreme nature of the violence erupting around me has demanded a more rapid response, which I have found morally inescapable.

Four of the most significant occasions for change in my life are tracked in the pages that follow. The first is the complex combination of experiences that took me from being an Orange Order chaplain in 1965 to a chaplain to Belfast's first Catholic and nationalist lord mayor in 1997. The second is the sequence of events at home and overseas that forced me to rethink my Christian beliefs, nudging me away from a cramped evangelical mindset towards more generous and encompassing perspectives, such as affirming both the Catholic and Protestant churches as integral branches of Christ's one church. The third came in the form of the violent deaths of three small children, out for a walk with their mother in Belfast in 1976, eight months after I began my ministry in Fitzroy Presbyterian Church. That tragedy propelled me to abandon forever my role as a passive spectator of Ulster's Troubles and to take to the streets with thousands of others as activists for a peace that could not be attained without sacrifice. Finally, it took a decade for the vision first birthed in me in Indonesia – of sharing my life in Belfast with a Catholic priest – to reach its miracle-strewn fulfilment in a friendship with Fr Gerry Reynolds.

Personal change is usually the ground from which the vocation to peacemaking grows. It is also the source from which it draws its encouragement and strength to persevere. Gainsayers readily dismiss the vision that accompanies it as ridiculously optimistic, particularly in a country blighted by a conflict-ridden history.

This memoir, therefore, will tell a lot about my own struggles and reflections as an Irish Presbyterian minister caught up in some of Belfast's most tormented times. But it is important to stress that featured actors in the story are also ordinary, grass roots, Christian bridge-builders who, at considerable cost to themselves, took action in the hope of turning their country around. Their concern found practical expression in the formation of the Clonard–Fitzroy Fellowship, which brought together members of two worshipping congregations – Clonard Monastery in west Belfast and Fitzroy Presbyterian Church in south Belfast. The result was a highly visible and resilient inter-church partnership, whose initiatives created an oasis of peace in a turbulent city. It also presented a glimpse of the reconciled future into which, we believed, God was calling churches too long estranged from each other and communities ruptured by rival political aspirations. Over the course of three decades (1969–98), when violence was commonplace and had spilled over into mainland Britain into the Republic of Ireland and as far afield as Gibraltar, we refused to submit to despair. With an intensity of desire born out of simple faith, influential friendships were formed between Protestant and Catholic, unionist and nationalist, loyalist and republican.

Thankfully, most of those who feature in this book lived to celebrate the demise of the Dark Ages and the dawning of a new era of political partnership in April 1998, with the signing of the Good Friday Agreement. Together with other peace activists throughout the country, they generated an ever-widening yearning for peace without which our best political minds could never have constructed the institutions of power with which we live today. This memoir documents and vindicates their investment in a vision that many considered unachievable.

As in other countries disintegrating under the weight of division and injustice, those who advocated a non-violent resolution of conflict in Northern Ireland and who championed the path of justice, dialogue, compromise and peace, inevitably met with determined resistance. Lamentably, religion itself played a major role in cultivating dogmatic and inflexible attitudes that manifested themselves in a stern distaste for reconciliation. The result was that both sides of the community, at their worst, resembled gladiators wrestling in a struggle for dominance. Those, therefore, who dared to question Ulster's entrenched culture of social estrangement, virtual spiritual apartheid and the intergenerational transmission of an enemy-consciousness, found themselves isolated in hostile terrain. Those who went further and were seen to transgress inherited boundaries or challenge one-sided narratives of the past entered an ideological minefield where survival skills were at a premium. It is often noted that in Northern Ireland we highly value stories of "religious conversion", but are not too keen on people changing. This book seeks, as honestly and sensitively as possible, to delve into what lies behind this culture of resistance to change and to shed some light on the wounds, fears, hopes, prejudices, beliefs and mistrust that fed into it and still do in some quarters. It is crucial to explore it because it will be impossible to sustain a vibrant peace if concepts such as mutual understanding, direct dialogue, power-sharing and reconciliation continue to be shunned by many as novel ideas that carry sinister connotations.

Despite dealing with the resistance factor regularly encountered by those working towards a more inclusive Northern Ireland, this memoir is an unapologetic Christian affirmation of hope. It emerges from the terrible period surrounding the hunger strikes of 1981, when violence seemed endemic and divided loyalties irreconcilable, and when Belfast had become an international byword for despair. Out of such gloom breaks a story within a larger story – of local people gripped by a vision of hope and healing.

It has been my privilege to work alongside many dedicated peacemakers who openly identify themselves as "non-religious" or "formerly religious". Wholehearted cooperation never presented any difficulties because it was founded on mutual respect, trust and a similarity of core values at the centre of our vision. But, as these pages reveal, a large percentage of those involved in peacemaking in Northern Ireland, as well as in southern Africa, the Balkans and the Middle East, have been motivated by a universal love for people inspired by the life, teaching, death and resurrection of Jesus Christ. If you asked them to say what they mean by "hope", they would probably resort to terms similar to those found in the prayer of Desmond Tutu, first black South African Anglican archbishop of Cape Town:

Goodness is stronger than evil;
love is stronger than hate;
light is stronger than darkness;
life is stronger than death.
Victory is ours, victory is ours
through him who loved us.
Victory is ours, victory is ours
through him who loved us.

Initiatives for conflict transformation inspired by religion are now an internationally recognised phenomenon, but they have long been undervalued – or worse, summarily dismissed – by writers and commentators who have presented a less-than-holistic interpretation of complex situations. While I do not for a moment wish to downplay the crucial role of secular peace activists or the courageous contributions made by agencies representing the Jewish, Muslim, Buddhist and other faiths, the witness of Christian peacemakers needs to be recognised and respected. The motive in doing this is not to attract some kind of public and vain celebrity status. It is rather to acknowledge that the institutional churches, despite all the good that flows from them, have largely failed at home to embrace the vocation to peacemaking that lies at the centre of the messianic mission of Christ. I live in hope that one day the churches in Ireland will rise up together to meet this prophetic challenge. One can only imagine the radical changes that could take place in the villages, towns and cities of the province if the churches bought into Christ's new commandment, "As I have loved you, so you must love one another" (John 13:34–5), and became local centres of spiritual and social transformation.

Finally, it is my ardent prayer that this book offers readers both a good read and a personal challenge to become active participants in making a difference in whatever part of the world they call home. The heady days of the 1998 Good Friday Agreement and the 2006 St Andrews Agreement are long gone, and many in Northern Ireland sense that we may be drifting backwards towards confrontational politics and social disorder arising from the unresolved issues of flags, parades and dealing with the past. To add to our concerns, we are also caught up in a decade of centenaries recalling events that polarised Ireland, north and south: the Ulster Covenant (1912), the Easter Rising (1916) and the partition of Ireland (1921). In contrast to the bitterness bequeathed by our history, this account of the determined efforts made to win peace is clear evidence that we are more than capable of transforming our own country. It will always require that "inner disarmament" that reduces our feelings of suspicion, hatred and hostility and turns us decisively towards our brothers and sisters who share this island with us. The path to healing the ancient rift between our peoples lies in respecting each other's cultures, cherishing each other's dignity and working together to strengthen every movement towards social inclusion, ecumenical cooperation, political partnership and – ultimately – reconciliation. May the vision that first seized St Patrick in the fifth century and captured my own allegiance in the latter part of the twentieth century present itself invitingly to all my readers as a vocation worth embracing.

CHAPTER ONE

# Growing Up Orange

Most people have no memory of their childhood before the age of three and only a sparse recall of the period between three and six. As a result, the retrieval of memories from the mists of infantile amnesia is notoriously difficult and those retrieved are not always reliable. My own earliest recollections are infused with the debris of the Second World War: a smelly "Mickey Mouse" gas mask being put over my head and a musty air-raid shelter with a clanking galvanised iron door ten metres from our home at 70 Shore Road, Belfast. I was four or five at the time.

In 1942 my father, Norman, had come to Belfast from Omagh on a double mission: to start work as a fitter in the Ulster Transport Authority Bus Depot in Duncrue Street and to check out a large two-storey family house nearby, which had been recommended to my mother by a Presbyterian minister in Omagh. It was owned by the Presbyterian Orphan Society and had recently come onto the market for rent. Like hundreds of other properties in the area, it had undergone extensive renovation following the Belfast Blitz of April 1941. It was ideal for a young, growing family and just a brisk 15-minute walk from the depot. When my mother, Eva, visited the city with my sisters, Margaret (then seven) and Audrey (then four), to scrutinise it, she was delighted. They all moved in a few months later. I was born in their first-floor bedroom on 14 May 1943. As was the custom during the war, when my mother went into labour, my father sprinted to the nearby surgery to alert the doctor and midwife. Shortly after their arrival I came into the world, screaming. Following a brief inspection from my two sisters, I was deemed worthy of their approval and presented with a shilling – an auspicious welcome.

My father and mother came from quite different social, economic, political and religious backgrounds. Dad was born in 1909 in the fishing port of Kilkeel,

County Down, the ancient capital of the Kingdom of Mourne. He and his brother Fred were twins, the eldest sons of the four children of William and Jane Newell, who lived in Newry Street with their maternal grandparents. Although that was a predominantly Catholic area, the town was staunchly unionist and proudly Protestant. The family of eight were associated with the local Mourne Presbyterian Church. Everyone in the street seemed to get on well with their neighbours, largely because many of them lived in the shadow of poverty and were bonded by a common struggle to keep body and soul together. In the midst of the economic difficulties, there was plenty of fun and genuine friendship. Parents and children would regularly be in and out of each other's small houses to chat, play and borrow things. At times of sickness they would gather around each other for care and support. When bereavement struck they would work alongside family members, providing tea, food and drinks for the crowds dropping in morning, noon and night to express sympathy during the three days of the wake.

Despite the genuineness of this neighbourly care, divergent and deeply held political and religious loyalties ran deep. These were respectfully and studiously avoided in daily interaction. Above the open hearth in my grandparents' house stood a large and revered picture of King William of Orange crossing the River Boyne on a white charger, holding aloft his flashing sword. For just one day each year – 12 July – the accustomed warmth between neighbours gave way to a distinct chill. Friends would walk past each other *en route* to a large Orange parade without casting a glance sideways or saying hello. The following day, however, the atmosphere of friendliness and practical support would return as if nothing had happened. A childhood friend of my father's, who lived five doors away and went on to become a Catholic priest, wrote to me much later in life, saying: "I shall always remember my good Christian Protestant childhood friends with great affection."

My grandfather, William, was a carter, a low-paid job involving heavy labour. It consisted in driving a horse-drawn cart laden with fresh fish or oats and potatoes from the farms to the local markets, or a load of locally mined Mourne granite to the harbour for export to England. Neither my sisters nor I have any memories of him. Sadly, he fell victim to the "big flu" epidemic that ravaged the area in the 1920s and claimed many lives, including some of the strongest young men in the town. From the moment of his death until the end of her life, my grandmother dressed in the black of widowhood and devoted herself to keeping the family afloat. At 14, my father left school and sought work to support his mother. He quickly became proficient as a car mechanic and was sought after by wealthy families – not only to fix their cars, but also to chauffeur them around the country. In his late teens, like most young and ardent Protestant men in Kilkeel, my father joined the Orange Order. This was almost certainly because his own father and grandfather had been members and retaining such family traditions was considered a key responsibility of the younger generation.

Such, then, were the experiences, images and deep emotional loyalties with which my father grew up in the shadow of the Mournes. Some of this legacy would permeate my own childhood and shape my teenage choices; but I have vivid and happy memories of family summer holidays in my grandmother's house in a Kilkeel whose beaches always appeared sun drenched and whose harbour was always busy with colourful fishing boats.

By comparison, my mother's early life was one of privilege. Born in 1908 into a relatively prosperous southern Protestant family in Belmullet, County Mayo, in the remote west of Ireland, she was baptised Evelyn Margaret, one of the seven children of William and Alice Redmond. They belonged to a tiny Church of Ireland community in a town that was overwhelmingly Catholic. My grandfather owned a drapery business in the square and also functioned as a justice of the peace, dealing with minor criminal cases at various local petty sessions. Just as the Mullet Peninsula is frequently battered by storms rolling in from the Atlantic Ocean, my mother's childhood was caught up in the political storms sweeping across Ireland. I remember her recounting an incident when a crowd of enraged townspeople swarmed around my grandfather's store at night with blazing torches, determined to burn it to the ground. As the whole family huddled together upstairs for safety, they believed they were going to be incinerated. Just as windows were about to be smashed and torches hurled in among the racks of suits and dresses and shelves of hats and scarves, the parish priest arrived and pushed his way to the front door. "Go home!" he shouted over the angry voices. "Leave these good people alone. They're part of our community too." With that they began to disperse and the family breathed a sigh of relief.

Given the fact that my mother was only 12 at the time, the historical context of the memory has proved difficult to pinpoint. However, it may well have coincided with the Belmullet Riot of 15 June 1920, during which police officers of the local Royal Irish Constabulary came under ferocious attack and sustained one fatality. The background to this incident was probably a "cleansing operation" against the Irish Republican Army (IRA) by the Black and Tans. They were composed largely of British First World War veterans sent over to Ireland to assist the Royal Irish Constabulary during Ireland's War of Independence (1919–21). They quickly developed a reputation for brutal and unprovoked attacks on civilians during their attempts to root out IRA volunteers. A few days before the attack on my grandparents' home they had stormed through various parts of west Mayo, including the Belmullet area, and vented their spleen on the local population. Some hotheads in the town may have conspired to retaliate by picking on a few vulnerable Protestant families who were sometimes privately supportive of the British presence in Ireland. My grandfather's business and family were assumed to fall within that category.

Shortly afterwards, the British government passed the Government of Ireland Act 1920, by which Ireland was finally divided into two distinct territories: the six counties of Northern Ireland, which remained part of the United Kingdom, and the remaining twenty-six counties of Ireland, which became an independent state. Two years later, probably for well-grounded security reasons, my grandfather sent my mother away from Belmullet to the owners of a large drapery store in Carlow, 200 miles away, where she could learn the business. They were a devout Methodist family and took her into their home to live with them. But leaving home as a 14-year-old proved to be a devastating experience for my mother. She felt ripped away from her family, particularly her mother, to whom she was very close. The last element of this story, which she often recounted to us in vivid detail, was watching her mother at the front door of the house, sobbing uncontrollably beside her husband, as my mother was lifted onto the horse and carriage that would take her to the nearest railway station. My only personal recollection of my grandmother belonged to the late part of her life, which she lived out with her son in England towards the end of the 1950s. By then she was very old and dying.

Two of my mother's three sisters married and settled down in the Republic of Ireland, and most summers we were taken south to see them. My mother never lost her strong Irish brogue, and spending part of the summer among my uncles, aunts and cousins in the republic created within my spirit affection for the whole of Ireland – its people and its natural beauty. It also engendered in me, almost imperceptibly, an appreciation of the Irish dimension of my developing personal identity. Like my mother and her brogue, I was never to lose it.

Around 1930, when my father and mother were in their early twenties, their paths crossed in the Lurgan/Portadown area of Northern Ireland, to which they had been drawn by a mixture of work opportunities and family connections. They fell in love and were married in St Saviour's Church of Ireland Parish Church on 26 September 1934. Shortly afterwards, they moved to their first home, in Omagh, where my father found work as a fitter in the Ulster Transport Authority Depot. Here my sisters, Margaret and Audrey, were born.

When they came to Belfast in 1942, it was a frightened and badly damaged city. On Easter Tuesday evening, 15 April 1941, German Luftwaffe bombers had blitzed the city with 200 tons of high explosives and 96,000 incendiary bombs. In one night 1,000 people had lost their lives; a further 1,500 had been injured and 50,000 homes – half of the city's housing stock – had either been flattened or rendered uninhabitable. Out of a population of 425,000, 200,000 had become refugees overnight and fled the city, many with nothing on them but their nightshirts. The Shore Road, which eventually became our home one year later, had been on the edge of the worst devastation; but houses that could be restored were becoming available again, either to returning families or to new families coming into the city to find work.

### Seaview Presbyterian Church

Fifty metres from our house was Seaview Presbyterian Church, which had opened its doors for worship in October 1940. It was said of its young minister, Rev Kyle Alexander, that no sooner had a new family moved into the area than he was on the doorstep to welcome them and offer any help he could. He was certainly quick off the mark in establishing contact with my parents; they immediately joined the congregation, which was experiencing rapid growth. As was the custom, Rev Alexander baptised me at home. My mother used to describe how, from the moment she discovered she was pregnant with each of us, she would lay hands on us in the womb and quietly pray that we would grow up to know and love Christ. In her keenness to have a son as well as two daughters, she promised the Lord that if a boy came along she would dedicate him to the service of the Lord, just as Hannah offered her child Samuel to serve at the ancient Israelite shrine at Shiloh (1 Samuel 1:1–28).

The faith of our parents and the bustling life of Seaview played a major role in our spiritual development. We loved its communal life, which was so rich in friendship that it became a kind of second womb in which our own faith was nurtured. Such sentiments chime with John Calvin's reminder to the readers of his *Institutes of the Christian Religion* that "those to whom God is Father the Church may also be Mother". We attended church every Sunday morning and Sunday school every Sunday afternoon. During the week we were involved in its burgeoning youth organisations. Seaview was a thriving evangelical congregation and by 1946 its membership had soared to 700 families.

My mother was without doubt the gentle driving-force in our spiritual upbringing – our first evangelist, our enduring teacher and our spiritual director. My father fully supported her in this role, but was hesitant to speak of his own faith. Like many working-class men, he would have a lie in on Sunday morning and get up in time for lunch. Then he would head off for a long walk through Belfast in the afternoon to listen to the street-preachers at the Custom House steps, and finally check into church for the evening service. He was very active in the trade-union movement within the Ulster Transport Authority and was later recruited by his colleagues in the Amalgamated Engineering Union to be their shop steward and one of their spokesmen in negotiations with management. I grew up with stories of his involvement in arguing for higher wages, pressurising management for better working conditions, challenging unfair dismissals, and threatening as well as terminating strikes that would bring his depot to a complete standstill.

The ethos of the church, however, seemed a thousand miles away from the social values and down-to-earth human concerns that faced him constantly at work. He certainly believed in the afterlife; but issues of justice, standing up to exploitation and voicing the concerns of a class that many took for granted or privately looked down on were rarely touched on in church circles. I do not think that anyone, including myself as a young evangelical Christian, ever affirmed his passionate concern for justice or suggested that such concern for ordinary people lay at the heart of God's mission in the world. I am convinced that he would have found himself more fully at home in the congregational life of the church if the teaching of the Hebrew prophets (Micah 6:8) and the Nazareth Manifesto of Jesus Christ (Luke 4:16–19) had been more prominent in its preaching and practice. Nevertheless, I respected him deeply and he taught me that having humanitarian convictions means nothing if one is not prepared to fight for them.

From our father there flowed quietly into us as children a stream of practical passion for social involvement; from our mother, a stream of personal devotion to Christ as Saviour and Lord. This was a combination that was later to blossom in us.

## Starting School

The newly built Seaview Primary School, complete with expansive playing areas and colour-filled classrooms, was just a five-minute uphill walk away and commanded a magnificent view over Belfast Lough. I quickly settled in and began the journey of learning under the skilful tutelage of teachers whose names I no longer recall. Year after year I ambled through the various classes and distinguished myself by being undistinguished – my mind and soul were somewhere else. By P5 I had only one consuming passion – playing football and supporting my childhood heroes, Crusaders, whose stadium was directly opposite our house. My proudest moment in school was being selected in my final year to play for our school team and winning the Belfast Primary Schools Cup in June 1955 at Cliftonville.

Needless to say, concentration on my studies coming up to the hugely important 11-plus examinations, which determined whether a child went on to grammar school or secondary school, suffered badly. My term results were consistently mediocre, despite my mother's stern conversations with me and my sisters' regular support with homework. When the headmaster wrote to inform my parents that I was not suitable for grammar school and should be streamed towards secondary school, my mother exploded. She went to see him and explained that both Margaret and Audrey had been successful in the 11 plus and had moved on to Ballyclare High School and Belfast High School, where they were doing well. She pleaded with him to give me the same chance. After some consideration, he reversed his decision, but insisted that I had to change my ways and to put into my studies the energy I had invested in football. When I realised the anxiety my lack of interest was causing the family, I slowly began to focus and this became evident in the grades I was getting. When finally I sat the 11 plus I was classified as "borderline" and was very fortunate to be accepted into Belfast High School.

Apart from providing us with a good basic education, Seaview School also gently reinforced our sense of Britishness. Each year, close to Remembrance Sunday in November, the Protestant clergy associated with the school would conduct a solemn service at our assembly to remind us of the sacrifices of those who died on the battlefields of Europe to safeguard our freedoms. Among the hymns we sang was "Jerusalem", with its patriotic lyrics celebrating "England's green and pleasant land". For a while I wasn't sure where Belfast was located.

### Community Rituals

The enclosed world I grew up in on the Shore Road was safe and friendly and I was always out and about: within 30 seconds I could be with the crowds on Saturday afternoon cheering on Crusaders football team or tearing around Seaview church halls. Within three minutes I could be with my chums playing games in the vast open spaces of the Grove Park. Boredom was not an affliction from which I suffered.

Only slowly did I become aware of the fact that our area was predominantly Protestant and loyalist. On 2 June 1953, the streets around us were deserted. Families huddled in front of their small black-and-white television sets to witness the coronation of the young and radiant Queen Elizabeth II as monarch of the United Kingdom, Canada, Australia, New Zealand, South Africa, Ceylon and Pakistan. We felt proud beyond words to be British. For weeks we had been preparing for this day: the houses were festooned with Union Jacks and the streets with red, white and blue bunting. Once the ceremony was over, everyone poured out into the streets and the party began. We children were given pride of place at the long tables in the middle of the road, which were laden with ice-cream, jelly, buns and cakes. Then with the adults we joined in various races and fancy-dress competitions.

The goodwill surrounding the coronation contrasted somewhat with the edge of uneasiness introduced at election times. Every four years there would be a cycle of elections: a general election for the Westminster parliament, a Northern Ireland election for Stormont, and a local election for Belfast City Council. My father regularly volunteered as a canvasser for the Ulster Unionist Party (UUP). In the preceding weeks a lorry bedecked with Union Jacks would drive through our area and the candidate would urge us through a crackly loudspeaker to "Keep Ulster British" by voting for him. Election fever instilled in our impressionable young minds a consciousness that our community and culture were under threat from the combined forces of Irish nationalism and Roman Catholicism. Since all my friends were Protestants, keeping Northern Ireland unionist seemed a worthy cause.

If election time heightened our awareness of division, the return of the marching season intensified those feelings. Between April and August each year up to 3,000 parades would take place across the province, of which 70 per cent were linked to the Loyal Orders. Only about 3 per cent of these would have been considered contentious because they passed right through or skirted around nationalist areas where local passions were easily inflamed and frequently issued in street confrontations. The season would reach its peak on 12 July, with mammoth Orange Order parades held in every county of Northern Ireland, the largest of which took place in Belfast.

In preparation for the Twelfth the streets around us would be swathed in Union Jacks, proudly asserting our cultural identity and marking out the political and religious allegiances of our territory. Our role as young teenagers was to collect discarded settees, chairs, tables, floorboards, wooden crates, branches and old tyres for the community bonfire. On the eleventh night the bonfire would be lit with great expectation and ceremony. Crowds would gather to enjoy the occasion, while on the fringes, excitable older teenagers would start to binge on cheap alcohol. Another of our preparatory activities was to paint the kerbstones red, white and blue and cover gable walls with large graffiti proclaiming "Remember 1690", "No Surrender", "Kick the Pope" – or stronger equivalents.

Loud and derogatory references to "Taigs" and "Fenians" usually peppered the bravado-inspired conversations of the few who were getting increasingly drunk. I knew exactly at whom these terms were targetted, but was too young to know to understand that "Taig" was Irish for "Tim", and that "Fenians" referred to the nineteenth-century forerunners of the IRA. We simply downloaded this language from the urban dictionary of religio-political abuse, which both sides of the community mined with great proficiency on occasions such as these. Sadly, the most popular insults were inscribed on the walls of our minds long before we replicated them on the nearest large gables. Indeed, our bonfire was not considered complete without an effigy of the Pope, our number-one hate figure. The nimblest climber among us would scale the bonfire and place him ceremoniously on the top, before the match was struck to set fire to the towering structure. As soon as the flames began to consume him, a roar of approval would go up as we cheered our way into a culture of religious contempt.

During the rituals associated with the marching season we also picked up, memorised and sang with gusto a host of anti-Catholic and anti-Irish songs, especially when accompanying a rousing flute band making its way down the Shore Road. We were far too young to reflect on the lyrics we sang, but without question they enlarged the boundaries of the zone of prejudice already within us. The most popular of the songs in our repertoire was "The Sash My Father Wore", which commemorates the Williamite Wars in Ireland (1690–1):

Sure I'm an Ulster Orangeman, from Erin's isle I came,
To see my British brethren, all of honour and of fame.
And to tell them of my forefathers who fought in days of yore,
That I might have the right to wear the sash my father wore!

(Chorus:)
It is old but it is beautiful, and its colours they are fine,
It was worn at Derry, Aughrim, Enniskillen and the Boyne;
My father wore it as a youth in bygone days of yore,
And on the Twelfth I love to wear the sash my father wore.

For those brave men who crossed the Boyne have not fought or
    died in vain
Our unity, religion, laws, and freedom to maintain;
If the call should come we'll follow the drum, and cross that river
    once more
That tomorrow's Ulsterman may wear the sash my father wore!

It was this ballad that awakened in me a desire one day to join the Orange Order; but I also picked up an uncritical attachment to its underlying ideology of conflict, which celebrates military victories over "the enemy". Both sides of our community have songs of a similar nature, and some of them can be quite innocuous, but others can definitely inculcate an enemy-consciousness that shapes sectarian attitudes. Most appealing to young minds and also most sinister is the call of the blood-sacrifice of our forefathers "to cross the river once more" and fight whoever might seem to threaten us. These ballads function as recruitment songs for the younger generation and it was this dimension that unconsciously influenced me most in the fervour and fun of the annual celebrations.

None of the songs ever hinted at the need to resolve our conflicts, banish the scourge of bloodshed or usher in a new era of respect for the rights and freedoms of both communities. It comes as no surprise to look back through the lyrics of what we sang and notice the total absence of any reference to what Jesus Christ taught about how we should relate to others. The sacred myths that God was on the side of Ulster or Ireland and would guide his chosen people to triumph over the other side offered only a future in which conflict appeared inevitable. The bonfire rituals were great fun, but one must recognise their contribution to the dysfunctional and segregated condition of life in Northern Ireland by generating and perpetuating a culture of mistrust.

When I was 13, my friends and I decided to spend a Sunday afternoon roaming around the spacious grounds of Belfast Castle. The route we took passed the Little Flower Oratory Catholic Church, where people were making their way into a service. For reasons I can scarcely fathom, we picked up stones, threw them at the worshippers and then sprinted towards the castle. Out of the side of my eye I noticed a man turning around and looking at us with an expression of sadness. In later years I wondered if he had prayed for us. Forty-five years later, I preached at an inter-church wedding in the Little Flower Oratory and told this story to a mixed congregation united in celebration of the gift of love.

Our parents and youth leaders in Seaview would have been horrified if they had discovered what we got up to. But in truth, much of this transmission of prejudice was taking place in us within the shadow of the church. I cannot recall the issue ever being addressed or any zealous evangelist ever suggesting to us that being "saved" involved viewing the faith and political convictions of the other community with the respect we claimed for our own.

## Belfast High School

Transitioning to grammar school in September 1955 did not sustain in me any desire to take my studies seriously, and as a result I was put into Form 1C. Indeed, within six months, I found myself in the headmaster's office: in a rugby match I had lashed out and punched an opponent who had deliberately stood on my hands. I was sent off and reported to Dr Harte. He informed me that I had let myself and the school down and as a result I was banned from playing rugby, which I had just begun to enjoy. I rechannelled my energies into playing football outside school, but my disconnection from study of any kind remained dominant right through to Form 4C, when I detected some unexpected stirrings within myself.

Some time between my fifteenth and sixteenth birthdays I noticed myself changing. Prior to the Twelfth I bought a flagpole, attached the Union Jack and proudly hung it out my bedroom window, overlooking the traffic and pedestrians of the Shore Road. My father said nothing about this sudden spurt of public patriotism, but my mother was surprised, embarrassed and annoyed. "Ken," she said softly but firmly, "there are other ways to express your loyalties than this." The flag remained out my window for weeks but she never brought the issue up again. She respected my choice, and I respected her for giving me the freedom to make my own decisions. The following year I heeded her advice and the flag did not appear. My awakening patriotism, however, continued to strengthen and took me in another direction.

I also noticed that in church on Sundays I was taking more interest and listening more attentively, especially to the recurring challenge of personally committing oneself to Christ as Saviour and Lord. Occasionally youth evangelists would preach to us about the satisfaction and joy that accepting Christ would bring. Older teenagers would give testimony to the sense of peace and purpose that Jesus had brought them. In the quietness of my own mind and in the privacy of my bedroom I followed the guidance they gave us and made a decision to commit myself to Christ. At first I experienced, as I had been assured, a quiet feeling of joy and peace, as well as a clearer sense that somehow my life mattered to God and that he would direct me along the path of his choosing. But slowly this initial impression of spiritual elation began to evaporate and my heart made a steady return to its default setting of restlessness. A year after these first attempts to connect with God, I confided my disappointment in another zealous evangelist, who advised me to accept Christ "the proper way". By this he meant that I should go over my sins one by one to make sure I was really sorry for them. To be honest, my sins were peccadilloes rather than dark, sinister habits, and after days of intense poring over them I ran out of subject matter to confess. To make matters worse, I grew increasingly sceptical of the advice being offered and wondered why it was proving hard for me to connect with God, who supposedly cared for all his children. Meanwhile, halfway through Form 4C, I started to concentrate on what I was being taught and my results steadily improved.

Around this time I attended a summer Christian Endeavour camp in Dundrum, County Down, along with several of my friends from Seaview, who assured me that sports events were very much part of the daily programme. I was now 16 and among the 50 or 60 teenagers present I found it impossible not to keep noticing a very attractive and vivacious 15-year-old girl called Valerie Ritchie, who was working in the camp kitchen. She had recently moved from the border town of Dundalk to Belfast with her parents, Harold and Renee, her older brother, Billy, and her younger sister, Janice. The dissolving of the Great Northern Railway Board in 1958 had brought numerous redundancies and many former employees, like Harold, had sought work in Northern Ireland. The family joined St John's Presbyterian Church, Newtownbreda, a short distance from their home on the Ravenhill Road.

At various times of the day I would drop in to the kitchen to ask the chef if there were any odd jobs that he needed done. From his smile I could see that he knew that my real interests did not lie in chopping potatoes and drying dishes, but he seemed not to mind. It gave me a chance to chat with Val and in the months that followed a teenage crush in Dundrum slowly turned into a real romantic friendship. She brought a joy into my life that counteracted a growing tendency to be over-serious and a gentler southern spirituality that contrasted with the sharper edges of my Ulster Protestantism. But most of all, as the friendship endured and matured in the months after Dundrum, it deepened my sense of emotional security and contributed to the sheer fun of being teenagers in love.

By the time I had reached 17 and entered my final year I had managed to make it into Form 6A. My greatest joy, however, was being invited again to play rugby, this time for the First XV, which went on to reach the semi-final of the Schools Cup for the first time in its history. My misdemeanours had long been forgotten.

Two of my closest friends in sixth form were devout Christians. Once, when I voiced some scepticism about the Bible, one of them asked me rather bluntly if I had ever studied it for my own personal benefit. I admitted I had not. "Well, go and read it," he said, "and then we can have an informed discussion!" His candidness punctured my pride, but thankfully it spurred me into action. For three months I went to bed each evening with a cup of tea, a hot-water bottle and the four Gospels. At first I was only interested in digging out inconsistencies in the story to justify my own nascent cynicism. Then a genuine curiosity about the person of Christ crept up on me. Finally, by the end of the third month, the increasing impact of his life, teaching, death and resurrection had captivated me. I knelt by my bedside, offered him the confusions of my inner self and asked for the strength to follow him and the path along which I knew he would lead me. In the quietness of my own room I experienced an epiphany moment, reminiscent of the Easter encounters of his disciples recorded in the Gospels. I felt embraced by a divine love I had not known in such a deep and intense way before; it enveloped me in a kind of luminous presence which I took to be the Risen Christ.

For months I kept my thoughts to myself, just to make sure I would not again be a victim of spiritual evaporation. Then, in January 1961, I joined the Scripture Union at school – not the coolest group for a rugby player to be associated with. Shortly afterwards I approached Rev SEM Brown of Seaview and asked to be received as a communicant member of the congregation by profession of faith.

### "The Sash My Father Wore"

Even as I was discovering a new spiritual centre to my life, I was keen to join the Orange Order when I turned 18 in May 1961. It was the culmination of many discussions with my father, who, when I was a child, would often take out his sash and let me try it on, even though his membership had lapsed decades earlier. I had also felt very proud of him as he and a colleague had patrolled up and down York Road and the Shore Road one evening a week in their Ulster Special Constabulary uniforms, equipped with pistols and batons. The Ulster Special Constabulary, or B-Specials, was a quasi-military reserve police force was set up in 1920 as an armed corps and was called out in times of emergency or insurgency.

Following in his footsteps was motivation enough for me, but I also felt that politically, culturally and religiously, I wanted to affirm my identity as an Ulster Protestant. In a simple yet formalised ceremony I was sworn into Loyal Orange Lodge 1322, which met in the nearby North Belfast Memorial Hall. Most of the lodge members were working-class men who took their Orangeism seriously but kept only a tenuous link with the local churches. It was a proud moment for me and I looked forward to striding out with the lodge on my first Twelfth of July parade through Belfast.

At eight o'clock on the Twelfth morning we assembled at the home of the worshipful master in North Queen Street and unfurled our lodge banner. Then we formed into ranks behind a 25-member flute band and marched up to Carlisle Circus to join 30,000 other Orangemen who, at 10 o'clock, would set off on the 7-mile walk through the city centre to "the Field" at Finaghy. It was a glorious occasion and I enjoyed every moment of it. The band stirred our patriotic pride; the waving crowds along the full length of the route cheered us on; and the sense of belonging to an order whose members stretched two miles in front of us and two miles behind created an unforgettable sense of solidarity.

But it also brought some surprises. Shortly after setting off from Carlisle Circus we passed the open doors of St Patrick's Catholic Church in Donegall Street. Suddenly the band ratcheted up the volume of the music and launched into "The Sash My Father Wore". The thump of the drums boomeranged into the empty church and out again. I caught sight of a few worshippers kneeling quietly in prayer. It didn't bother me greatly at the time – the adrenaline flowing through my veins mitigated its impact.

As the parade snaked its way along Royal Avenue, the numbers of those who had crowded into the city centre to enjoy the festive occasion increased considerably and our band quickly picked up a group of "young supporters" on the pavement, who attached themselves to us and escorted us all the way to the Field. Most of them were swigging beer and holding aloft their dripping cans while singing traditional songs with boisterous intensity. As their feet grew sore and their mastery of the words dimmed with drink, the usual expletives were slipped into the lyrics damning the Pope, questioning the parentage of Fenians and mocking the mother of Christ as revered by Catholics. I put it down to the effects of too much alcohol and shelved any deeper questioning of the carnival atmosphere.

By the time we reached our destination our feet were sore and we headed for food and refreshments in the hospitality tents, followed by an hour's rest before the return leg of the journey. Most people in the Field were well behaved, but a minority of the supporters continued to consume large quantities of alcohol and stagger around. After lunch I made my way to the raised platform for the religious ceremony, which I assumed was the central purpose of our gathering. I was surprised to discover that no more than 60 out of the thousands milling around took the time to listen to the prayers of the grand chaplain, the speech of the grand master and the presentation of the resolutions affirming our reformed faith and loyalty to the Queen.

Over the next seven years Orangeism loomed large in my affections and I rarely missed the monthly lodge meetings. But the underbelly of Belfast Orangeism that shocked me on my first Twelfth continued to trouble my conscience and I became convinced that the order needed to purge itself of some unwelcome but rarely discussed features. I also began to realise that Orangeism could not be reduced to the simple categories of religion or politics, as I had initially assumed. It was a complex amalgam of interlocking elements – cultural, political, religious, ethnic and national – held together by a communal memory and a strong territorial sense of the need to protect the state it had helped to create. All of these factors were constantly re-energised by annual parades whose primary purpose seemed to be to commemorate historical conflicts; this, in turn, reinforced a vibrant ideology of separateness. This religio-political cultural cycle preserved Protestant identity over and against Catholicism and declared the dominance of unionism over and against Irish nationalism. The core values of the Orangeism to which I had sworn my allegiance had little or no room for reconciliation or dialogue. But, like most of my colleagues, reconciliation and dialogue were concepts that I viewed with suspicion and distaste. My grasp of Christianity's insistence on love of neighbour and love of enemy was still gravely underdeveloped.

The summer of 1961, however, brought me some good news. I had done well enough in my A-level examinations to get a place at Queen's University, Belfast. My parents were delighted: Margaret was settling into her career as a teacher in Lowood Primary School and Audrey into nursing at the Royal Victoria Hospital. I had no idea where I was heading; I was just excited at the prospect of further education.

**Strange New World**

It was with a mixture of excitement and trepidation that I travelled across town at the beginning of October for Freshers' Day at Queen's. A friend in Seaview Church had arranged for me to meet John Dunlop, president of the Christian Union (CU), who was studying philosophy and planning eventually to become a Presbyterian minister. He welcomed me to the campus, showed me around the library and took me to the Latin, Geology and Philosophy Departments that I would soon be frequenting. Little did I realise at the time that John's friendship, example and support would mean so much to me when, in the 1970s, we both found ourselves working in an almost unrecognisably different Belfast.

I then headed off alone to explore the centrepiece of the university, the Lanyon Building, completed in 1849 by the architect Sir Charles Lanyon. This Tudor-Gothic red-brick edifice exuded such a sense of academic presence and expectancy that I wondered whether I could cope. Adjacent to it was the Whitla Hall, buzzing with dozens of organisations competing for adherents among hordes of fresh-faced newcomers. I squeezed my way through to the Rugby Club stand and signed up for the year, then on to CU to pick up a programme of events. I had made up my mind to keep my life at Queen's simple so that I could seize the opportunity for study that had come my way.

The Northern Ireland Education Act (1947) had opened up university education to those from less well-off backgrounds who could attain the required standards. This was part of the unionist government's bold strategy of economic and educational modernisation at a time when the traditional industries of shipbuilding and linen manufacture were in decline. Unemployment was running high in working-class Protestant areas and even higher within the burgeoning nationalist community, which constantly complained of job discrimination. Unionists usually denied these allegations but subsequent investigations revealed that Catholic men were two and a half times more likely to be unemployed than Protestant men. The flow of young nationalists into Queen's was steadily increasing. Education was highly prized by their teachers and parents as a route out of economic and social disadvantage in a state with which they felt little connection.

It was through the Latin Department that I formed my first meaningful relationship with someone from "the other side" – a Catholic student who rejoiced in an Irish name I found hard to get used to and still harder to spell. He loved Gaelic sports, attended Mass regularly and socialised most of the time with the hundreds of students who crammed into the Catholic Chaplaincy in Elmwood Avenue for lunch. Over numerous cups of coffee in the Great Hall, our friendship deepened to the point where we could converse openly about our backgrounds, beliefs and values. For both of us it was like crossing a frontier and travelling into a strange new world that was actually only millimetres away but felt extremely distant. It was bizarre that I had reached the age of 18 and was just starting out on this journey, such were the powerful self-segregating influences at work within our compact little country. For the most part, even in the crowded Great Hall, students tended to fit into the patterns prevailing outside Queen's and to socialise mainly with those who were culturally, politically and religiously similar to themselves.

As our friendship grew over the months that followed, I noticed that my negativity towards Irish nationalism was softening and some of the rough edges of my anti-Catholic prejudices were being smoothed away. But these were only micro-changes. Underneath, I was still loyally Orange and believed that Protestantism was the purest form of Christianity on earth. I had not yet cultivated the capacity to critique my own religio-political tradition or feel burdened by the depth of Ulster's divisions.

## Philosophy and the Unexamined Life

My decision to concentrate primarily on Classics and Philosophy during my three years at Queen's was motivated by an eagerness to learn how some of the world's greatest minds addressed life's most basic questions. In first year our study of metaphysics raised questions about the fundamental nature of all reality – what it is, why it is and how we can understand it. As part of that process we asked questions such as "Is there a God?", "Can the truth about ultimate reality ever be known?", "Is the world exclusively composed of matter?" and "Do people have free will?" The simplicity and magnitude of the questions always seemed to overshadow the hesitancy of our answers, but we had started to think for ourselves.

In second year we turned our attention to moral philosophy and the ideas that shape conscience: good and evil, right and wrong, obligation and responsibility. We examined the major moral codes by which people live and sought to weigh up whether morality is objective and absolute or subjective and relative, the cultural product of communities which protect themselves from chaos by requiring certain standards of civilised behaviour.

For a few months prior to starting my final year, Rev Brown of Seaview had been urging me to consider going into the ministry. At first I was reluctant, but gradually he persuaded me with this assurance: "If it's not God's will, he'll stop you." Since Philosophy and Classical Studies were considered good preparation for Theology, I selected Latin, Ancient History and a course on Greek Philosophy taught by an American professor, Marjorie Glicksman Grene. She introduced us to the towering trio of the Athenian School – Socrates, Plato and Aristotle. Their writings exerted considerable influence over some early Christian thinkers, such as Clement of Alexandria (AD 120–50) who asserted that "Philosophy acted as a schoolmaster to the Greeks, preparing them for Christ, just as the laws of the Jews prepared them for Christ."

I was particularly intrigued by the *Dialogues of Plato*, in which the philosopher Socrates interrogates the religious beliefs and moral perspectives of people with a reputation for expertise in these areas. The experts get lost in confusion before they are receptive to Socrates' guidance about true wisdom – namely, that it is only through self-questioning that we can truly know ourselves and choose to pursue the path of knowing God and espousing goodness. In his final speech before the jury that condemns him to death he declares: "The unexamined life is not worth living."

Dr Grene adopted the Socratic method of interrogation with us, particularly in seminars. We loved her sense of enthusiasm and commitment to our intellectual development, but she could also slay us with a single phrase or question. It was she who provoked me into seriously examining my own beliefs and presenting them with some sort of reasoned reflection. In short, while the rigour of philosophy bequeathed to me the courage of honest thinking, it also rooted the Christian beliefs and values I had inherited in the soil of personal conviction. It was a legacy that was to accompany me into the painful process of questioning what my faith in Christ was really about when confronting the powerful cultural pressures of Northern Ireland to conform to what is expected by one's own side.

## Maturing Evangelically

University proved to be an important time of transition in my life and during it the CU grounded me in the verities of orthodox Christianity and gifted me with a set of friendships with some deeply spiritual students. It also afforded me the privilege of listening to renowned theologians such as Rev John Stott, the Anglican rector of All Souls, Langham Place, London. In hindsight, however, while the CU reflected the best in Ulster evangelicalism, it also shared its weaknesses. I cannot recall a speaker ever urging us to cross the sectarian divide so evident even in Queen's, or to apply the social-justice agenda of the Hebrew prophets to the smouldering grievances of the Catholic community. Nor was any opportunity created to frame a Christian response to the titanic political struggle going on around us between Captain Terence O'Neill, the unionist prime minister, and the firebrand fundamentalist Belfast preacher Rev Ian Paisley, then 37 years old.

In March 1963 O'Neill was chosen as the fourth unionist prime minister of Northern Ireland and set out to modernise the economy and challenge the "crude and unthinking intolerance" that kept the province divided. A tentative thaw in intercommunity relations was already underway. In 1962 the IRA had decided to hang up its guns after a futile five-year guerrilla campaign; Dr William Philbin became the first Catholic bishop to be invited to Belfast's City Hall as a guest of the unionist lord mayor; and then, following the death of Pope John XXIII on 3 June 1963, the Union Jack on the dome of the City Hall was lowered to half mast in an unprecedented mark of unionist respect. That very evening Ian Paisley convened a rally in the nearby Ulster Hall and roundly condemned the sending of condolences to the Catholic Church. "This Romish Man of Sin is now in hell!" he roared, to shouts of "Hallelujah" from the 500-strong audience. When O'Neill began visiting Catholic schools and was seen on television drinking tea with nuns and priests, Paisley was determined to remove him. "The ecumenists, both political and ecclesiastical, are selling us out," he declared, "and every Ulster Protestant must unflinchingly resist these modern Lundies." (Robert Lundy, governor of Derry during the siege of 1688–9, won lasting infamy as a traitor when he attempted to betray the loyal citizens of the city in the face of the Irish force of the Catholic monarch James II.)

I felt a growing kinship with Captain O'Neill's progressive political thinking and was shocked by the strength of Paisley's anti-Catholicism. Nevertheless, his identification of ecumenism as the dominant threat to Ulster's survival struck a chord, in a milder form, within my own spirit. The atmosphere at Queen's, however, seemed little concerned with O'Neill's openness or Paisley's extremism; our preoccupation with study, romance, socializing, sport, career and the rock music of the Beatles and the Rolling Stones insulated us somewhat from the world outside. But this general air of apathy was slowly being pushed from centre stage by a cataclysm waiting in the wings. I graduated from Queen's in June 1964 and looked forward to crossing the road to study Theology at the Presbyterian College. My parents and Val's parents attended the graduation ceremony in the Whitla Hall and afterwards enjoyed strawberries and cream in the quadrangle with hundreds of other celebrating families. They were happy and supportive of the new direction in which my life was heading.

## Entering Assembly's College

Hardly a week went by at Queen's that I didn't look across College Park East and wonder what was going on behind the stately Renaissance facade of the Presbyterian College, with its four large Doric columns. It faced directly into University Square and transmitted an impression of the independence and strength of the PCI at the zenith of its position as Northern Ireland's largest Protestant denomination, with over 400,000 members. But as the summer gave way to autumn, tension was rising on the streets. The province headed into a Westminster general election in October 1964. Unionists were panicking at the prospect of losing their West Belfast seat to a republican Labour candidate, and when an Irish tricolour was spotted in the window of the Divis Street headquarters of a rival republican candidate, Paisley threatened to march his supporters into the area and remove it. When the police took action on 28 September to preempt this possibility, it sparked Belfast's worst week of rioting since the 1930s.

It was during that week that I arrived at Assembly's College, as it was generally referred to, to meet up with Rev James Boyd, professor of Practical Theology. He took me on a guided tour of the historic building, during which I discovered that the college was another of the architectural brainchildren of Sir Charles Lanyon. Furthermore, when the Government of Ireland Act 1920 had partitioned the island, the college had offered its facilities to the newly formed government of Northern Ireland until a permanent home was found at Stormont. Professor Boyd also showed me around the quaint Gamble Library, the large chapel and the Gibson Chambers, where the unmarried ministerial students were accommodated. I was allocated room 13. Despite being less than a mile from Divis Street, I slept soundly on my first night. Like most Protestants, I felt that the police would soon quell the riots and that the strident extremism of Paisley would not capture the sensible citizens of Ulster and would eventually wane.

A spirit of camaraderie prevailed among the 30 ministry students, most of whom were evangelical in outlook. But that label was sometimes withheld from any who, during lectures, questioned the inerrancy of Scripture or inadvertently confessed to benefitting from the writings of liberal scholars. I was never sure who was "in" or "out" of the sound group, but apparently there were indicators: a stirring testimony of conversion, a passion for evangelism, and an ample display of Banner of Truth books containing the writings of the peerless Puritans. I began to dislike this preoccupation with boundary-drawing among colleagues who were devoutly orthodox and eager to voice their questions.

As I made preparations to return to Assembly's College in September 1965 to begin my second year of study, the lampposts of Belfast were being festooned with posters as the province headed into yet another electoral battle, this time for the 52 seats in the Stormont parliament. Everyone wondered if Prime Minister O'Neill's attempts to heal the religious divisions in the north and normalise political relations with the south would hold up against the incessant sniping of Ian Paisley. The newly-formed Campaign for Social Justice was also giving voice to nationalist demands for an end to gerrymandering, unfair employment practices and discrimination against the Catholic community in the allocation of public housing. As it turned out, the Ulster Unionists under O'Neill captured 36 of the 52 seats, two more than previously. I was relieved.

Shortly after the opening of the autumn term, Professor Ted Russell called me into his office and encouraged me to undertake a two-year bachelor of divinity degree in Queen's University alongside my ministerial studies. This would mean, he explained, dropping Hebrew and concentrating on New Testament Language and Literature. Then, unexpectedly, some third-year colleagues asked me to take on the role of Irish coordinator of the Theological Students Fellowship (TSF), a branch of the UK Inter-Varsity Fellowship of Evangelical Unions. The purpose of TSF was to promote an evangelical perspective on the Christian faith and a commitment to biblical scholarship and research among ministry students throughout Ireland. Over the next two years I got to know many of the trainee ministers in the Edgehill Theological College of the Methodist Church, the Church of Ireland Theological Institute in Dublin and, of course, my own colleagues in Assembly's. I listened to their hopes for the future as well as their theological struggles and passed on to them the *TSF Bulletin*, a high-quality triannual theological journal in which evangelical scholars addressed the issues with which we were all wrestling. Prominent writers included the American philosopher Francis A Schaeffer and Dr FF Bruce. The friendships I formed helped me to appreciate the life of other churches beyond the confines of Presbyterianism.

Then, out of the blue, another request arrived. My brethren in LOL 1322 asked me to consider taking on the role of lodge chaplain. This would involve opening our meetings with prayer and a Scripture reading, walking at the head of the lodge beside the worshipful master and lodge secretary on the Twelfth and every three months giving a 15-minute mini-lecture on the "Qualifications of an Orangeman". I felt honoured to be invited and agreed to undertake the responsibilities.

My notes for some of the talks I gave offer a reliable insight into how my thinking was developing at that time. Firstly, I stressed the primacy of personal faith: "An Orangeman should have a sincere love for his heavenly Father and a steadfast faith in Jesus Christ ..." Secondly, personal faith must be accompanied by the adoption of evangelical attitudes: "He should cultivate truth and justice, brotherly kindness and charity ... ever abstaining from all uncharitable words, actions, or sentiments towards his Roman Catholic brethren ..." I stressed that this meant abandoning any displays of sectarianism towards the Catholic Church and community. Thirdly, and perhaps most revealingly, I steered clear of all reference to the bald anti-Catholicism of the "Qualifications": "he should strenuously oppose the fatal errors and doctrines of the Church of Rome, and scrupulously avoid countenancing (by his presence or otherwise) any act or ceremony of Popish Worship ..." Privately I was questioning how any of us in the lodge could oppose the numerous and complex "doctrines of Rome" without ever having studied them with the help of an articulate Catholic theologian. Were we expected just to parrot the belittling sentiments of our forefathers? Furthermore, the few Catholics I had got to know well exhibited in their lives the same love for their heavenly Father and steadfast faith in Jesus Christ that were viewed as the indispensable evangelical virtues required of every Orangeman. I was loath, therefore, to voice the nascent hesitancy growing within me about the anti-Catholic sentiments embedded in the "Qualifications" that each of us as Orangemen had subscribed to. I was not sure if my reservations were valid and I had no desire to cause unnecessary tension in the lodge.

Throughout the rest of my second and third years at Assembly's College I worked really hard at juggling study preparations for my BD exams in May 1967, fulfilling my responsibility to other ministerial students as TSF representative and living up to the lodge's expectations for me as chaplain. It was a relief for me from these pressures to run onto a rugby field or cricket pitch on Saturday afternoons with Belfast High School Former Pupils and to spend time relaxing with Val and my family at the weekends.

Underneath all my activity, friendships and enjoyable study during three years at Assembly's College, a very big personal and spiritual issue swirled, and I tried to resolve it in an intellectually honest and thoughtful manner. The issue was this: how could one be theologically evangelical and anti-ecumenical, but avoid the manner of Ian Paisley, who had launched his weekly *Protestant Telegraph* newspaper in February 1966? For months I read it from cover to cover, trying to identify the sinister forces he believed were threatening Protestantism and traditional unionism. These turned out to be trends towards reconciliation emanating from within the Protestant churches and the UUP. No longer did he restrict his denunciations to the

Catholic Church: the traitorous bridge-builders of the UUP, the Church of Ireland, the Presbyterian Church and the Methodist Church were now firmly in his sights. I grew tired of his scaremongering and abusive polemics.

On another level, my study of the New Testament was convincing me that Christ had established only one church and that its visible unity in diversity was clearly his desire for it. On the eve of his arrest, as the Gospel of John reminds us, Jesus repeatedly prays: "Father, may my followers be one just as you and I are one, so that the world will believe that you sent me." Interpreting Christ's prayer within my own theological framework, I had started to believe that unity among evangelicals in the Gospel was highly desirable, just as the proliferation of Protestant denominations was seriously flawed. However, several of the evangelical ministers I looked up to shared Paisley's antipathy to what they labelled the "unbiblical ecumenism" of the World Council of Churches (WCC). In their view, it was mired in "compromise", "liberalism", "heresy" and "apostasy". I just took their word for it.

The book, however, that clinched my commitment to anti-ecumenism was the 1964 Banner of Truth publication *Unity in the Dark* by Rev Donald Gillies, minister of Agnes Street Presbyterian Church, Belfast. His arguments were charitably expressed, widely researched and logically well presented. Moreover, he was unafraid to commend much in the ecumenical movement, which he thought was "inspired by a lofty ideal [of unity] which shames much of our evangelicalism, stricken by the blight of negative criticism and internecine strife". Nevertheless, he identified three serious errors in the functioning of the WCC. It devoted more concern to social and political matters than to the salvation of souls; it was more sacramental than evangelical; and it set aside in practice the authority of the Bible. But his primary charge against ecumenism was that "it bids to become the greatest menace to the truth of the Gospel since the time of the Reformation" because its leaders sought union with Rome as their ultimate goal. "In view of the admission of the Greek Orthodox Church to the WCC," he wrote, "there is no valid reason for refusing entry to Rome. The recognition of Orthodoxy and Rome as Christian Churches is a serious departure from the historic Protestant position."

Despite being convinced by Gillies, two reservations stilled niggled away in the back of my mind. Firstly, his position, though shorn of Paisley's polemics, led to the same conclusion – ecumenism was evil and must be resisted with determination. Secondly, my rejection of ecumenism was primarily based on the religious and cultural conditioning of my Ulster evangelical outlook and the impact of reading Gillies's book. I had never met a Greek Orthodox believer or crossed the threshold of a Catholic church. Something within me felt uneasy about drawing conclusions about churches of which I had little or no personal experience.

## An Unexpected Opportunity

Midway through my final summer term in 1967, a circular from the WCC posted on the college noticeboard caught my attention. It was offering ministry students a one-year postgraduate scholarship to study Theology in a different country. The more I thought about it, the more I felt I should apply, for three reasons. I felt it would be good to broaden my horizons and spread my wings after six years of study within the narrow confines of Northern Ireland. It would give me an extra year to prepare for a master of theology degree in New Testament Studies at Queen's, which, once again, Professor Russell had urged me to undertake. And finally, I could investigate ecumenism directly and from the inside, and thereby equip myself with the capacity to oppose it with integrity and not from a biased distance. I sent off my application form to Geneva and then buried my head in my books as exam-time loomed.

## Spectre of Antichrist

The public closing of the college at the end of May is always a big occasion. Students who have successfully completed their examinations are presented with graduation certificates, which allow them to proceed to their licensing as "probationers for the ministerial office". On 26 May 1967, the chapel was packed as 15 of us sat at the front, ready to graduate. A lecture of general interest was customarily delivered by one of the professors, and on this occasion Dr John Barkley's theme, "The Antichrist: A Historical Survey", was highly relevant and controversial in view of the rise of Paisleyism and the surge in support for him among Presbyterians. It was widely publicised in the press, as Dr Barkley, Professor of Ecclesiastical History, knew it would be. Anti-Catholicism was making a comeback. In January, when the Anglican bishop of Ripon, Dr John Moorman, was due to speak in St Anne's Cathedral on the role of the papacy in a future united church, Ian Paisley and Belfast Orangemen combined forces in a call for 100,000 protesters to oppose it. The dean was forced to cancel the event for fear of violence. Furthermore, a witch-hunt was in progress in parts of the Orange Order and a worshipful master in Larne was expelled for attending a Catholic wedding. The toxic mix of suspicion and confrontation was breathing new life into the "Christ versus Antichrist" ideology lying in the basement of the Ulster fundamentalist psyche.

Of more immediate concern to us as students for the ministry was that we would shortly required at our licensing to sign the Westminster Confession of Faith (1646) as "founded on and agreeable to the Word of God". This included the contentious assertion that "There is no other head of the Church but the Lord Jesus Christ: nor can the Pope of Rome in any sense be head thereof; but is that Antichrist, that man of sin, and son of perdition, that exalteth himself, in the Church, against Christ and all that is called God." It was a belief I had never questioned. Sitting just a few metres from the lectern where Dr Barkley was standing, we listened with rapt attention.

Beginning with the three scriptural proofs offered by the Confession of Faith to justify its charge of Antichrist, he argued that in the thirteenth chapter of the Book of Revelation, "the beast symbolises both the Roman Empire and the demonic Nero coming from the abyss – an expectation prevalent from AD 90 onwards in many Christian communities". The "Man of Lawlessness" in the Second Epistle to the Thessalonians was "a false Messiah sent to punish the Jews for having rejected the true Messiah". The text from the Gospel of Matthew, he claimed, "makes no reference to the Antichrist". In short, there is no credible biblical basis for the Confession's declaration that the Pope is the Antichrist.

Turning then to the early church fathers of the first six centuries, he concluded: "They viewed the Antichrist as one of the Jewish false Messiahs. No one ever suggested that he would rise out of the Christian Church." During the Crusades (1096–1270), which were intended to wrest the sacred sites of Christianity in Palestine from Muslim control, some within the western Catholic Church claimed that Mohammed was the Antichrist. It was not until 1318 that a pope was, for the first time, branded Antichrist. That pope was John XXII (1316–34), who burned at the stake hundreds of the Spirituals – strict Franciscans who sought to live by the rule of evangelical poverty. It was noted that "the term is used descriptively, not ontologically, as it was still possible to believe in a good pope".

It was during the Great Papal Schism (1378–1417) that the two popes, and later three, vied for supremacy over the Catholic Church and frequently hurled charges of "Antichrist" at each other. This currency of contempt continued into the Reformation of the sixteenth century, argued Barkley, but now went beyond "bad" popes: "Luther came to hold that every pope was Antichrist even though personally exemplary, because Antichrist is collective; it is now an institution, the papacy, a system." John Calvin (1509–64) took a similar view. The papacy, in turn, gave the Reformers as good as it got and Pope Hadrian VI pulled no punches in declaring that Martin Luther was the real biblical Antichrist.

Professor Barkley completed his lecture by inserting two highly relevant conclusions into the increasingly rancorous religious discourse of the province. The first was that theological abuse should have no place in Christian conversation. We should engage with members of the church of Rome, he argued, just as Calvin did at conferences in Haguenau, Worms and Ratisbon, but only to if we are prepared to "speak the truth to each other in a spirit of love", as Paul commends in his letter to the Ephesians. The second was that the belief that the Pope was the Antichrist did not exist for 1300 years: "Should anyone seek to make this a fundamental doctrine of the Apostolic Faith he can have little objection to others making their additions thereto." In other words, it is a late arrival on the battlefield of ecclesiastical conflict. Subscription, therefore, to the Confession of Faith "does not involve acceptance of the statement that the Pope is the Antichrist and should anyone suggest removing it there could be no valid objection".

It would take two or three years for the impact of Professor Barkley's lecture to percolate into the depths of my anti-Catholic belief system, but the graduation ceremony in the college marked a definite progression in that process. Two days later, on Sunday evening, 28 May, I was officially licensed in Seaview Church by the Presbytery of North Belfast as a probationer for the ministry and signed the Westminster Confession of Faith. I felt increasingly sure that serving Christ within the life of his church was what God intended for me. A month later, having passed my BD examinations, I graduated from Queen's, this time along with Val, who had successfully completed her honours degree in English. Shortly afterwards, I headed off excitedly to Bangor, County Down, to spend the summer with the congregation of Hamilton Road Presbyterian Church, to which I had been appointed as assistant minister to Rev David Burke.

# CHAPTER TWO

# Expanding Horizons

Around the time when I was preparing to leave Assembly's College in June 1967, a letter arrived marked "British Council of Churches". As I opened it, the first word to catch my eye was "Cambridge". It set my mind buzzing with excitement. I was being offered a WCC scholarship to study the New Testament for an academic year at Cambridge University's Divinity School. I would be living at Ridley Hall, one of Anglicanism's foremost Evangelical Colleges.

I checked into Ridley at the end of September and had a few days to explore the most famous locations of the university city on my doorstep. For me, the jewel in the crown was King's College Chapel, founded in 1446 by King Henry VI. From the moment I crossed the River Cam at the Backs I was captivated by this massive white edifice dominating the skyline and standing like an ethereal, gravity-defying cathedral of light.

The student community at Ridley was quite diverse, not just in age, intellectual ability and social background, but also in churchmanship. Most were evangelical, some were middle-of-the-road and a few were passionately liberal – a diversity that frequently sparked exchanges of good-humoured banter as well as offering penetrating insights into the strengths and weaknesses of the various perspectives. The evangelicalism nurtured within the college was often referred to as "open" – the Scriptures were respected, intellectual thoroughness was encouraged and the disciplines of daily worship were dutifully observed. Within that ethos, space was also created for discussing the theological, cultural and political issues of the day, without impairing relationships.

## Acclimatizing to Anglican Worship

Our days would begin with Matins in the chapel at 8.00 am. Then, after breakfast, we would disperse, either to lectures on pastoral ministry within the college or to the Divinity School. At 5.30 pm we would reassemble for Evensong before donning our academic gowns for dinner in the Refectory. At our first communal meal I found myself sitting beside John, a 35-year-old mature student from Cornwall, who kept recommending the health benefits of West Country cider. Assuming it was non-alcoholic, I ordered three glasses during the course of the dinner. As the evening progressed, I became endowed with a sense of benign goodwill towards the whole world!

On Wednesday evenings and Sunday mornings everyone gathered in the chapel for Holy Communion. This frequency of the Lord's Supper was new to me as an Irish Presbyterian, for whom a quarterly celebration was the norm, but I was surprised how effortlessly I adapted to the simplicity and spiritual depth of the service. The Prayer of Humble Access (1548) never failed to move me, especially the words: "We do not presume to come to this thy Table, O merciful Lord, trusting in our own righteousness, but in thy manifold and great mercies."

When I got up out of my seat, approached the altar rail and knelt to receive the body and blood of Christ, I often thought of the words of Calvin when he described the Eucharist as "too lofty for either my mind to comprehend or my words to declare. I rather experience than understand it."

In time I eased into the rhythm of the Anglican liturgy and found it helpful that a clear theme ran through every service and blended with beautiful prayers, appropriate scriptural readings and moments for silent reflection.

## The Privilege of Learning

Most mornings would find me in the Divinity School listening to two world-class New Testament scholars, Dr Charles Moule and Dr Dennis Nineham. When Professor Moule issued an open invitation to an evening seminar for postgraduate students in his rooms at Clare College, I jumped at the prospect. There were five of us in the group and each week one was assigned the task of evaluating a recent New Testament publication that Dr Moule considered significant. My first assignment was *Memory and Manuscript* (1961) by Professor Birger Gerhardsson of Lund University, Sweden. It traced the process by which the words and actions of Jesus were remembered within the earliest Christian community, transmitted through teaching and preaching and finally written down in the Gospels. After summarising and critiquing the author's arguments we were thrown to the lions – the other participants were given free rein with questions and comments. The seminar concluded with Professor Moule offering his own appraisal.

## Rhodesia and Renewal

My closest friend at Ridley was Roger Maggs, who had grown up in Rhodesia before coming to Cambridge to read Theology. Our conversations often turned to the unrest back home. Rhodesia was descending into civil war; in 1965 the 200,000-strong white minority of a population numbering 4,000,000 issued its Unilateral Declaration of Independence from the British Crown. Meanwhile, in Northern Ireland, the Civil Rights Association was challenging discrimination against Catholics while Rev Ian Paisley spearheaded a campaign against the modest liberalising gestures of the Ulster Unionist prime minister, Terence O'Neill.

Another issue on which Roger and I frequently exchanged thoughts was the growing Charismatic Movement among younger Anglican evangelical leaders like Rev Michael Harper. Roger invited me to a meeting at which Harper spoke about how his life had been transformed by being "filled with the Holy Spirit". He gave us examples of discouraged pastors finding new joy in their faith and seeing signs of growth in their parishes. The evangelicalism in which I had been nurtured at home centred on knowing Christ personally as Saviour and Lord; here now was a stream of faith that also tapped into the life-giving ministry of the Holy Spirit. The Charismatic Movement, however, seemed excessively emotional to me. I could see how it was definitely enriching Roger's spiritual life, but it was not something I felt I needed at that stage.

With the approach of Christmas, Ridley emptied. I was excited to be going home, for a special reason. Val and I were planning to get engaged. We headed downtown into Belfast's pre-Christmas shopping frenzy and visited several jewellers until Val spotted the ring she wanted. The price – £125! I kept my imminent student insolvency to myself and splashed out on the best investment I ever made. It was a Christmas full of joy for us and our families.

## Learning from Exile

Early in January 1968 I flew back to London to attend a four-day conference on the south coast of England organised by the BCC for 20 ministry students, mostly from Asia and Africa, who were studying in the United Kingdom on

WCC scholarships. Each of us had to make a presentation about the countries we came from. It was, in a way, reassuring to discover that Northern Ireland was not alone in facing problems. The interest in Rhodesia that Roger had aroused in me took on a new dimension when a black student told us how he had had to flee for his life from Bulawayo. He was one of the first of 250,000 refugees to flee Rhodesia in the years following the Unilateral Declaration of Independence. His only crime was that he had become involved in student protests for democratic rights. In one of the refugee camps he was befriended by an English volunteer who, on discovering that he was planning to become an Anglican priest, accessed a WCC scholarship to enable him to pursue his dream in England. His exile, however, felt like a nightmare and it was eating him up emotionally.

He and I were able to fit in several long walks, during which he explained to me the humiliation and exploitation endured by the Zimbabwean people. As I began to understand both sides of the Rhodesian conflict, I realised how ill informed I was about the nationalist narrative of Northern Ireland. I still tended to view the crisis at home through one eye – that of my own Protestant-unionist perspective.

## Holland and Secularism

On returning to Ridley at the start of the Lent term, I immersed myself once again in the familiar routine of lectures, seminars, and research for my MTh. Shortly afterwards, another BCC invitation arrived, this time for a conference in Holland entitled "A Christian Response to Secularism in Europe". It would be held in April in two venues, Driebergen and the University of Amsterdam. The background to the conference was that following the Second Vatican Council (1962–5) the Dutch Catholic and Reformed Churches decided to address together the growing secularism within their own country, where 30 per cent of its citizens classified themselves as non-religious. We met up in London and travelled across by train and ferry.

For three days in Driebergen, Catholic and Reformed professors explained to us how modern secularism had evolved out of the sixteenth-century European Renaissance, with its flowering of philosophy, science, literature and art. It was a reactive movement, turning away from the excessive otherworldliness of the Middle Ages, which had downgraded the value of human life. It re-emphasised the goodness of human beings and the creative achievements of humanity. In time, elements of this trend hardened into criticism of religion itself.

Driebergen carried an added significance for me. I had never before been in the same room as a Catholic priest giving a lecture. At first I listened with a wary politeness but, as time passed, his pleasant manner, command of the subject and reverential use of the Scriptures coaxed me out of this instinctive attitude. He and his Reformed counterpart also related to each other extremely well, as if they were friends who had lectured together before – a novel concept for me to get my Ulster head around. As we were preparing to leave for Amsterdam I thanked them for what I had learned, but was not confident enough to disclose the small changes happening inside me.

## Studentenekklesia

In Amsterdam, the Reformed and Catholic chaplains welcomed us to the university and showed us around a teeming campus. Our group was particularly intrigued by Studentenekklesia (Student Church), a highly successful initiative by the Catholic chaplains to capture the imagination of a new generation of young people who were drifting away from faith of any kind. To experience it for ourselves, they invited us to a student Mass at noon the following day.

Once again, this presented difficulties for me. I was almost 25 and had never set foot in a Catholic church. Moreover, the mere mention of "Mass" brought to the surface much of the anti-Catholic sentiment lodged deep within me. I was also anxious about what my fellow Orangemen and some of my evangelical peers back home might think if they discovered that I was breaking a much-venerated taboo. I came within inches of declining the invitation and walking away. But part of me felt uncomfortable at such a cowardly response. Why should I be cowed by the fear of what others thought? Should I have just meekly nodded in agreement at the hand-me-down interpretations of others when I had an opportunity to judge for myself what happens at Mass? Slowly my spirit tilted in favour of attending, albeit with a certain theological reservation.

When we entered the brightly-lit Dominicuskerk I explained to the group that I preferred to sit not in the body of the church with them but in a small, unoccupied gallery I had spotted. Thankfully they did not press me for an explanation. I made my way up to it and sat back to observe the scene below. Perched high in splendid isolation, I felt sad at being such a divided being – eager to explore the new horizons beckoning me, but equally feeling the pull of old loyalties.

By noon the church was full and the service got underway. It was led mostly by students: they made up the 20-piece orchestra and 30-member choir, as well as taking part in the Scripture readings and the offering of prayers from the lectern. When the young worshippers streamed forward to receive the Eucharist, priests in open-necked shirts offered them both bread and wine, a practice advocated by the Reformers. All aspects of the worship seemed bathed in beauty, prayerfulness and joy, and despite the language barrier I was drawn into its flow. The whole experience collided head-on with the negative slant on Mass instilled in me over the years – and, while differences of interpretation remained to be resolved, I wondered whether I had been looking down on the Catholic Church for too long.

Afterwards we enjoyed lunch with the students in the chaplaincy and I sensitively enquired about what they believed was happening inside themselves at the service. Their most common response could be summarised as follows: "We go forward to encounter Christ's love and receive him afresh into our lives." I began to recognise that despite the Herculean efforts of theologians to define how Christ engages us in Communion, this personal testimony captures its inherent dynamic. Light can shine through broken windows as well as inadequately framed theological definitions. Whether the Lord's Supper is celebrated in a Byzantine basilica, a Catholic cathedral, a Presbyterian meeting house or in the front room of a house-church in São Paulo, Christ always comes to meet us, just as he promised.

On return to the UK, I had little time to process all these new experiences. My mind was preoccupied with the start of the Easter term, my ordination was coming up in July, and Val and I were planning a wedding for Christmas. But there was one outstanding matter I needed to attend to before leaving Cambridge.

## Leaving the Orange Order

My lodge wanted to know if I was intending to march on 12 July, as I had done in the previous seven years. It took me time to clarify my thoughts. I was moving away from the Orange Order's view of the Catholic Church, and I also felt strongly that being ordained as a minister of the Gospel required a transparent loyalty to Christ alone, as well as an unqualified commitment to love all people. I did not want to be wearing an Orange vest under my clerical collar or to be attached to an organisation with robust political overtones. I therefore penned a letter of resignation, thanked the lodge members for their comradeship over the years and paid my outstanding dues. With that, the Orange phase of my life was over.

## A Call from Bangor

A week after returning to Belfast, I attended my home presbytery, the Presbytery of North Belfast, to receive a call from Hamilton Road Presbyterian Church, asking me to become their ordained assistant minister for the following two years. It was presented to me by the moderator, Rev Donald Gillies, the most astute and compelling anti-ecumenical spokesperson within our church. We knew about each other, mainly because we moved in the same evangelical circles. The straight-talking Scotsman was aware of my role as TSF representative in Assembly's College and of my progress through the presbytery towards ordination. He knew that I held him in high regard as a theologian and author because of the intellectual armoury with which he had provided me to justify my own anti-ecumenical convictions. But as he handed me the call and then proceeded to pray for me, he was totally unaware that I was undergoing change. Moreover, what none of us at the presbytery meeting had the slightest inkling of was that he too was in the process of re-examining his views. He had formed a thought-provoking friendship with an Irish Jesuit theologian and ecumenist, Fr Michael Hurley, and was engaged in a private dialogue with him about the issues on which he had written so convincingly.

With my ordination now just nine days away, I needed space to let the significance of it sink in, so I decided to set aside a day for a walk along the north-Down coastline. Sitting on the rocks looking over Belfast Lough, I recalled how eight years earlier, when some friends at Seaview had encouraged me as an 18-year-old to think about becoming a minister, I had laughed at the idea. Now, as I strolled along the coastal path, I knew that this was what I wanted to do with the rest of my life. On Sunday evening, 7 July 1968, I knelt before the Presbytery of Ards in Hamilton Road and felt the moderator's hands on my head invoking the Holy Spirit and ordaining me as a minister of the one, holy, catholic and apostolic church. I also felt enveloped in the affection of my family, friends and colleagues as they sang over me the Aaronic blessing from the Book of Numbers: "The Lord bless you and keep you. The Lord make his face to shine upon you and be gracious unto you. The Lord lift up his countenance upon you and give you peace."

The transition from Cambridge to Bangor was now complete and I could begin to pour my energies into what I looked forward to most – getting to know the members of a congregation of over 800 families, preparing sermons to encourage them in their faith, being mentored by the vastly experienced Rev David Burke, visiting hospitals, planning new initiatives with our youth leaders, and joining Bangor Rugby Club, one of Ulster's most successful teams.

## Settling into Married Life

On Friday, 27 December, in a Belfast blanketed with snow, Val and I were married in St John's Presbyterian Church, in the company of our parents, siblings, extended families and friends. We had packed so much into the previous six months that following the service and reception it felt great to be heading off directly to the international airport for two weeks in the warmth of Ibiza. We set up our first home in a small bungalow on the outskirts of Bangor and life returned, to some extent, to being pleasantly uncomplicated. We had busy but not-too-onerous jobs. In ten minutes Val could be at the Down County Welfare Offices in Newtownards, where she was employed as a social worker; I could be at church in five minutes. My "boss", Rev David Burke, was an invaluable and generous source of pastoral advice to me and also offered helpful feedback on my preaching.

The year 1969 flew in and by the summer of 1970 change was in the air. My MTh thesis for Queen's was accepted in May; in June Val announced that she was pregnant; and from July I was eligible for a call to a congregation of my own. Then, out of the blue, a letter arrived from Rev Cyril Young, the PCI's Convenor of Foreign Mission, who had just returned from a visit to the Christian Evangelical Church in Timor, Indonesia. Its membership was rising steadily towards the 1,000,000 mark and its 1,500 congregations were scattered across the islands of Timor, Semau, Rote, Savu, Alor and Pantar. In response to this rapid expansion, the Timor Church, in partnership with the Christian Church of Sumba, was launching a new theological college, Akademi Teologia Kupang, to train additional ministers. The academy was searching for a lecturer in New Testament Studies and an English teacher. Would we willing to consider it? We were flabbergasted.

Within minutes we had pinpointed Timor in an atlas, the last island of the Indonesian archipelago, 450 miles north-west of Australia, but it took several months before we felt sure it was the right step for us. We discussed the invitation with our families, and especially our parents. Though they were fully supportive of us, it was hard for them to hide their feelings of disappointment. They had naturally assumed we would settle down somewhere in Northern Ireland, which would allow us to continue sharing each other's lives, particularly with a new grandchild on the way. We also held extensive conversations with Rev Cyril Young about language-learning facilities, departure dates, accommodation and medical facilities in Timor and eventually wrote to the Mission Board declaring our intention to accept the appointments. However, with Val being pregnant, we wanted to wait until after the birth before finally confirming our decision. Our first child, Timothy, was born on Wednesday, 27 January 1971, in Belfast's Royal Maternity Hospital.

Leaving the hospital late that night, I went out into a bitingly cold wind and, with no one around, jumped with joy and punched the air at having become a dad. I hadn't noticed a cleaning lady who had nipped outside for a quiet smoke, but once I caught the whiff of her cigarette I turned around and she greeted me with a huge smile. I beamed back and headed home.

**Return to Holland**

The congregation of Hamilton Road hosted our commissioning service on Sunday evening, 27 June 1971, and within days we were *en route* to the Dutch Reformed Mission College near Leiden for orientation and language study. Over the next six months we learned all we could about Indonesia, "the emerald of the equator", the fourth-largest nation on earth (with 124 million inhabitants), home to the world's biggest Muslim community (111 million). It was an ideal location, for Indonesia had been a colony of Holland up until 1949. Our courses included The Theology of Mission, Coping with Culture-Shock, How to Stay Healthy in the Tropics and The Religions of Indonesia and the Story of the Church. Most of our time, however, went into learning the language with Dr FS Eringa. I recall the shock I got when translating for him parts of the Indonesian Bible and discovering that "God" was translated as "Allah"; I had always assumed this was an exclusively Islamic name for God. But the highlight of our week was undoubtedly the conversation classes with local Indonesians, whose melodic accents, facial expressions and hand gestures showed us that there was more to communication than finding the right words. We returned to Belfast in April 1972 to complete our final preparations for heading to Timor.

## Grim Farewell to Ireland

Gunfights between the IRA and the British Army had now become commonplace. The previous year the Ulster Unionist prime minister, Brian Faulkner, had introduced internment without trial and, in a one-sided swoop against the "men of violence", as they were known, the security forces had rounded up 342 republican suspects. On "Bloody Sunday", 30 January 1972, the British Army shot dead 14 unarmed civilians during a civil-rights march in Derry; in March the British prime minister, Edward Heath, dissolved the Northern Ireland government and introduced direct rule from Westminster. This came as a body blow to the unionist community. At night, as we lay in our beds in the mission house in south Belfast, we could hear gun battles raging two kilometres away in the west of the city. The situation seemed to be spiralling out of control. Then, the day before our departure, it suddenly got worse.

On Friday afternoon, 21 July, Belfast was bathed in sunshine, but an air of apprehension hung over the city. I drove into town to make some final purchases and walked quickly about my business from store to store. Then, suddenly, all hell broke loose. At 2.10 pm a car-bomb exploded nearby in Smithfield Bus Station and caused a stampede of shoppers and workers into the streets. Everyone started racing to the car parks and bus stops. Within 20 minutes, three more bombs rocked the inner city. All the roads out were blocked up with traffic or debris. It was like being trapped in a war zone under heavy artillery bombardment. I had inched my car into the northern end of Oxford Street, 300 metres from one of the busiest bus stations in the province. It was crammed with terrified men, women and children. Seconds later, at 2.38 pm, it was blasted to smithereens by a car-bomb driven into the rear of the station. My car shuddered under the impact and I found myself praying: "Lord, what can I do to stop this madness?" Thick smoke was billowing everywhere but it could not muffle the screaming and the crying. Nine people lost their lives and the one hundred and thirty who were injured were ferried quickly to the Accident and Emergency Departments of our local hospitals.

Over the next 45 minutes, a further 17 explosions blasted the city before an eerie silence finally descended around 3.30 pm. This heartless barbarity had been masterminded by the Belfast Brigade of the IRA in response to the collapse of secret talks with the UK government, which rejected their demands for a withdrawal from the province by 1975. "Bloody Friday" was their way of teaching the British a lesson. They had the capacity to turn Belfast and, by implication, London, into a theatre of war if they did not get their way.

When I finally got home around 4.00 pm I was shattered but also consumed with guilt. The next day we were leaving Ulster as it was lamenting its lost. I felt as if a chunk of moral shrapnel had ripped through the remaining layers of my detachment from the conflict and lodged itself in my conscience. I knew that some day I would get involved in doing something.

## Slow Journey East

After a three-week journey, with stops to visit serving PCI missionaries in Lebanon and India, we arrived in Jakarta before travelling on to Bali, the "Island of a Thousand Temples". After a four-day wait we boarded the Merpati Airways flight to Kupang Airport in Timor and, two hours later, caught our first glimpse of the island. It was dry, brown and desolate, like the surface of the moon. There to meet us were Rev Andreas Yewangoe, principal of the Academy and Rev Homo Reenders, a Dutch missionary, and their families. Within ten minutes we were pulling into the new college with its shining white bungalows, dormitories and teaching block. The Reenders family hosted a reception for us, during which they gently broke the news that our bungalow, just opposite, was not finished. The college faculty had decided, therefore, that after a few days of rest we should travel inland for one month's orientation among the Atoni Pah Meto, the "People of the Dry Land", who constituted the largest ethnic group in the church.

The academy was a joint initiative between the Christian Evangelical Church in Timor (GMIT) and its smaller partner, the Christian Church of Sumba (GKS). When the GKS gained its autonomy from Dutch missionary control in 1947, its membership stood at 5,000 out of a population of 250,000, but by 1970 it had risen to 200,000. The first batch of ministerial students from both churches, 30 young men and women, had been received in September 1971 to undertake a three-year Bachelor of Arts degree in Theology. The GKS provided two lecturers: Rev Yewangoe (Systematic Theology) and Rev Reenders (Church History). GMIT supplied a Dutch Reformed missionary, Rev Kees Oppelaar (Old Testament) and me (New Testament).

## Life at the Academy

Our principal, Rev Yewangoe, was a gifted administrator and ensured that the college was well managed. Lectures began promptly at 8.00 am and finished at noon, when concentration levels faded in the heat. Between 4.00 pm and sunset at 6.00 pm everyone relaxed and then, after dinner, the campus would fall silent for private study until the generator was switched off at 10.00 pm. In January 1973 Val and I began our teaching. I delivered two lectures each day from Monday to Friday, while Val taught three English-language classes per week. Preparing ten new lectures per week was gruelling, but my fluency in Indonesian improved rapidly. With the commencement of the academy's second academic year in 1972, our numbers reached 60, 30 per cent of whom were young women. It started me wondering why no women had yet been ordained in our own church at home.

As I taught through the New Testament curriculum I became intrigued by those passages of Scripture that awakened an instant interest in our students – genealogies, healings, sacrifices, curses and blessings. For example, when we were studying the death of Christ in the context of the Jewish sacrificial system, it prompted floods of questions about the details of ritual slaughter. "Some of our village elders who follow the old ways still perform these kinds of sacrifices," they would exclaim. In the light of their comments I set them summer research projects designed to explore the connections between *agama asli* (the original animistic religion of their ethnic groups) and the teaching of Christianity. This involved them interviewing the guardians of these rituals, who still lived in communities where churches had now been built. These assignments were the most pertinent I ever set, but they also raised big questions. If the Jewish sacrificial system foreshadowed the sacrifice of Christ, had the creator of all humankind left any glimmers of his love, forgiveness and mercy in the shadows of other faiths? Paul's speech in the Acts of the Apostles to the devoutly religious Athenians took on a new light: "God is actually not far from any one of us … 'In him we live and move and exist'" (Acts 17:27–8).

At weekends most of our students headed home, leaving the rest hanging around the campus with little to do. Sundays could be particularly long and boring once worship in our village church at Oesapa was over at 10.30 am. On the Sunday following the arrival of our new jeep, we let it be known that we were going for a swim after church and if anyone would like to join us they would be welcome. A queue quickly formed outside our front door. We squeezed everyone in and headed off to one or other of the magnificent sandy beaches close to the academy. On one occasion we arrived to find students from a local Catholic college in Kupang playing football under the supervision of an Indonesian priest. He invited us to join in and we did so with great enthusiasm. It became a regular fixture for us and a great way to make new friends. Many of the students had never had a conversation with a Catholic priest or a Protestant minister before, never mind playing soccer on the same side as one. After the game we would all splash around in the waves and then dry off, sitting side by side on logs, chatting away under the palm trees.

## Ireland Meets in Oesapa

One day in April 1973 we were having our normal afternoon siesta when we heard a knock at the front door around 4.30 pm. Val got up and answered it. From a distance I heard "Dundalk" mentioned several times and then some bursts of laughter.

"Hello!" the stranger began. "I'm Noel Carroll from Dundalk. I believe there are three Irish Presbyterians living here. I've heard that one of you was brought up in Dundalk." Noel (then aged 31) was a missionary with the Society of the Divine Word; he had arrived in Timor two years before us and had been appointed by Bishop Manteiro as parish priest in the remote village of Putain. He had driven for six hours down to the coast to meet us. Val introduced him to Tim and me, and the two of them chatted excitedly about the places and people they knew in Dundalk. He stayed for dinner and became a regular guest. We loved to see him coming. Often, after dinner, as Val got Tim ready for bed, he and I would sit outside in the cool of the patio and talk until the lights went out. Gradually our friendship deepened as we began to understand something of the loneliness of a single man living in the mountains and the strength of his commitment to parishioners whose daily lives were overshadowed by poverty. He struck us as a male version of Mother Teresa of Calcutta.

Noel was an avid student of Scripture, who had studied Theology in Ireland at St Patrick's College, Maynooth, before being ordained in 1970. Many of our early discussions, therefore, were about the Bible, but eventually we got around to the more sensitive terrain of the differences between Protestants and Catholics. At times he would correct my perceptions of Catholicism, and I would rectify his observations on Protestantism. These wholesome exchanges convinced me that the only way to understand another person's faith is through direct contact – not from a safe and polemical distance. It was sad that we had to get out of Ireland to find the space and opportunity to do this.

I often wondered why Noel and I got on so well. Was it just because we were Irish people thrown together in a strange land? Perhaps, but I don't think that is the complete answer. The real reason was that we had come to see each other not as religious opponents but as brothers in Christ. That crucial discovery affected also how we viewed each other's churches – not as sub-Christian offshoots of the church, but as fully participating branches of the one, holy, catholic and apostolic church of Christ. By 1975 I had reached a conviction, soon to find expression at the Second National Evangelical Congress in Nottingham (1977), chaired by Dr John Stott: "Seeing ourselves and Roman Catholics as fellow Christians, we repent of attitudes that have seemed to deny it."

Those late-night conversations instilled in my mind something else – the idea of one day developing in Belfast the same kind of friendship with a priest that I had enjoyed in Timor. I knew it could be controversial as well as difficult, given the reactionary nature of Ulster's religious culture and the unresolved political conflict and violence. But in the cool sea breezes of an Oesapa evening, such dreams seemed a long way off.

## Brave New Initiative

Indonesian Christians are acutely conscious of being a small minority in a country that is 85 per cent Muslim. As a result, they view cooperation between the Christian churches within Indonesia and beyond as eminently desirable. The Second Vatican Council, with its openness to other Christian traditions, intensified that instinct even further. In June 1974, our faculty discussed the possibility of developing a lecturer and student exchange programme with St Paul's Catholic Seminary at Ledelaro on the island of Flores, 200 miles north-west of Timor. As it happened, I had already planned to travel to Flores in August as part of the Kupang City football team, which was taking part in a regional soccer competition in Maumere, the capital of Flores. St Paul's was located in the hills, 20 kilometres outside the city. In correspondence with the president of the seminary our principal had received a positive response to our initiative and dispatched me to discuss the details of the exchange with their faculty.

The landscaped setting of St Paul's Seminary with the tall Kapela Agung (Solemn Church) at the centre of the campus was a breathtaking sight. The German president and three Polish priests welcomed me and gave me a quick tour of their facilities before getting down to business. They were all missionaries with the Society of the Divine Word. When I was explaining to them that our academy was the result of cooperation between the Reformed Churches of Timor, Sumba, the Netherlands and Ireland, I mentioned that I was a minister of the PCI. Some eyebrows were raised, for in the Indonesian media the conflict in Northern Ireland was depicted as a religious war in which extremist Protestants were persecuting Catholics. I took a moment to describe the complexity of our situation at home, and then mentioned that one of their own order, Fr Noel Carroll, was one of my closest friends in Timor. They breathed a sigh of relief and relaxed.

After an extensive discussion we agreed to set up a month-long exchange programme each year involving a lecturer and up to three students from each institution. We hoped that the long-term benefit of such a programme would be that trainee ministers and priests would get to know each other as friends and in their future parishes work together to reduce the inherited distance between the Christian churches of south-east Indonesia.

When we considered the areas of expertise we could offer each other, St Paul's requested help with Biblical Studies, in which they felt we were traditionally strong, while our faculty had already pinpointed Christian Philosophy and Apologetics as one the strengths of St Paul's. Finally, we agreed that we should get the exchange underway in February 1975, but before that we needed to report back to our respective faculties and receive the approval of our church leaders.

When I submitted my report to our principal and faculty, they agreed unanimously to the initiative. Then, to my surprise, they decided that I should return to Flores and deliver the first course of lectures on the New Testament. Unfortunately, it took longer than anticipated to get the approval of the Sumba and Timor churches, but when it did come through in May 1975 it was wholehearted. Unfortunately our time in Timor was fast running out. Val was six months pregnant and we needed to be on a flight home for our furlough before she exceeded the permitted travel limit for an expectant mother. I was disappointed not to be able to see the project get off the ground. Shortly afterwards our principal travelled to Flores and launched it with lectures on Systematic Theology.

Remarkably, some of those who benefitted from the exchange have gone on to extend its influence even further. In 2007, on the island of Flores, a Catholic priest and a minister of the Christian Evangelical Church of Timor set up a joint project in which 38 trainee priests spent a week living and worshipping with families of the local Protestant congregation. When interviewed about it, they said, "We hope this activity lets the whole church in Flores, and throughout the whole world, know that we are one in faith, hope and love."

## Controversy within the PCI

The milder Christian climate prevailing among the churches in south-east Indonesia seemed a million miles away from the increasing tensions around ecumenism within Irish Presbyterianism. Once again, our membership of the WCC was due to be debated at the General Assembly in June. A few weeks before leaving Timor I received a letter from one of the leaders of the pro-WCC group within the PCI, asking if I would write a letter supporting membership of the WCC from the perspective of Timor. I was happy to do so and in my letter offered four reasons. Firstly, the clear teaching of Christ mandates us to strengthen the bonds of cooperation with other Christians, not to sever them. Secondly, our partner churches overseas in India, Africa, the Caribbean and Timor play an active part in the global Christian fellowship of the WCC and view it as a blessing, not a threat. Thirdly, several ministry students at our academy were receiving WCC scholarships, which enabled them, in a poverty-ravaged community, to access theological education. Finally, I recounted my experience of standing at the largest harbour in Timor, watching tonnes of emergency food supplies being hoisted onto trucks for transportation to the central mountains during a critical period of famine. The sacks were marked "CWS" (Church World Service, USA) – a partner agency of the WCC.

I was conscious when posting my letter from Timor that, when Rev David Lapsley made reference to it during the assembly debate, some of my evangelical colleagues would be surprised at my reversal of attitude. Yet I knew that the time had come for me to be open about what I believed, rather than to play games of charades just to win approval. I hoped that we would all be mature enough to continue to value each other's friendship and affirm each other's ministries as before.

## A Welcome Furlough

When Val, Tim and I arrived in Timor in August 1972, only the Yewangoe and Reenders families had been there to meet us. Now, at the end of May 1975, 30 of our friends accompanied us to the airport. We watched them wave as our flight taxied for take-off and we returned their goodbyes. We had grown to love them. Without their support we would have found Timor much more testing. As the plane climbed into the clear blue sky and the now-familiar shoreline disappeared, I remember praying: "Lord, it will be great to come back here in six months' time. Our language has improved, our effectiveness as teachers has increased and we feel more at home in ourselves and in Timor. We'll be able to give you a better three years when Val and I return with our two children."

Without a doubt, Timor had changed me for good, by stretching the horizons of my heart and mind in ways that were to shape me for the rest of my life. We learned more than we ever taught, and we received more than we gave. I now felt more fully part of the worldwide human family and more deeply connected to the universal and vibrantly diverse church of Christ. The cramping boundaries of my past were giving way to bridges that I was no longer hesitant to cross. In the remoteness of Timor, God prepared me for the challenges of being a minister of Christ in my own home town.

CHAPTER THREE

# Settling In and Holding On: Fitzroy 1976–83

The journey in May 1975 from Timor to Bali, Bali to Singapore, Singapore to London and finally London to Belfast was long and tiring, especially for Val, who was well over six months pregnant. When our plane touched down at Belfast International Airport, a welcome party of family and friends was there to meet us. It was great to be home again, even though it would only be for a short time. The Overseas Board made available to us a mission residence in east Belfast, where kindly neighbours invited us to their homes for coffee. Local children were keen to meet Tim, who chatted to them in a mixture of Indonesian and English. It was a relaxing summer for us as we eased back into the generosity and hospitality of our families.

On Tuesday, 12 August Val was admitted to the Royal Maternity Hospital. Two days later we experienced the inexpressible joy of holding in our arms another baby – this time a daughter, Jennie. As we were preparing to leave the hospital, two consultant paediatricians called us into their office. The screening procedures for all newborns had picked up some medical complications that needed to be closely monitored. "Under no circumstances," they advised, "should you return to Timor." We sat motionless on our chairs, stunned. We knew it was the right course of action for us as a family, but it was still with a heavy heart that we sat down a few days later and wrote letters of resignation to the Overseas Board and the Theological Academy in Timor.

Prior to a preaching engagement in Great Victoria Street Presbyterian Church in mid-September, Rev Harold Graham phoned to talk over the service and casually enquired about when we were returning to Indonesia. I explained to him briefly the reasons why the doctors had advised us against it. Unknown to me, he was the convenor of a vacancy in Fitzroy Presbyterian Church, and a few days later he was on the phone again asking if I would consider a call to Fitzroy. I asked whether I could get back to him in a few weeks – we were still struggling with all the changes that had engulfed us. After a lot of discussion with Val, we decided to pursue the invitation. I phoned Harold to confirm my interest.

At the end of September we were interviewed by a group from Fitzroy led by the clerk of session, Frank Jenkins, and the congregational secretary, Harold McCollum. They gave us an overview of the history of the congregation since 1813 and how it had recently integrated into its life two neighbouring churches that had sadly had to close – Donegall Pass (closed in 1973) and the Crescent (closed in 1975). They spoke affectionately of Rev Roy Alexander, who had retired after 32 years and was bequeathing to a successor a very large and united congregation of 600 families. The ethos of Fitzroy was evangelical, they explained, but not in a narrow sense.

Saying yes proved easy. The warmth of the delegation and the profile of the church attracted us. In time the congregation issued me with a unanimous call to be their minister; it was processed through the Presbytery of South Belfast and a date was set for my installation – Thursday, 15 January 1976.

To sit in the beautiful sanctuary of Fitzroy, surrounded by our families and close friends, was an affirming experience. But I was worried about Val. Ten days earlier she had been admitted to the Fever Hospital with malaria and the doctors had only given her permission to attend the installation provided she returned immediately afterwards. The service was followed by several light-hearted and generous speeches; as was customary, the final one was reserved for the new minister. I expressed our thanks that the people of Fitzroy and then reflected on the challenge of ministry in the city:

> We feel honoured to be associated with a congregation so steeped in the history of Belfast. Bishop Stephen Neill insists that a Christian undergoes three conversions: to Christ, to his church and to his world. First of all, the faith of Fitzroy will be continually refreshed as we drink together from the river of grace that flows from the Risen Christ. Secondly, he calls us to cherish his whole church and to invest ourselves in the local manifestation of it to which we belong. Thirdly, he orientates us to be outward-looking in embracing the world for which he gave his life. Our primary arena of mission, therefore, is this parish – where murders occur in University Street and bombs go off in Rugby Road. In the sound

of the explosions and in the lament of the suffering let us together
listen for the voice of Christ pleading with us to work for peace.

The prayer I made on Bloody Friday in 1972, when caught up in the Oxford
Street Bus Station bombing before leaving for Indonesia, was still working its
way through me, but living it out on the streets around Fitzroy was going to
require a lot of sensitivity. Furthermore, my core faith was no longer couched
in the polarised categories of Ulster evangelicalism. In Timor it had become
integrated around being evangelical (treasuring Christ's Gospel) and
ecumenical (embracing Christ's one, holy, catholic and apostolic church). I
saw no contradiction in holding both perspectives together.

My first task was to get to know our 600 families, many of whom were
elderly. I spent an inordinate amount of time each week visiting Belfast's
three main hospitals and numerous nursing homes. But underneath my
excitement at forming new friendships was a gnawing grief at the collapse of
our plans to return to Timor. For months I would walk through the beautiful
old church or sit quietly in its empty pews, wrestling with dark moods that
stifled my capacity to bond with the place. Val and I talked a lot together, but
looking back, I wish I had sought professional counselling. I had buried my
distress behind an all-concealing smile. In addition, I was finding it difficult,
like many returning missionaries, to squeeze back into the religio-political
mould of Ulster culture. When I decided not to let that happen to me, I
began picking up a sense of suspicion from those who seemed to carry its
prevailing assumptions.

It wasn't until the summer of 1976 that I began to appreciate the skilful
way in which Rev Alexander had woven together the three strands of Fitzroy,
Donegall Pass and the Crescent. The congregation's form of spirituality
expressed itself through traditional Presbyterian worship, a commitment to
local evangelism and world mission and strong support for humanitarian
causes. But alongside these strengths were also reasons for concern. Our
youth organisations, especially the Boys' Brigade and Girls' Brigade, had
dedicated leaders but numbers were dropping. Our Kirk Session consisted of
35 elders, all men, with many closer to 70 years of age than 30; and half of our
600 families were non-attending, through either age, infirmity or habitual
disconnection. I seemed to spend my first year burying people: I conducted
35 funerals and started having premonitions of a "for-sale" notice going up
outside Fitzroy in 25 years' time.

When I voiced these concerns at Kirk-session meetings, some elders thought I was being unnecessarily alarmist, but I could not help noticing a real dearth of creative alternatives. I wondered whether the large numbers on our books were inducing a false sense of security or whether, perhaps, some felt depressed after having presided over two church closures. Privately, I dreaded the prospect of ever having to officiate at the funeral of this calm and beautiful congregation. So, in order to tip the balance in the direction of hope, I kept repeating to myself the mantra, "God has not invested the life of his Son in the death of the church." I also set myself to preach chronologically through the four Gospels, convinced that exposure to the total range of Christ's life would revitalise ours. Apart from an occasional hiatus to celebrate Christmas, Holy Week, Easter and Pentecost, I pursued this goal throughout my first ten years in Fitzroy.

## The Peace Movement

In the summer of 1976 a tragedy occurred that affected me very deeply. On Tuesday, 10 August, Anne Maguire was walking along Finaghy Road North in Belfast with her three children when a car driven by an IRA man veered out of control and plunged into them. It claimed the lives of six-week-old baby Andrew in his pram, two-year-old John by her side and eight-year-old Joanne on her bicycle. Anne's sister, Mairéad Corrigan, described on television the devastation inflicted on the extended Maguire family and made an impassioned plea for the violence to end. Within a week the Northern Ireland Peace Movement was born. Thousands from both sides of the community poured onto the streets to reassert their togetherness and to reaffirm the sacredness of human life. Over the next few months I joined them on the marches. I kept scanning through the sea of faces around me, looking for other evangelical colleagues, but they were disappointingly few in number. I was mystified, especially in the light of the words of Christ in Matthew's Gospel: "Blessed are the peacemakers: for they shall be called the children of God." I was pleasantly surprised, however, to meet up with Rev Donald Gillies of Agnes Street Presbyterian Church, one of the PCI's most competent evangelical thinkers. We enjoyed each other's company on the long and sometimes hazardous marches through areas where angry residents hurled abuse, rocks and flour-bombs at us to let us know we were not welcome. Many of the other ministers I met on the marches had also worked overseas.

When the Peace Movement organised itself into regional street meetings, the Presbyterian Community Centre became the venue for our parish area, known affectionately as the Holyland. In September 20 members of Fitzroy joined me for meetings hosted by Rev John Morrow, the PCI chaplain at Queen's University. Among the 70 local people who turned up were Rev Sydney Smart, the Anglican rector of All Saints Parish Church, Rev Robert Clarke of Rugby Avenue Congregational Church and Fr Denis Newberry, the 30-year-old curate in St Malachy's Catholic Church.

I quickly realised that I had an important decision to make. Fitzroy would have no difficulty developing relationships with All Saints and Rugby Avenue, but cultivating a friendship with Fr Newberry and St Malachy's Catholic Church was an altogether different matter. It would involve crossing a religious boundary that would inevitably expose me to serious criticism. In Timor such friendships were natural – and indeed encouraged – but in Ulster the e-word ("ecumenical") was viewed as a threat to traditional Protestant values. I took time, therefore, to think clearly through the consequences of my actions. Was this a God-given opportunity to share my life with a priest as I had done in Timor? Or should I back off from living such a spiritually inclusive lifestyle out of fear? The more I entered the deep silences of my spirit, the more the voice within, which I took to be Christ's, remained clear and persistent: "You can't change your country, but you can change your own lifestyle. Go for it!" I finally yielded to this inward prompting and one morning, a few days later, I walked the 75 metres down Magdala Street, which is adjacent to Fitzroy, and rang the doorbell of Fr Newberry's house. A most pleasant friendship developed between us that resulted in some groundbreaking initiatives in our area.

The most visible of these was the Holyland's first ever united Christmas carol service – led by all five local clergy – which took place on Sunday afternoon, 19 December 1976. We had to hold it outdoors and down by the River Lagan because the churches were not yet ready to host such an overtly cross-community event. Nevertheless, we flooded the community with posters and, despite the incessant rain and bitingly cold winds, around a hundred local people turned up and sang their hearts out. We conducted the service from the back of a lorry. I could not help but smile at the encouraging signs of unity unfolding before our eyes – Belfast Protestants and Catholics clustering together under large umbrellas to keep each other dry and huddling closer to keep each other warm. The miserable weather made us determined to come up with something better in 1977.

## Affirmation

As part of the pastoral oversight of the 25 churches under its care, the Presbytery of South Belfast would visit each congregation once every seven years to conduct an audit of its life. In March 1977 they came to Fitzroy and one month later presented their finding to the congregation. It was very affirming, even though I had only been in Fitzroy for 15 months:

> Today more than ever the Church is being challenged by the mission field on its door-step and by the necessity for evangelism and community reconciliation. We need to develop the courage to become the Sign of the Gospel we preach – the Sign that in Christ men and women from different political and religious traditions become brothers and sisters. In his attempts to lead the new Fitzroy along this road the new Minister is assured of Presbytery's support. But we also echo the concern of your Kirk Session that the Church will die if we stand still.

## Hint of Unease

By the summer of 1977 I detected some disquiet over my friendship with Fr Newberry, mainly among a few rank-and-file members of the congregation who had connections with the Orange Order or had been brought up with anti-Catholic attitudes. On a sunny Monday morning, as I was walking into Belfast, I bumped into one of the senior citizens who lived in the parish area. After exchanging the normal pleasantries, she seized the moment.

"Reverend Newell, we've gone off you! I've seen you going into a priest's house."

"That's right," I replied. "We're friends. We drink coffee, chat, pray together, and plan some joint initiatives for the area. Wouldn't Christ do the same if he lived in Belfast?"

She went quiet for a moment, smiled courteously, looked up at the sky and said, "It's getting a bit overcast, isn't it?" With that we wished each other well and headed off in different directions.

## Breakthrough at Christmas

After nearly two years in Fitzroy I asked the Kirk Session if we could host the second community carol service on Sunday, 18 December 1977. With the support of some prominent elders already involved with me in the street

My maternal grandparents William and Alice Redmond, Belmullet, Co Mayo.

Our family: *(standing l-r)* dad, mum, uncle John Walker, *(front row)* Margaret, Ken, Audrey and cousin at John's farm near Richill, 1948.

Wedding of my father and mother in St Saviour's Church of Ireland Parish Church, Portadown, 26 September 1934.

Val's parents, Harold and Renee Richie, with their children *(l-r)* Billy, Janice and Val, Dundalk, 1951.

Seaview Primary School football team – winners of Schools Cup in 1955 *(second row standing fourth from right)*.

Belfast High School Chess team *(top, standing third from left)* and 1st XV Rugby Team *(bottom, standing fourth from right)* in 1961.

Ministry students, Faculty and Staff at the Presbyterian College, Belfast, 1967 *(first row standing, sixth from right)*.

Ridley Hall, Cambridge, Faculty and Anglican Ministry Students *(first row standing, extreme right)*.

Val and Ken, Graduation Day, Queen's University Belfast, 1968.

Wedding Day 27 December 1968: *(l-r)* Harold Richie, Evelyn Newell, Roger Maggs, Maud Hoey, Ken, Val, Janice Richie, Reverend Sam Millar, Renee Richie, Norman Newell.

Wedding Day 27 December 1968, at Conway Hotel, Dunmurry.

Hamilton Road Presbyterian, Bangor: Robin's Display 1969. Striking a few chords with a youthful singer.

Bangor 3A Rugby Team, winners of Harden Cup at Ravenhill, 1970 *(standing fourth from left)*.

Timor, Indonesia, 1972. Val with Tim outside our college bungalow.

Central Timor, Indonesia, 1973. Ken and local Catholic Nursing Sister visit one of Timor's regional kings.

Central Timor, Indonesia, 1973. Ken with Elders and Evangelists of the Christian Evangelical Church in Timor at a training conference.

Central Timor, Indonesia, 1973. Local families and children of the Timor Church come to see what's going on at the conference.

Ballymena Presbytery, 1975: Ken visits local church to introduce the work of PCI in Indonesia.

Ken installed as Minister of Fitzroy Presbyterian Church, Belfast, January, 1976 and robed by Mrs Nell Jenkins and Mrs Norah Lowry.

Fitzroy Presbyterian Church shortly after its opening in 1874.

Fr Denis Newberry, a Curate in St Malachy's Catholic Church, became a close friend and colleague in Northern Ireland Peace Movement, 1976.

1978: After a Children's Address in Fitzroy about making tea, Ken and Val were interviewed by the Belfast Telegraph and their photograph appeared on the front page.

Granny Newell celebrates another birthday with Audrey, Ken and Margaret, 1984.

A frequent winter scene at the manse in Maryville Park, Belfast BT9.

World Cup 1982: Ken and Val meet the Northern Ireland team at Zaragoza Airport, Spain. Martin O'Neill surprises Tim and Jennie by giving them his tracksuit.

1983: David 'Packie' Hamilton (UVF) *(front row third from right)* and Liam McCloskey (INLA) *(front left of Ken)*, preaching at the Morning Service in Fitzroy with James McIlroy, Director of Prison Fellowship NI *(front row fourth from right)*.

Falls Road peaceline, 1983: Argentine Evangelist Luis Palau *(left)* tours West Belfast with Ken and Fr George Wadding, Rector of Clonard Monastery *(right)*.

1984: Bishop Desmond Tutu pays the first of two visits to Fitzroy. *(l-r)* Jonathan Bradford (USA), Graeme Fowles (Youth Worker) and Mary Seeger (USA volunteer).

1987: Ken and Fr Gerry speaking at Corrymeela Summerfest.

1991: A Political Dialogue Evening in Fitzroy with *(l-r)* Ken Maginnis (Ulster Unionist), Dr John Alderdice (Alliance), and Mark Durkan (SDLP).

September 1992: Some of the Presbyterian members of the Clonard–Fitzroy Fellowship meet with President Mary Robinson in Aras an Uachtarain, Phoenix Park, Dublin.

meetings, it was agreed. Once again, we publicised the event widely in the area. This time 400 people turned up and threw themselves heart and soul into the celebration. What encouraged me most was that a third of those who came belonged to Fitzroy; their presence boosted the expanding core of those members who believed that our witness should include a reconciliation dimension. Many of those at the service hoped that the elusive peace for which we all longed might be somewhere close on the horizon. The murder rate had been dropping and Mairéad Corrigan and Betty Williams, the founders of the Peace Movement, had recently been awarded the 1976 Nobel Peace Prize.

But away from these scenes of international recognition, another tragedy was unfolding. Mairéad Corrigan's sister Anne could take no more. The incident that engendered the Peace Movement had left her physically and psychologically damaged. "In her own mind," Mairéad was later to write, "she refused to accept the deaths of her three children and often talked about seeing them playing in the back garden. Their deaths and the brain-bruising she suffered resulted in psychotic depression. She seemed to lock herself in a private world with her dead babies." In January 1980, Anne took her own life.

The annual united Christmas services took a significant step forward in 1982, when Fr Newberry invited us all to St Malachy's. The participation of a hundred schoolchildren from Presbyterian, Catholic, Methodist and Church of Ireland backgrounds captured a headline in the *Belfast Telegraph*: "Children Get Together in Prayer for Peace". "I believe we should be coming together all year round, not just at Christmas," Fr Newberry told the *Telegraph*. "We should not forget our own identities, but we are called to love and respect each other; we hold much more in common than what divides us."

Sadly, this was his last involvement with us before being transferred to a parish in south Down. One of the long-term consequences of the united services was that increasing numbers of Catholic residents in the parish would stop me on the street and talk with me. They had begun to view the other local churches not as spiritual no-go areas but as friendship zones where they would experience a warm welcome. Fr Newberry's departure saw our links with St Malachy's fade until the arrival of Fr Anthony Curran as parish priest in 1997, but our cooperation with All Saints and Rugby Avenue continued to deepen.

## Gender and Leadership

An issue that had been simmering for a decade arose in the Kirk Session in 1978 – the legitimacy of women sharing equally with men in the ordained leadership of the church. Several elders were now too old to fulfil their responsibilities and it was agreed that we needed to bring in some new blood. But what should we do, it was asked, if women were chosen? At the previous election in 1969, long before my arrival, some highly respected women were voted for by the congregation in significant numbers. The all-male Kirk Session, however, had blocked their path to ordination by six votes to five, despite the 1928 ruling of the General Assembly that women were eligible for election "on the same basis as men". This time round the elders sought my advice. I recommended that we proceed to ordain whomever the congregation decided to nominate. Only one of the twenty-one elders dissented.

In October 1978 the Presbytery of South Belfast returned to ordain six new elders, two of whom were outstandingly loyal women, Molly Duncan and Renee Pelan. I was delighted and became much more vocal within the PCI whenever the issue of the ordination of women as ministers and elders reared its head. Sadly, progress on the matter has been snail-like in the face of a re-energised conservatism within the PCI that appeals to a selection of biblical proof-texts – often, in my opinion, divorced from their context in an ancient world where the role of women was much more restricted than is the case today. As a result, the appeal of the ministry to gifted Presbyterian women who are used to an ethos of equality in the workplace and at home has dimmed. Equally serious is the restriction this conservatism places on the reservoir of talented leadership available to a denomination now experiencing decline for reasons sometimes of its own making.

## Colliding Musical Cultures

By the end of 1978, a momentum for change was building up in Fitzroy. I believed that if we were to attract more young people to the church we had to create forms of worship more culturally attuned to them, rather than always to expect them to adapt to the traditional forms being used Sunday upon Sunday. The renewal movement, which had spread across Ireland during the 1970s, had brought with it a gentle beauty and fervour in worship which had felt like a breath of fresh air. Its appeal to teenagers and those in their twenties and thirties was evident. New songs were being sung to the accompaniment of violins, cellos, flutes, clarinets, drums, guitars and saxophones.

With the help of our organist, Marie Crawford, I started introducing some renewal-style music into Fitzroy. But it proved more difficult than we had imagined and drew fire from those who preferred only organ-led music and psalms and hymns selected exclusively from the *Presbyterian Hymn Book*. When a musical group made up of Fitzroy students armed with guitars sought to lead the congregation in singing, a determined silence ensued. The young people felt embarrassed. Then, in August 1978, Chris Blake, a young, classically trained English musician, turned up out of the blue at one of our evening services. He had recently got a job with the Ulster Orchestra. In time he became involved with the group and its musical quality steadily improved. But the rumblings in the choir continued and some members refused to sing when the group was playing. When we met to discuss our concerns I explained that my goal was to strike a balance between traditional and contemporary forms of worship, but given the ageing profile of Fitzroy it was crucial to draw younger people into the life of the church. Some did not want to follow me down that road and sadly went elsewhere.

At the same time as things were unravelling in Fitzroy, another impetus towards renewal was making itself felt nearby. Rev David Lapsley of Fisherwick Presbyterian Church had invited Canon David Watson of York, England, to lead a "week of festival" in March 1979. His talented parish musical team from St Michael le Belfrey played a prominent role in the worship, which came as a surge of spiritual refreshment to mostly younger Christians of all branches of the church who were, in varying degrees, wearied by formality and traditionalism. Ireland was just one destination in Watson's international mission to promote reconciliation and renewal on five continents. His other destinations included South Africa, Canada, the USA, New Zealand and Australia. He had come to Belfast at a time when the city was gripped with fear. The previous month a former prison officer and his wife had been shot dead by the IRA at their home on the Oldpark Road; and 11 members of the notorious loyalist gang, the Shankill Butchers, had just been sentenced to life imprisonment for 112 offences, including 19 sectarian murders. The crowds that packed into Fisherwick night after night were a testimony to the courage of ordinary people longing to find a way through the morass of violence.

Canon David Watson's appeal lay in the fact that everything he sought to communicate flowed from his integration of evangelical passion, ecumenical inclusivity, charismatic openness and a vision for peace. I immediately recognised in him the same strands of conviction that had been woven together in me over the previous seven years. Furthermore, his journey into this position parallelled my own. He was almost 40 when he found himself, in 1971, guest speaker at the international Fountain Trust conference in Guildford, Surrey. The other speaker happened to be a popular Catholic theologian. The evangelical environment in which the young Watson had come to faith had instilled in him the idea that Catholicism was an aberration to be avoided. At the conference he was surprised how much he had in common with his Catholic counterpart and gradually he grew to respect the new reality he was discovering. After Guildford, he started building bridges towards believers in other branches of the church that affirmed the same core beliefs as his own Christian orthodoxy – but this landed him in hot water. Some of his more stringent evangelical colleagues accused him of being a lily-livered compromiser. In time he realised that he was part of something new and deeply significant that was happening within British Christianity and that a whole swathe of Anglican evangelicalism was moving in a similar direction. Meeting him at Fisherwick, therefore, assured me that I was not some kind of spiritual oddity or evangelical maverick. It also allowed me to discover that he had studied at Ridley Hall a decade before I arrived!

Perhaps his strongest appeal to ministers in their thirties, like me, was his belief in church growth. From his own experience as a parish minister he had become convinced that the Holy Spirit could reverse the decline of the church in the face of advancing secularism. He had seen it happen. When he was assigned to St Michael le Belfrey Parish in York it had been facing imminent closure, with an elderly congregation of less than 20 worshippers. Through sheer faith, a lot of patience and the courage to get out into the community, he had turned it into a vibrant congregation of several hundred active members. Given Fitzroy's background, having lived through the trauma of closure, his story filled me with hope. I listened to him with rapt attention, distracted only by the depressing realisation that perhaps Fitzroy was drifting towards the rocks.

**Low Point**
The rumbles of discontent building up over reconciliation and worship came to a head between November 1979 and September 1980. After a series of difficult session meetings, 7 of our 29 elders resigned and 12 families left the congregation. Before their departure I visited their homes to thank them for

all they had put into Fitzroy over the years and to pray with them. I knew that their decision to leave was not easy; stepping away from a congregation they had loved and faithfully served was like bereavement. My inability to hold on to people of such quality churned up within me currents of self-doubt and feelings of failure. Friends urged me not to take it so personally, but that was impossible. I was the minister and inching forward slowly was still too fast for some.

For months I lost sight of the positive things happening around me. Of the elders, 75 per cent were still supportive of my ministry. Half of our congregation was keen to move forward, one quarter being resistant and a further quarter being unsure what to think. Affecting our situation may also have been the growing sense of insecurity within the unionist community. In 1978 the Irish prime minister, Jack Lynch, had called on the British government to issue a "declaration of intent" to withdraw from Northern Ireland. Threatened by a seemingly united Irish nationalism, and under siege from an IRA responsible for 104 of the 125 deaths in 1979, it is not surprising that peacemaking was viewed negatively among many unionists.

Within Fitzroy, however, there was nothing more I could do except relinquish my longing to see change and turn the clock back to where we all had been in January 1976. But that would mean disappointing those who had weighed in behind the leadership I was trying to give. Caught between a rock and a hard place, I felt like I was sinking, like the disciples in the boat with Jesus during the tempest on Lake Galilee. The lure of milder climes proved increasingly tempting. Should I apply for a congregation down south, or transfer to the Church of Scotland or the United Reformed Church in England? Should I suppress who I really was and just fit into what people expected? My spirit was clogged up with guilt.

To make matters worse, my father died suddenly on 17 September 1981 as he was walking home after visiting some former work colleagues in the Ulster Transport Depot. His death came as a devastating blow to us all; it was the first break in our family circle. Margaret, Audrey, her husband, Dr Ken Kerr, Val and I gathered around my mother to comfort her and help organise his funeral in Seaview Church – where, in later life, he had been received at Communion on profession of his faith in Christ. The last decade of his life had been perhaps the most fulfilling. He had loved being part of the wider family circle and watching his four grandchildren (John and Andrew, Tim and Jennie) growing up. With the private reflections generated by grief, I realised just how much I loved and admired his quiet manner, his gentle nature, his concern for social justice and the value he placed on his friends.

In the midst of this swirl of heavy emotion there came once again from somewhere deep inside me a whisper: "You are not alone in this storm. Hold on to the mast and you will come through into a great calm. Make no decisions about moving somewhere else until you have completed ten years." I took these promptings to heart and refocussed my energies on preaching, visiting the sick and burying the dead. It was only well into 1984 that my confidence returned and with it the first faint traces of Fitzroy entering the calmer phase I had been assured would come.

But events unfolding within the wider Presbyterian Church also contributed to my descent into the doldrums. A storm over the WCC was sweeping through the church and would not abate until the summer of 1980. Since settling into Fitzroy I had been drawn into the middle of the controversy. It was complex, painful and revealing.

### In or Out: The WCC Debate

The General Assembly of June 1975 witnessed two groups locking horns over our church's membership of the WCC: the Inter-Church Relations Board and a group calling itself calling itself the Campaign for Complete Withdrawal from the WCC. The case against our membership of the council was constructed largely on three allegations. Firstly, the council's Programme to Combat Racism (PCR) had given grants to "terrorist organisations" in Rhodesia, Namibia and South Africa. Secondly, this funding was motivated by "liberation theology", which clashed with the Reformation principal that salvation was personal, not societal. And thirdly, membership involved us in "doctrinal ambiguity" with some churches that did not hold the same confessional beliefs as Irish Presbyterians.

A spirited defence of the council was made by Rev Robert Brown, convenor of the Inter-Church Relations Board. He argued that disagreeing with any policy of the council, or indeed of our own General Assembly, was a reason not for withdrawal but for robust discussion, hopefully leading to change. The real issue, he maintained, was a difference in the way we viewed the universal nature of Christ's church and the call of Christ for unity among his followers. He drew attention to what he identified as the underlying agenda of the WCC:

> Withdrawal from the WCC is but the starter for withdrawal from the British Council of Churches, the Irish Council of Churches, the World Alliance of Reformed Churches, and, indeed, to schism within our own church in the pursuit of a purist concept of the church.

This goal mirrored the agenda being pushed by Ian Paisley, with whose views (but not with whose belligerent attitude) a significant number of WCC evangelicals privately sympathised. I was later informed that, when my letter from Timor was referred to during the debate, some friends who had come through Assembly's College with me reacted more strongly than I had anticipated. Sadly, the debate itself had begun to degenerate to the point where opposition to the WCC was almost considered a mark of evangelical orthodoxy.

In 1976, as I began to circulate within the wider life of the Presbyterian Church, the subject surfaced repeatedly in personal conversations and I found myself giving information about the WCC that was not generally known. Many were genuinely surprised to discover that the WCC had grown out of the 1910 Edinburgh Missionary Conference, which had drawn together 1,300 international delegates from Protestant denominations and missionary societies who sought to "evangelise the world in this generation". Alarmed, however, at divisions among Christians that were hampering this purpose, they pleaded for greater unity. The 1910 Edinburgh conference led to the formation of the WCC in Amsterdam in 1948, when 147 churches, including the PCI, committed themselves to work together in mission and for unity.

The word "ecumenical" (from the Greek "*oikoumene*" meaning "universal", or "worldwide" in reference to the church of Christ or the whole human family) was regularly dropped into our conversations with considerable loathing. As a result, I found myself explaining that in early Christianity the term was revered currency and was used of the great Ecumenical Councils and creeds of the church. In addition, the word indicated the universal scope of Christ's mission and the universal and unifying nature of his church.

Again, it was frequently mentioned that the WCC had ambitions to become a world super-church to be used by Satan in spreading godless apostasy across the globe. I suggested that this was pure misinformation and asked if those present had ever read the WCC's basis of membership. When most conceded that they had not, I would quote it directly:

The World Council is a fellowship of churches which confess the Lord Jesus Christ as God and Saviour according to the scriptures and therefore seek to fulfil together their common calling to the glory of One God, Father, Son and Holy Spirit.

After hearing this simple Trinitarian affirmation of faith there would often follow a few moments of silence, in which I detected hints of genuine surprise.

Finally, most of those I chatted with admitted that they knew little or nothing about the global nature of the WCC. It came as a revelation to them to discover that it was the largest non-Catholic Christian organisation on earth and represented half a billion Christians belonging to 285 churches in 140 countries. It came as an even greater shock to them when they realised that the largest denomination in the council was Presbyterian (28 per cent) and that 85 per cent of all Reformed Christians on the face of the earth were associated with it. The other denominations represented included Lutherans, Methodists, Orthodox, Anglicans, Baptists, Congregationalists, Mennonites, Disciples and Pentecostals. The Catholic Church, I explained, was not a member but worked closely with the WCC on various initiatives. "I didn't realise that!" was the most common response to emerge as these conversations drew to a close.

But why had the issue of ecumenism come to such heated prominence in Northern Ireland? Why was it viewed as such an imminent threat to Ulster Protestantism and a political menace to the security of Ulster unionism?

### The Background

The process that led to this state of alarm is complicated and multifaceted, but certain components are clear. Firstly, during the 1950s, more generous attitudes towards the Roman Catholic Church and community began to emerge within the Protestant churches, and in particular the PCI. In 1950 the General Assembly declared, "We need to manifest a spirit of reconciliation and goodwill if there is to be any hope of healing in Ireland." In 1956, when the unionist government was considering proposals to restrict family allowance to the first three children in a family, the assembly commissioned a deputation to Stormont to oppose the proposals because they would adversely affect Catholic families, which were generally larger. Their representations proved effective.

Secondly, the personal charisma of Pope John XXIII (1958–63) had the effect of prising open the cumbersome doors of the Catholic Church to fraternal relations with other Christian churches, including those of the Reformation. In December 1960 Pope John welcomed to the Vatican Dr Geoffrey Fisher, the Anglican archbishop of Canterbury, in the first meeting of its kind since the fracturing of western Christendom in the sixteenth century. Most British churches welcomed this groundbreaking initiative, but a considerable section of non-Anglican evangelicalism reacted negatively, particularly in Northern Ireland. If the Catholic Church was no longer an enemy to be resisted but a "sister Christian church" to be embraced, then the religious fault-line demarcating the community was being called into question. So also were the validity of the Reformation and the Protestant version of the Gospel.

Thirdly, no sooner had these evangelicals begun to make common cause to counteract this watershed moment than another encounter of seismic proportions took place. In May 1961, Queen Elizabeth II visited Pope John in the Vatican – the first non-Catholic British monarch ever to do so. She wore a long black dress and a cascading veil – the customary protocol of modesty for female monarchs of the Protestant faith and those of non-Christian religions. Concerned evangelicals seized on this custom and read into it "a sign of Protestant penitence" by the Queen as the supreme governor of the Church of England. But the irrepressible smiles on the faces of the Queen and the ageing pontiff belied this overly suspicious interpretation. Elizabeth II had set herself to be a reconciling monarch on the national and world stage.

Fourthly, the most internationally influential project of Pope John's brief pontificate was the calling together of the Second Vatican Council (1962–5). The council gave the reading and preaching of the Scriptures a central place in every Eucharist and encouraged the search for the unity of Christians by "seeking pardon for Catholic contributions towards separation". Furthermore, it urged the faithful to engage with the modern world as "a constitutive element in the Church's mission for the liberation of the human race". Vatican II was a defining moment for the Christian world: it broke through highly entrenched religious boundaries and crystallised new ideas to create fresh horizons. Prominent Irish Presbyterians were heartened by these changes and were at the forefront in welcoming them publicly.

When news of Pope John's death broke during the 1963 General Assembly, the moderator asked everyone to stand as a mark of respect, but the following year the first rumblings of disquiet were sounded. Seventy ministers petitioned the assembly over "trends in the Ecumenical Movement in which we are involved by virtue of our membership of the WCC". But the prevailing mood within the PCI was still positive. The 1965 assembly welcomed Vatican II's *Decree on Ecumenism* with its unprecedented affirmation of Reformed Christianity:

> The daily Christian life of these brethren is nourished by their faith in Christ and ... shows itself in their private prayer, their meditation on the Bible, in their Christian family life, and in the worship of a community gathered together to praise God ...This active faith has been responsible for many organizations for the relief of spiritual and material distress, the furtherance of the education of youth ... and the promotion of peace throughout the world.

But when the same assembly passed a resolution expressing "penitence for past uncharitableness towards Roman Catholics", it struck a raw nerve and letters from irate Presbyterians poured into the press, rejecting any suggestion of guilt.

Into this swirl of discontent stepped the intimidating figure of Ian Paisley. He led a picket to the opening of the General Assembly in June 1966, during which rioting broke out, church officials were roughed up and four policemen were injured. During his subsequent three-month imprisonment, an opinion poll revealed that 200,000 Protestants supported Paisley. Many of them were loyal Presbyterians registering their anger at the emergence of more benign attitudes to the Catholic Church and community within their own church.

Paisley was simultaneously waging the "O'Neill Must Go" campaign against Captain Terence O'Neill, the Ulster Unionist prime minister of Northern Ireland (1963–9). O'Neill's moderate brand of liberalism and his personal determination to transform relationships with the estranged Catholic community in Northern Ireland was unnerving many unionists. In 1965 he welcomed Taoiseach Seán Lemass to Stormont for the first time since partition in 1921, and a month later travelled to Dublin to discuss economic cooperation. But street confrontations between rival loyalist and republican factions added to his woes, as did the creation of the Northern Ireland Civil Rights Association in 1967, highlighting the long-standing grievances of the Catholic community. They demanded major reforms: "one man, one vote" in local council elections; an end to gerrymandering; the end of discrimination in the allocation of government jobs and council houses; and the disbandment of the B-Specials, a 100-per-cent Protestant constabulary.

In response, O'Neill introduced a modest five-point reform programme, but it failed to satisfy reform-hungry nationalists and concession-rejecting unionists. When a civil-rights march to Derry in October 1968 was attacked by the police in full view of the world's media, the province was plunged into widespread rioting. O'Neill made his "Ulster at the Crossroads" speech on television just prior to Christmas; four months later he resigned. Ulster had already travelled beyond the crossroads and was now heading towards a precipice. This context of social, political and religious upheaval and the conservative reaction it generated helped ignite and fuel the controversy over the WCC.

As the debate over the council's PCR and its humanitarian grants to liberation movements in southern Africa raged, the civil war in Rhodesia assumed ever greater prominence in the international media, often running in parallel with coverage of the conflict in Northern Ireland. Within church circles in Ireland, the situation in southern Africa was regularly viewed through the lens of our own deteriorating situation. Those most opposed to the WCC often held views sympathetic to the white regimes. In addition, the liberation movements were routinely dismissed by unionists in the same breath as the IRA. One vociferous Belfast city councillor labelled Nelson Mandela "a black provo" and an anonymous fundamentalist leaflet that circulated widely in the province declared that "an IRA spokesman claimed that the IRA had benefitted from the WCC Special Fund to Combat Racism".

The implication behind this fanatical fabrication was that if the PCR humanitarian grants could be given to the "terrorist" liberation movements, then there was no reason whatsoever that they would not be made available to the IRA. The simple facts, however, were enough to debunk this prevailing myth. The truth was that no republican or loyalist paramilitary groups had ever been given a grant by the WCC. If they had, Irish Presbyterians, Methodists and Anglicans would have been the first to know, since the list of proposed grants was routinely sent out each year to the 285 member churches of the council in the hope that individual churches might fund them. No republican or loyalist groups had ever appeared on any list since the grants were first awarded in 1970. Furthermore, the IRA could never qualify for a grant because the conflict in Ireland was political in nature, not racial. Finally, republicans and loyalists alike had available to them democratic alternatives to armed conflict waiting to be embraced – the freedom to organise politically, to commend their views publicly and to seek support through elections. These indispensable human and democratic rights had long been denied the black communities of southern Africa.

Early on in my conversations with colleagues about these issues I came to the conclusion that discussing Africa was really a coded way of discussing what was unfolding in Ulster. An embattled Protestant community, digging in against change and fearful of the future, empathised with the besieged white minority communities of southern Africa. Then, unexpectedly, the debate lurched to a new level of intensity.

### The Elim Mission Massacre

On Friday evening, 23 June 1978, in the Vumba Mountains of eastern Rhodesia, guerrillas stormed the Elim Mission School and hospital complex and carried out the worst massacre of white missionaries of the 14-year civil war. Eight British missionaries and four children were bayoneted to death. Among the victims were Pastor Roy Lynn, his wife, Joyce, and their three-week-old daughter, Pamela Grace. Roy had grown up in the County Antrim village of Cullybackey, a strongly Presbyterian area.

The murders sparked an international backlash against the WCC and its humanitarian grants to the Patriotic Front parties led by Robert Mugabe (Zimbabwe African National Union) and Joshua Nkomo (Zimbabwe African People's Union). Both vehemently denied that their organisations had been involved, and even David Owen, the British secretary of state for foreign and commonwealth affairs, admitted in parliament that he did not know who was responsible. The Rhodesian government laid the blame squarely on the "terrorists" of the liberation movements, while the Catholic Institute of International Affairs pointed the finger at the Selous Scouts, a notorious African counter-insurgency force managed by the Rhodesian Army.

Over the next few months I scrutinised reports of the incident emanating from the white-minority government, the main Rhodesian churches and interviews with Mugabe and Nkomo. I was particularly moved by the testimony of survivors who spoke of living constantly in fear of small groups of guerrillas, usually intoxicated, looting homes and mission compounds. In the preceding two years the lives of one Southern Baptist, two Dutch Reformed, two Salvation Army and sixteen Catholic missionaries had been taken. All of them had been utterly devoted to serving the Zimbabwean people. The Elim Mission Massacre was the latest in this sequence of savagery and its gruesome circumstances plumbed new depths of depravity. The accumulating weight of evidence pointed unmistakably, in my view, to rogue elements within the liberation movements. I became convinced that the WCC should side with the victims, terminate all grants to the Patriotic Front and seek other ways to expose the injustice of the illegal white regime while supporting the aspirations of the Zimbabwean people for national democratic self-determination.

## Straight-Talking in Geneva

Such was the revulsion felt throughout the PCI at the Elim Mission Massacre that an emergency meeting of the Inter-Church Relations Board was called in September to consider a proposal to suspend our membership of the WCC. It was defeated by 24 votes to 13 in favour of an alternative course of action. Firstly, a strongly worded letter would be written to the WCC's general secretary, Dr Philip Potter, urging the WCC to "take into account lessons learnt from our own tragic experience in Northern Ireland. While the WCC's concern to combat racism was thoroughly justified, the operation of the PCR was open to serious criticism. Racism is both the cause and excuse for great evils in the world." Secondly, a six member delegation, headed up by our general secretary, Dr Jack Weir, would travel to Switzerland to drive home our opposition to the PCR grants.

A few weeks later we were sitting in the WCC headquarters in Geneva with Dr Potter and those responsible for managing the PCR. We pulled no punches in registering our abhorrence at the humanitarian grants made to the Patriotic Front, just as other member churches in the UK, Switzerland, Germany, France, Holland and the USA had done. Dr Potter, a West Indian Methodist minister, and his team listened respectfully, but their response took us by surprise:

> The western churches which have been the fiercest critics of the PCR belong to countries that have been the most involved in creating and sustaining the racist system in southern Africa.

> Third World churches, on the other hand, believe it is their duty to
> help racially oppressed groups which have exhausted all peaceful
> means of winning their freedom.

There was no meeting of minds, but we were assured that our representations
would be brought to the WCC Central Committee in January 1979.

## The Special Assembly

The actions of the Inter-Church Relations Board were never going to quell
the outrage felt across the church and a special assembly was convened in
November 1978 to debate a proposal to suspend our membership. Every seat
in the house was taken and journalists lined the front rows of the gallery
as speaker after speaker queued up to command their five minutes at the
rostrum. The debate was heated and weighted towards the Rhodesian
conflict. The case against the WCC was that it "supports those who commit
acts of crime and uses the issue of racism to achieve its Marxist political
ends: the overthrow of capitalism and the communisation of Western society
in pursuit of a collectivist world state"; that "the Roman Catholic Church is
now determining the goals and theology of the WCC"; and that "leaving the
WCC could herald revival in our church".

Those seeking to retain our membership contended that "we should
continue to lobby the WCC about the grants, but not cut ourselves off from
Christians who think differently from us"; that "being evangelical and
ecumenical are not mutually exclusive"; and that "the WCC is motivated not
so much by the social implications of the Gospel as by the conviction that
God in Christ is actively involved in the redemption of the world".

Understandably, a torrent of anger was unleashed in relation to the murder
of the white missionaries in Rhodesia – but, in my opinion, it was seriously
unbalanced. There was barely any reference made to the enduring plight of
the black African community that made up 95 per cent of the population. My
speech, therefore, was an attempt to correct this imbalance by bringing into
the discussion the real but carefully screened-out reasons for the civil war.
They were: firstly, the illegal and brutal seizure of the land in 1893 by heavily
armed white colonists, which claimed the lives of thousands of the native
community; secondly, the 1930 Land Apportionment Act, which granted
whites (3 per cent of the population) 49 million acres of the best land and
handed the black majority 28 million acres of much inferior quality; thirdly,

the abolition of African political rights in 1962 by the white Rhodesian Front Party, which repressed peaceful dissent, banned the ZAPU and ZANU parties and imprisoned their leaders (this slamming of the door to peaceful change in the faces of 95 per cent of the population forced them to consider and adopt a policy of armed resistance); fourthly, in November 1965 the issue of the white minority's Unilateral Declaration of Independence, an act of rebellion against the British Crown and an act of war on the human rights of six million Africans. After that, the regime moved quickly to establish a police state which saw 15,000 Africans detained without trial, tens of thousands of refugees fleeing across the border and the Rhodesia Air Force carrying out hundreds of bombing raids on the refugee camps, in which thousands of innocent civilians were killed. This, I contended, was the immediate background to the PCR's decision to give humanitarian assistance to the liberation organisations managing these overcrowded and vulnerable camps in 1970. The result was that the refugees were provided with food, clothing, medicine, education and basic housing.

Many in the assembly that day assumed that the PCI was actively funding these grants through its membership of the WCC. It came as a shock, therefore, when I explained that our church had never contributed a penny to the PCR. When I went on to draw attention to the fact that as a church we had never offered any kind of moral support or humanitarian assistance to the economically exploited and racially oppressed communities of southern Africa, some delegates were surprised. Finally, in the face of allegations that the civil war was about safeguarding Christian civilisation against the rising tide of Marxism sweeping through Africa, I reminded the house that Zimbabweans were overwhelmingly Christian and desired equality and democracy, not atheistic communism, as was alleged.

After an intense debate, the assembly decided by 561 votes (64 per cent) to 318 (36 per cent) to suspend our membership of the WCC. The decision to withdraw completely could not be taken until June 1980. As Christmas 1979 approached, however, the situation in Rhodesia took a dramatic turn for the better.

## The Birth of Zimbabwe

In December 1979 a diplomatic breakthrough in the 14-year war was achieved by the British prime minister, Margaret Thatcher, and her foreign secretary, Peter Carrington. They succeeded in getting all parties to the conflict together in London for round-table talks. The remarkable outcome was the signing of the Lancaster House Agreement. A ceasefire was secured, which enabled the fundamental elements of democracy to be put in place. A date for elections was set, every adult was given the right to vote, parties were free to draw up their manifestos and parity of access to the media was guaranteed.

In the country's first general election in February 1980, the Patriotic Front parties won a landslide victory, gathering in 87 per cent of the votes, with the ZANU-PF party of Robert Mugabe topping the poll at 63 per cent. On Friday, 18 April, Mugabe was sworn in as Zimbabwe's prime minister and in a historic speech he called for national reconciliation, quoting the prophet Isaiah about "beating swords into ploughshares". Celebrations broke out across the country and the leaders of the liberation movement attended services of thanksgiving in the Catholic and Anglican cathedrals in Harare to acknowledge the moral support of the churches throughout the nation's struggle for freedom. On Sunday in villages, towns and cities, millions of smiling Zimbabweans streamed into their local churches to thank God – not for the triumph of Marxism, but for escape from oppression and the prospect of a better future.

I found it thrilling to watch, but my joy was tempered by the thought of the families of the 32 white missionaries who had lost their lives. But would the sight of Zimbabwe's first exhilarating taste of democracy cause some Irish Presbyterians, six weeks before the final decision about the WCC, to question the slanted interpretation they had been given of events in southern Africa?

### The Decisive Vote

As delegates arrived at the opening night of the General Assembly in June 1980, a vociferous crowd of Free Presbyterian pickets was there to help sway the vote in their direction. On Thursday the house was once again packed and the debate flowed backwards and forwards for five hours, with a stream of speakers covering every angle of the matter with forcefulness and respect. While criticism of the WCC touched on other matters, the crux issue remained the role of the WCC in Rhodesia and southern Africa. The well-rehearsed arguments against the liberation movements and the PCR humanitarian grants were once again expressed with the customary passion.

My contribution was again to call into question what I considered to be a biased interpretation of the events unfolding in southern Africa. The Campaign for Complete Withdrawal from the World Council of Churches (CCW) group had put itself on record as dismissing Rhodesia's first ever democratic elections:

> The WCC has played a major part in the support of the Marxist terrorists of the Patriotic Front who have now, with the connivance of Lord Carrington and the British Government, taken over power in Rhodesia after a cruel campaign of murder and violence.

Their views continued to chime ominously with those of the white regime that had just been voted out, while international opinion, led by the UK and USA, moved swiftly to recognise the newly independent nation. "If the resolution of this conflict has been achieved by introducing the same democratic rights that all of us in Ireland enjoy," I contended, "how can we remain so churlish at the outcome of free elections?"

After several speakers underlined the moral principle that "no Christian organisation can offer humanitarian assistance to groups which arm themselves for political purposes", I felt obliged to remind the house of our own not-too-distant past:

> In April 1914 Presbyterians were at the forefront of the gun-running which smuggled 25,000 rifles and three million rounds of ammunition into Donaghadee and Larne for the Ulster Volunteer Force. The circumstances may be different, but should the similarities not make us hesitant about passing intemperate judgments?

This uncomfortable reference to the smuggling of large quantities of military hardware into the province, as distinct from humanitarian assistance for refugee camps, provoked audible murmurs of disapproval.

My final observation was:

> Leaving the WCC will change nothing in southern Africa, for there is something God-given in the hearts of the victims of oppression that will never allow injustice to triumph. By their own blood, sweat and tears they can and will achieve their own liberation.

Our Lord himself has warned us that houses built on sand always crumble. The tragedy is that so many innocent people, black and white, get hurt in the falling debris. Despite its weaknesses, the humanitarian assistance offered by the Programme to Combat Racism is a courageous attempt to pick up the pieces and build something on a better foundation.

I was convinced that the river of freedom now flowing through Zimbabwe would soon cross the border into Namibia and eventually reach apartheid-ridden South Africa.

After a long debate, the moderator called on the assembly to vote and by 448 votes (54 per cent) to 388 (46 per cent) it was decided to withdraw completely from the WCC. Even though emotions were running high, no one clapped or cheered; I was proud that our church could display this depth of sensitivity. We filed out, tired but respectful to the end. Some were elated, others bitterly disappointed. As a hundred pro-WCC ministers and elders streamed forward to register their dissent, I slipped out, stopping on the way to congratulate some of my anti-ecumenical colleagues whose company I had enjoyed for four years as together we had debated the issue from every conceivable angle. I headed back up to Fitzroy with a heavy heart, feeling sad about the direction our church seemed to be heading in relation to world Christianity.

**Sequel**

With the passage of time the consequences of our decision became more and more apparent. First of all, we found ourselves on the wrong side of one of the biggest political debates of our time. By adopting an agreed international process of installing democratic freedoms for all, the liberation movements brought to an end their long servitude under the forces of racial exploitation. Zimbabwe won its freedom in 1980; Namibia followed in 1990. Then, in April 1994, South Africa held its first ever multiracial election. Twenty million voters went to the polls and Nelson Mandela's African National Congress party captured two-thirds of the votes. In a moving ceremony, watched on television by the whole world, he was subsequently sworn in as the rainbow nation's first black president. The man labelled "a black Provo" by extreme Protestant-unionist propaganda emerged as one of the twentieth century's great leaders.

The PCI was the only church of the 285 member churches of the WCC to withdraw completely. The Salvation Army, which lost two missionaries in Rhodesia, reduced its involvement to fraternal status. Revealingly, none of the other 80 reformed churches in the council followed us out the door. Our dismissal of the legitimate political aspirations of the liberation movements of southern Africa because of our own moral abhorrence at the Provisional IRA's campaign of violence will remain forever a historical embarrassment for Irish Presbyterians.

I became increasingly conscious, too, that some Presbyterians felt uncomfortable about being part of the vibrant diversity of the global Christianity represented by the WCC. I detected a tendency in certain quarters to view other Christian traditions with considerable suspicion because they were different from us in some ways. Handling the reality of such cultural, theological and historical diversity with a positive and grace-orientated approach is far from easy. It requires the wisdom advocated by the seventeenth-century Lutheran theologian Peter Meiderlin, who wrote, "If we hold to Unity in essentials, Liberty in non-essentials and Charity in all things, our affairs would certainly be in the best condition." I envisaged a future in which the PCI would be tempted to embark on the easy path of searching for new ecclesiastical partners resembling itself, rather than embracing the rich diversity of Christ's church in our world today. Such limited acceptance of other Christians would mean reducing the content of the Gospel of sheer grace and shrinking the boundaries of Christ's church. Thankfully, however, our church has retained its membership of the Irish Council of Churches, the Conference of European Churches and the World Communion of Reformed Churches. But, if Christ's church is truly universal, then being in fellowship with only a part of it is a choice that excludes the rest of God's family.

Moreover, the energy driving much of the anti-ecumenism within the Presbyterian Church appeared to be an anti-Catholicism resurrected by the Troubles. The similarity with the fundamentalism of Ian Paisley was too close to be accidental, though it must be emphasised again that it differed considerably in intensity and tone. Nine years after the vote to leave the WCC, when the racism issue was well and truly *passé*, the assembly decided not to join the new Churches Together in Britain and Ireland – solely because the Catholic Church would be involved. The underlying dynamic was unmistakable.

I now understood why relatively few Presbyterian evangelicals identified with the Peace Movement in 1976. If they harboured reservations about identifying with a global fellowship of largely Protestant Christians, then there was bound to be little or no motivation for building bridges with the local Catholic community. As a consequence, our villages, towns and cities seemed doomed to live with high levels of prejudice and segregation far into the future. The same old attitudes would continue to overpower any youthful dreams of reconciliation.

I always sensed that at the heart of the WCC debate was a clash of fundamental belief about what kind of church Christ was calling us to be in Northern Ireland, and what kind of country we desired to live in. From a Protestant perspective, was it to be one where anti-Catholic attitudes and anti-nationalist sentiment continued to reinforce our divisions? Or could something healthier emerge: a community where Catholic and Protestant, unionist and nationalist could team up to construct an integrated future built on respect and friendship? Sadly, this was a hope I only occasionally encountered on the radar of many of my evangelical colleagues. The debate about our future, however, was destined to continue.

## Jaded Heart

Disappointment over our withdrawal from the WCC stayed with me over the summer and intensified the gloom that had already settled within me over the tensions in Fitzroy. Even during our family holiday I was anguished with the guilt of personal failure, feelings of alienation from the PCI and a struggle to fit into a Protestant-unionist culture seemingly inured to progressive thinking. Month after month, Val had to listen to my rambling and tormented thoughts, which emotionally had turned me grey inside.

However, I came to know one of the most courageous leaders of the renewal movement, Rev Cecil Kerr, a gentle Anglican minister who had founded the Christian Renewal Centre at Rostrevor in 1974. Realising the exhaustion and isolation of ministers involved in reconciliation work, he started organising clergy-renewal conferences to enable them to take time out in the beauty of the Mourne Mountains. Each month, therefore, early on Monday morning, I would drive down to Rostrevor along with two or three other Presbyterian ministers to listen to Cecil. He constantly encouraged us to let the Holy Spirit take us more deeply into the life of God, where, he assured us, we would discover a place of greater self-acceptance, healing and peace. He always seemed to exemplify what he was talking about.

In theory, I believed what he was saying, but in practice I found it hard to reveal the details of my disillusionment to anyone except Val. After one of the sessions, when the room had emptied as everyone headed for coffee, he came over and sat down beside me.

"Ken," he began, "are you OK? You look so alone and burdened."

I instantly retreated into my default position of smiling defensiveness, "Sure, I'm fine."

"If you don't mind me asking," he continued, "what's going on inside you?"

His gentle persistence coaxed me out of a deep reserve about revealing anything personal and over the next hour I poured out my heart to him. When I finally heaved a sigh of relief at the end of my story, he asked if he could pray with me. It was the first time I let him do for me what I had repeatedly done for others in Fitzroy. I cannot recall what he prayed, but for me it was a moment of epiphany: his warm hands resting upon my head felt like the hands of Christ imparting to me, almost physically, a most beautiful sense of God's love. I felt as if I was standing under a waterfall that was refreshing my body and cascading down into my soul. A boil within my spirit had been lanced and healing had begun.

In the weeks that followed the gloom began to dissipate and I started to be happy again with the person I was and the views I held. I identified with the seventeenth-century English poet George Herbert who, in the poem "The Flower" (1633), wrote:

> How fresh, O Lord, how sweet and clean
> Are thy returns! even as the flowers in spring …
> Who would have thought my shriveled heart
> Could have recovered greenness? It was gone
> Quite underground; as flowers depart
> To see their mother-root, when they have blown …

### The Tide Turns

By the spring of 1981 the quality of Sunday worship at Fitzroy had been lifted to new levels through the skilful musical leadership of Marie Crawford and Chris Blake. Other talented musicians joined our music groups, as did a steady stream of gifted singers. In time, the worship dimension of our services became one of the most attractive features of Fitzroy's spirituality. By patiently working through the tensions, we had reaped rich rewards. Young people were turning up at worship in greater numbers and, when their non-church friends came along with them, few of them felt as if they had landed in a foreign country.

Away from the tension of denominational controversy, I turned my mind to the writings of David Watson and pored over his book *I Believe in the Church* (1979). It offered biblical principles and practical advice on how to build a healthy and growing congregation and I sought to find out how to integrate them into the life of Fitzroy. My confidence was slowly returning.

Over the next 12 months I presented the Kirk Session with a vision for renewing the life of Fitzroy so that it could become a place of greater influence in the city and beyond. This would involve setting ourselves clear goals and identifying gifted members of the congregation to pursue them in what we termed "ministry-groups". These goals included the development of worship, fellowship, evangelism, reconciliation, overseas mission, prayer, ministry among the young and care of the elderly. By 1983 Fitzroy was buzzing with creative thinking and a host of practical new initiatives began to unfold as we set ourselves to transform the life of congregation. The Reconciliation Ministry Group, led by Jim Boyd, Harold McCollum, Heather and Philip Mateer, Sandra Rutherford and Ian McMurray was to have a significant impact on how Fitzroy lived out its mission within the turbulence of Belfast.

### International Meeting Point

In 1982 David Bleakley, the general secretary of the Irish Council of Churches (ICC), invited me to take on the chairmanship of its Overseas Board for three years. It was composed mainly of former missionaries, mostly from an evangelical background. It was an exciting time. On the one hand, the ICC had become a target for the Free Presbyterian Church, which regarded it as "apostate", while anti-ecumenical activists within the PCI were dismissing it as an example of "unbiblical ecumenism". But, in truth, its eight member churches represented 85 per cent of Irish Protestantism. The Catholic Church was not a member, but since the 1970s there had been joint working groups dealing with drug abuse, mixed marriage, doctrinal differences, conflict and peace. I was keen to take the overseas dimension of the council's life out of its secluded existence in the ICC's offices in Elmwood Avenue and into a public place, where ordinary people could meet some of the international Christian leaders visiting Northern Ireland.

In January 1983 we held our first public meeting in Fitzroy and welcomed a two-man delegation from the churches in Russia: Pastor Alexei Bychkov, the general secretary of the All-Union Council of Evangelical Christians-Baptists, and Bishop Nerses Bozabalian of the Armenian Orthodox Church. At a time of Cold War tension between the USSR and the west, we selected "From Russia with Love" as the theme of the service. We were not surprised when a small group of fundamentalist pickets stationed themselves at the gates of Fitzroy to harangue our visitors as "communist agents" as they made their way into the church. The hundreds who turned up for the event, however, were intrigued to see a senior Baptist pastor from Moscow speaking side by side with the bishop of an ancient Christian church that traces its roots back to the apostles Bartholomew and Thaddeus. Pastor Bychkov informed the congregation that, while some believers continued to suffer persecution in the USSR, the general situation was improving. The soft-spoken bishop confirmed this:

> The number of children being brought for baptism by their parents has risen to 65 per cent of all the children in Armenia. Though atheism is officially taught in state schools, it is in the home that children are being taught the Gospel.

Most of those present had never attended an ICC event before and the feedback we received was heartening.

At Easter 1983 we hosted an evening with the Argentine evangelist Dr Luis Palau. In Latin America he preached regularly to crowds of up to 70,000 and each day 18 million listeners tuned in to his radio broadcasts. Few of the 600-strong congregation will forget the fervour with which we sang the great hymns of the resurrection. In his address, Dr Palau gave us three key principles which he believed could help to turn our situation around – dream great dreams of peace; pray great prayers in confidence that God will answer them; and live by the Great Commandment of Jesus to love thy neighbour as thyself. This, he stressed, was the path to peace and reconciliation.

When I discovered that Bishop Desmond Tutu, general secretary of the South African Council of Churches, was coming to Ireland, I was keen to get him to Belfast to speak at another ICC public meeting. He was on a whistle-stop tour of the British Isles to encourage the British and Irish churches to lobby their governments to disinvest from South Africa and thereby erode the economic foundation of apartheid. The multifaceted overseas anti-apartheid campaign had seen the rand plunge in value by 35 per cent. As a black Christian leader within South Africa, Bishop Tutu had been denounced by his white right-wing detractors as "sympathetic to terrorism and communism", while sections of Ulster unionism and Irish Presbyterianism viewed him with similar suspicion. On Saturday evening, 16 June 1984, the diminutive 53-year-old prophet ambled into Fitzroy an hour before the service, smiling from ear to ear, but also looking exhausted. After welcoming him, I suggested that he spend half an hour in a comfortable armchair in my office and snooze. I would wake him ten minutes before the service started. "A good idea!" he answered wearily. I locked the door of my study from the outside to make sure he was not interrupted. When I eventually woke him up, he took a few moments to come around and then asked me to pray with him.

As we entered Fitzroy's pulpit, a reverent hush came over the excited congregation and he sat subdued as I led the congregation in some hymns and prayers. Then, when I invited him to address us, he exploded into life with a gush of new energy. Within minutes we were convulsed in laughter at his impish good humour, poking fun at the apartheid government's recent attempts to bring mixed-race and Asian people into parliament but exclude the black majority, 72 per cent of the population:

> In South Africa political rights are dispensed on the basis of the colour of a man's skin. What a ridiculous way to decide a person's value. It's as ludicrous as deciding to give people the right to vote if their noses are the right size and shape! Those with long slim noses qualify to go to the polls; those with large and broad noses like mine can stay at home!

Just as suddenly, we collapsed into silence as he recounted story after harrowing story of the effects on the black community of living under such an arrogant and intolerant racist regime. He explained that he was travelling the world to explain why thousands of his compatriots are languishing in jails without justice or under house arrest for organising Christian opposition to apartheid. He declared:

I am a voice for those organisations silenced by banning orders and arrested for engaging in peace marches ... The South African Council of Churches, which I represent, is made up of 19 member churches, 1,500 affiliated black independent churches, and almost 15 million black Christians. We refuse to be silent about the political abuse of our people. The governing National Party may be able eventually to gag me, but be assured, someone else will take my place. God is not mocked.

He then turned his attention to the white Dutch Reformed Churches, which were using Christianity to shore up apartheid:

The Christian church has always taught that God became a human being in the person of Jesus Christ, whose own faith was grounded in the Old Testament Scriptures. These Scriptures stress that God is on the side of the widow, the alien, the orphan and the marginalised. That's why the driving force in my faith is not politics but what I read in the Bible. Eighty per cent of the Bible is about political issues. Jesus did not die because people got tired of him, but because he rejected the way in which his opponents steered the ordering of their society to their own advantage. When Jesus hobnobbed with prostitutes, sinners and outsiders and preached that some of them were closer to God than the religious leaders they couldn't take it. Christianity can never be an excuse for escapism; rather, it provides the dynamic for us to get involved in social and political transformation.

His exposition of the Gospel was electrifying and ended on this prophetic note:

We will have a black prime minister in five to ten years. We are going to be free. The only questions remaining are how and when. Why am I so confident? I know that a lie cannot prevail forever over the truth; darkness cannot extinguish the light; and death cannot overcome the power of life.

The time-frame expressed in his prophecy was well chosen. Six years later, in 1990, President FW de Klerk released Nelson Mandela from jail and together they charted a new path for the "rainbow nation". Apartheid was abandoned and plans for multiracial elections were set in motion. In April 1994 the African National Congress party swept to power, and with the rest of the world I watched as Mandela became president on 10 May. Moments after taking his vows, Mandela's hand reached out to Tutu's and, beaming with joy in front of a crowd of over 100,000 people, they raised them together into the air in a salute of joy and triumph. The new president then spoke to the crowds:

> The time for the healing of the wounds has come ... Never, never and never again shall it be that this beautiful land will again experience the oppression of one by another.

It was an exhilarating moment. But I couldn't stop longing to see such a joyous outcome in my own country. Southern Africa was resolving its massive problems, but we in Northern Ireland were still mired in despair. Keeping hope alive was far from easy.

For those who crowded into Fitzroy in 1984 to meet Bishop Tutu, it was one of those inspirational encounters that linger for a lifetime. I was glad that in face of considerable misinformation I had sought to present to Presbyterians a more balanced perspective on the liberation struggles in southern Africa. But, more than anything else, my conviction was restored that I was being called to work through Fitzroy for the transformation of our own community. The Northern Ireland conflict was exacting an outrageous cost in terms of human lives and, after almost 17 years, showed little promise of abating. I was sure that those from Fitzroy who had attended the service were thinking along similar lines.

### New Buoyancy

By the end of 1984, the tensions that had characterised Fitzroy over the previous six years had given way to the season of calm I had been promised. We had learned to respect the diversity of perspectives within the congregation and to affirm the integrity and worth of those who held them. There were also heartening signs of spiritual vitality and progress – a sustained upsurge in financial support for the overseas work of the Presbyterian Church, a growing army of volunteers keeping the church's activities moving forward, an increasing warmth of friendship among us which visitors were quick to notice, and between 15 and 20 new families joining us each year. I was greatly encouraged and content to let the future unfold in its own way and at its own pace.

CHAPTER FOUR

# Building the Kingdom of Peace:
# The Clonard–Fitzroy Fellowship

Winter had well and truly settled into the city as I made my way down Magdala Street in October 1982 to have coffee with Fr Denis Newberry. We were putting the final touches to our sixth inter-church Christmas carol service, soon to be held in St Malachy's. Towards the end of our discussion he broke the news to me that his bishop had reassigned him to a parish in south Down. Since 1976 he had begun to fulfil my hope, first cherished in Timor, that one day I could developing a working relationship with a Catholic priest in Belfast. But as our links with St Malachy's were loosening, something new and unexpected was germinating in the background.

**In the Beginning Was a Dream**
BBC Radio Ulster had invited me in April 1981 to contribute for a week to its three-minute *Thought for the Day* slot on the early morning news. I selected five sayings of Jesus about "true happiness" and related them to the stories making the headlines. One story was dominating the news – the IRA hunger strike in the Maze Prison outside Belfast. Bobby Sands, the officer commanding the IRA in the Maze, had refused food on 1 March and nine other prisoners were timetabled to join the strike at intervals in order to maximise publicity for their demand for the restoration of "special-category" or political status. This had been phased out by the UK government in 1976 with the result that IRA prisoners were treated as ordinary criminals rather than as prisoners of war entitled to specific rights under the 1949 Geneva Convention.

The Maze was becoming a volcano. Part of the H-block compound housing republican prisoners was burned down and 300 inmates refused to don the prison uniform. They were demanding five rights: not to wear prison uniform; not to undertake prison work; free association; one visit, one letter and one parcel per week; and the restoration of remission lost through the protest. A head-on collision was about to take place between the "Iron Lady", Prime Minister Margaret Thatcher, and republicans, who were as resolute as steel. Five days after Sands began his hunger strike, the independent republican MP for Fermanagh and South Tyrone, Frank Maguire, died and a by-election was set for 9 April. Republicans seized this opportunity to intensify their campaign and nominated Sands to fight the seat as an "Anti H-block, political prisoner" candidate in opposition to the Ulster Unionist Harry West.

On Friday morning, 10 April 1981, an anxious province woke up and tuned in to catch the latest speculation about the election's outcome, which was to be declared later that day. Would it deliver an affirmation of democratic politics or an electoral boost for the armed struggle? It was into this explosive mix that my *Thought for the Day* was dropped:

Recently we have all taken a long hard look at ourselves as we watched Robert Kee's *Ireland* and ITV's *The Troubles*. If Irish eyes can be smiling, as the song says, they can also glare with bigoted contempt and ice-cold cruelty. The repeated sight of fingers on triggers, bricks in people's hands, businesses going up in flames, mobs confronting each other in the streets, pavements stained dark red with innocent blood and a community divided and estranged all add up to one thing – a future without hope.

While these programmes were being shown, I went to a meeting in Belfast where 700 people from different political and religious backgrounds gathered together in the name of Jesus Christ. The hall was beautifully decorated with large tapestries, one of which I just couldn't take my eyes off. It was of two people, one dressed in orange, the other in green, embracing each other with outstretched arms ... In contrast to the depressing TV programmes, there were no clenched fists, no hooded heads, no pointed guns; just two people, two communities, reaching out and embracing each other in warm friendship.

When Jesus says, "Happy are those who work for peace; God will call them his children," he makes it clear that the mark of a Christian, a child of God, is an active concern to promote peace.

Wherever you are going to spend the rest of this day – at home, at school, at work, with friends – let your life and your words contribute to bringing back the summer of warm friendship towards everybody in this country.

In the hard-nosed climate of Ulster politics, my contribution must have sounded like the naïve ramblings of an inveterate optimist. A few hours later the result was declared: Sands had won by 1,400 votes. His election agent jubilantly declared, "It's time for Britain to get out of Ireland. The nationalist people have voted against unionism and against the H-blocks." The unionist community was devastated. Sands, now in the forty-first day of his strike, was harvesting international support for the republican cause and with it the promise of increased funding for its armed struggle. The community braced itself for new eruptions of savagery.

The following day my phone rang and I found myself talking with an American.

"Pastor Newell," he began, "could you send me a copy of your Radio Ulster talks for use among our young people in Clonard Monastery?"

He explained that, having been demobbed from the US Army, he had felt called to give a year to working with young people on the Falls Road. When he dropped into the conversation that he was part of a Bible-study group of Protestants and Catholics in Clonard, led by a 70-year-old priest, Fr Christy McCarthy, my ears pricked up. "Could you arrange for me to meet him?" I asked.

A week later I arrived at the cathedral-like Church of Christ the Most Holy Redeemer. At reception I was informed that Fr McCarthy was not in great health but was looking forward to meeting me in his room upstairs. I was surprised to find him in a wheelchair, looking frail and requiring a neck brace to support his head, but his sparkling eyes and radiant smile put me at ease. Over the next two hours, despite a 30-year age gap, we discovered that we had a lot in common. He had served overseas in Sri Lanka, taught Theology in a Catholic university in the USA and had a passionate love of Scripture. With great pride he pointed out to me a shelf full of Daily Study Bible books written by William Barclay, Presbyterian professor of Divinity at Glasgow University. Eventually our conversation turned to what he referred to as his "dazzling vision": "If only England and Ireland could unite to resolve their differences, what hope they could give to every hopeless situation in our world!" Then he made a suggestion: "Could we develop links between Fitzroy and Clonard based on our mutual love of the Scriptures? The only condition I would add is that if we study Christ's message together that we also commit to living it out together on the streets of Belfast."

I could hardly believe my ears. He was voicing a vision that blended perfectly with mine. We decided to set up the Falls–Fitzroy Bible-Study Group, but first to clear our plans with the leaders of the Redemptorist community at Clonard and the Kirk Session of Fitzroy.

Just before Christmas 1981, 40 of us gathered together in Fitzroy to study the Gospel of Luke's account of the birth of Christ. The atmosphere was one of nervous excitement. We sang traditional carols and pored over the nativity story with its message of God building a bridge towards humankind in the gift of his Son. As we looked around at the gathering of virtual strangers, we sensed that God was still constructing bridges, even in the bleak midwinter of Belfast. Towards the end of the evening, some residual fears began to surface. Over a cup of tea a Clonard member said to me, "I hope you don't secretly harbour thoughts of trying to convert us. We love our own church and our own faith." That kind of honesty marked our interactions from the beginning. In January Fr Christy wrote to me:

> All my thanks for the glorious evening you provided for us. Your people are beautiful, beyond all praise. The undivided verdict of our group was that we fell in love with you all. One of my most memorable experiences was having your wife in my group. I will let you know in a short time when we will be ready for your visit to Clonard. I wish you all an abundance of Divine Graces. Begging a prayer. I remain yours in Christ.
>
> Christopher McCarthy

The more we got to know Fr Christy, the more we all admired him. His constant pain and restriction to a wheelchair in no way constricted his yearning for peace. As I sat beside him at those early meetings, my mind turned to God's ancient promise in the Book of Joel: "I will pour out my Spirit on everyone … your old people will have dreams" (Joel 2:28). After less than 15 months of this cooperation between Clonard and Fitzroy, on 28 July 1983, Fr Christy passed away quietly. At his funeral those closest to him in Clonard expressed the belief that his most influential years came towards the end of his life. He was the prime mover behind the invitation in 1980 to the first Protestant minister to preach in Clonard, Canon John Baker, the Anglican chaplain to the British House of Commons. His brief initiative with us also helped to construct a fragile rope-bridge between Fitzroy and Clonard. In an obituary carried in the *Irish News*, a colleague, identified simply as "AR", wrote:

> The truly Christian joy which so many Protestants and Catholics have experienced in worshipping together at the Clonard Service and the deep Christian hope for the future which this experience has inspired in their hearts, are living signs of the presence of the Holy Spirit ... and God's blessing on the work of the man who inspired it all – Father McCarthy.

The author was Fr Alec Reid, a priest not widely known outside west Belfast. Drawn into his older colleague's "dazzling vision", he was to carry it to fulfilment in ways that nobody could have foreseen.

## Someone Is Coming towards You

While it lasted, the fledging relationship between Clonard and Fitzroy had been lit up by the example of a remarkable old man. Now that he was gone, our meetings were suspended and we wondered if our initiative would fall apart. Unbeknown to us, the rector of Clonard, Fr George Wadding, was already pursuing plans to consolidate the Redemptorist community's reconciliation ministry. He convinced the Irish provincial of the order to transfer from Galway to Belfast a 48-year-old Limerick priest, Fr Gerry Reynolds, to inject new energy into Clonard's peace vocation. It was an inspired choice. Within a month Fr Gerry was settling into his new surroundings.

Gerard Reynolds was born in 1935 into a farming family in Mungret Parish, a few miles west of Limerick city, the second of four children cared for by devoutly Christian parents, Bartholomew and Mary. His father's two brothers were Redemptorist priests. Tragedy struck the family in 1941 when his father died, but his mother's faith and hard work provided the children with an environment of stability and love. The first Protestants Gerry met were among his mother's friends, who regularly visited the farm to buy eggs. Occasionally in the kitchen questions of faith would arise. On one occasion Gerry intervened in a discussion with a suitable quotation from the

Catechism, only to be reminded by his mother that little boys should be quiet when their elders were speaking! By the age of 18 he sensed a calling to the priesthood and, following graduation from university in 1956, he undertook theological training at the Redemptorist seminary in Galway city. It was from one of his lecturers, Fr Sean O'Riordan, that Gerry gained positive insights into the nature of Protestantism. Fr O'Riordan shared with his students conversations he had been involved in with Protestants of various hues in Belfast. He confessed to a growing admiration for their emphasis on a personal relationship with Jesus Christ as Lord and Saviour, a relationship that was also central to Gerry's faith and to his spiritual formation as a witness to Christ the Redeemer.

Following his ordination in 1960, he was appointed to Redemptorist Publications in Dublin and the Catholic Communications Institute. In September 1973 he was invited to attend the first meeting of the ICC (representing 85 per cent of the Protestant churches in Ireland) and the Irish Catholic bishops at the Ballymascanlon Hotel, outside Dundalk. Its purpose was to create a Christian forum to initiate common action for peace in the face of a conflict that was spiralling out of control: the previous year 4,876 people had been injured and 497 killed in the Troubles. Over lunch he met Rev Jim McEvoy, minister of Rathgar Methodist Church. They discovered that for a decade they had been living within a kilometre of each other in Dublin but had never met. They became friends and went on to form the Rathgar–Terenure Fellowship, which over time drew in other clergy and congregations. In 1975 Fr Gerry was appointed rector of the Redemptorist community in Limerick.

Other influences were also working through him before his arrival in Belfast, especially the fresh perspectives of faith emanating from the Second Vatican Council and gradually spreading throughout the wider Catholic Church. He was particularly taken with the concept of the befriending grace of God, which infused many of Vatican II's weighty documents. One specific sentence was to impact his future ministry in Clonard as he crossed the border in August 1983 *en route* to Belfast: "The invisible God, from the fullness of his love, addresses all people as his friends, and moves among them, in order to invite and receive them into his own company."

It took Gerry time to grasp the complexities of a troubled city, but he was fortunate to have good mentors. Fr Alec Reid, who had worked among the nationalist community of west Belfast for 25 years, advised him to develop a holistic approach to peacemaking, taking seriously the unresolved political issues that fuel conflict and the religious influences that reinforce the boundaries of division. "Peacemakers," he insisted, "should be open to dialogue with groups engaged in violence in order to bring it to an end and replace it with inclusive and democratic politics."

Another wise mentor was 80-year-old Brother Hugh Murray. He brought Gerry up to the third floor of the monastery that overlooks the peace wall and beyond it the streets of the Protestant Shankill Road. "They're all the same people as those on this side of the wall," he said. "For generations the same factory hooters ruled their lives, calling them to the mills. They were exploited and their differences were exaggerated to keep them divided. Neither group got a fair share of the wealth they created."

Shortly afterwards Gerry ventured through the gate in the peace wall to visit the Shankill. For a Catholic priest, this was a risky thing to do. He recounted:

> I walked along the road dressed as a clergyman and in the Community Information Centre I met an elderly man named George.
>
> "You're up from the Free State, Padre," he asked, latching on to my southern accent. "Where are you ministering?"
>
> "Over the wall there at Clonard," I replied.
>
> The game was up. He knew who I was, but we went on talking at length. Before parting I asked him, "Have you any advice for me as newcomer to Belfast?" His answer still rings in my memory: "You clergy will have to get together to bring the church to the people again."

Gerry became a frequent visitor to the Shankill and a familiar face in its churches.

It wasn't until May 1984 that he phoned in order to invite me to Clonard. As we walked and talked in the monastery garden, it became clear that we both shared a simple belief that God could transform the depressing realities around us. In other ways we were very different. His rural background manifested itself in an unruffled calmness, while I was utterly urban, constantly on the go and churning over new ideas. He was quintessentially Irish, Catholic and nationalist, whereas my roots were in the soil of an unsettled unionism and the perpetual strivings of conservative evangelicalism. Why, then, did our friendship become so strong and enterprising? Certainly, the natural ease with which we got along with each other played a big part, as did our willingness to learn from each other's experience and faith. But the essential reason we bonded was that we both sensed that we were brothers in Christ with a common passion and God-given vocation for peace.

## Surge of New Life

The news that Fr Gerry and I would be reactivating the Clonard–Fitzroy Fellowship brought a lot of excitement to Fitzroy. We invited several members of Clonard to join us on Sunday morning, 2 December 1984, for an Advent service being televised by the Independent Broadcasting Authority. During it we prayed for those caught up in the IRA bombing of the Brighton Hotel in October, which claimed five lives and left thirty-one others injured; in particular we remembered Prime Minister Margaret Thatcher and her husband Denis, who narrowly escaped injury. When it came to my sermon, one passage reflects the early joy we felt at the restoration of the links with Clonard:

> May every Protestant and Catholic in Ireland today so encounter Christ that all bitterness, arrogance, selfishness and hatred may be removed, and the love of Christ be implanted in us. I have benefitted hugely over the last few years from the friendships we have developed with Clonard Monastery through our joint Bible-study group. It makes me so happy that some have come this morning to worship with us.

The following evening 60 of us gathered in Fitzroy for a Christmas Bible study based on the first chapter of John's Gospel. It revealed how God breached the barrier between divinity and humanity to become an infinitesimally small foetus in the womb of the Virgin Mary. This message steadied us for the future and our sense of smallness in a barrier-burdened province no longer felt so intimidating.

Other joint initiatives followed quickly. In January 1985 I took part for the first time in the public worship of Clonard when Fr Gerry included me along with Methodist and Anglican colleagues in a service marking the Week of Prayer for Christian Unity. Another step forward took place on the sunny but chilly Sunday afternoon of St Patrick's Day, 17 March 1985. Twenty of us travelled to Downpatrick Anglican Cathedral for a thanksgiving service in honour of our patron saint. Local Free Presbyterians threatened massive protests because the service would be led by the president of the Methodist Church, the Anglican primate, the Presbyterian moderator, Dr Howard Cromie and, controversially, Cardinal Tomás Ó Fiaich, the Catholic archbishop of Armagh. A local newspaper warned that a ring of steel would be needed around the cathedral to hold back the protesters. After finding car-parking space we unfurled a ten-metre-long banner that read "Come Spirit Come" and joined the hundreds of cheerful pilgrims processing up the sweeping ascent to the cathedral. There were no rings of steel in sight, just 30 respectable male protestors glaring at us with stony faces. We seemed to be on different planets. With reference to space, however, there was one unexpected sighting: Colonel James Irwin, pilot of the 1971 Apollo 15 lunar module and the eighth person to walk on the moon, joined the pilgrims. His most memorable comment was, "Jesus walking on the earth is more important than man walking on the moon."

By the end of the year the friendships within the fellowship had been well and truly cemented. In the wake of the hugely unpopular signing of the Anglo-Irish Agreement on 15 November by Prime Minister Margaret Thatcher and Taoiseach Garret FitzGerald, we organised an all-night prayer vigil in Fitzroy in December. During the slow-moving hours of the night, a prayer formed within me that summed up the common yearning of those present:

> We are a people made one by the love of Christ. We have been changed by his grace. Gone is the pride that desires to dominate and the anger that wants to undermine. We want to listen to each other's hurts and fears, and build together a community furnished with the generosity, justice and compassion of Jesus Christ.

### Building a Team

Among those attending the fellowship on a regular basis, it became clear that some were natural leaders. By November 1987 we had formed a strong committee: the four representing Fitzroy were Sandra Rutherford, Philip Mateer, Ian McMurray and William Rutherford, an eminent Belfast medical consultant. Clonard provided five: Monica Curran, Marie McMullan, Marie Crothers, Helen Moran and Jim Lynn. The challenges we faced were formidable. The fellowship was a small group of never more than 25 from Fitzroy out of a congregation of 400 families, and 30 from Clonard out of almost 1,500 who attended Mass on Sunday. How, we wondered, could we bring our larger worshipping communities into the process? In addition, once we got beyond the normal pleasantries, how would we navigate our way through the differences we detected in each other in terms of denominational, cultural, social and political backgrounds?

Several factors contributed to our survival and foremost among them was our resolve to centre our life together on Christ. To some this might appear unduly pious, but a consideration of the durability of the group and the practical outcomes of this decision display its strengths. Our shared faith bonded us at a spiritual level and, like iron filings drawn towards a magnet, we clustered together in the process. Furthermore, we designed most of our early meetings around getting to know each other and understanding the journeys we had made to prepare us for this joint venture. As our trust in each other grew, so did our willingness to be honest – which, at times, did not make for easy listening. Some of the Clonard members revealed how humiliated they felt in their early lives when applying for job after job, only to be turned down because of their Irish-sounding name, the nationalist area they lived in or the Catholic primary school they had attended. But other stories from childhood, which spoke of friendships and good neighbourly relationships across the sectarian divide, were inspiring. These often left a legacy of affection and respect, which explained the eagerness of these people to be part of a group like the Clonard–Fitzroy Fellowship.

Another element in the bonding process was our daily experience of living through the bleakness of a conflict that appeared almost insoluble. Instead of driving us to despair, it sharpened our sense of responsibility for the city and country we were living in and spurred us into championing the sacredness of life. In fact, the Troubles created within us a true clarity about our vocation to be peacemakers.

Finally, the "craic" factor cannot be underestimated. Belfast people love humour and frequently use it to poke fun at religious taboos and political rivalries. Time and again this gift rescued us from an overindulgence in the emotional intensity that sometimes characterises those involved in peacemaking. Our objective, however, always remained clear and uncomplicated. In the words of Professor Nico Smith, a Dutch Reformed minister and opponent of apartheid in South Africa:

We have to build a new society in which people learn to trust one another; to trust one another, we need to love another; to love one another, we need to accept one another; to accept one another, we need to know one another; to know one another, we must go and meet one another.

## Evolving Goals

The sinking of the Belfast-built *Titanic* in 1912 is an uncomfortable reminder of the vulnerability of optimism. It is easy for people to be caught up in the initial vision and thrill of an exciting project, but if that vision is not galvanised with clear goals it can steadily corrode to the point where it disappears without trace. With the formation of a committee in 1987 the purpose of the fellowship began to crystallise around "promoting contact, mutual understanding, respect and common witness between people from the various Christian traditions in Northern Ireland". In time we identified the five goals which defined our mission:

1. Nurturing the faith of our members
2. Creating space for inter-church dialogue
3. Drawing close to those directly affected by the Troubles
4. Integrating more fully into each other's congregations
5. Connecting with the Loyal Orders.

These turned out to be deep and lengthy commitments.

### *Nurturing Faith*

It was an inspired choice when the rejuvenated Clonard–Fitzroy Fellowship decided to let all of its activities grow out of the soil of a shared spirituality. The quality time set aside for Bible study and prayer transformed our relationships from polite association to genuine friendship. When we tackled the obvious differences that existed among us, the respect we had cultivated at a spiritual level accelerated our acceptance of diversity as part and parcel of life. Furthermore, our spirituality always had a practical orientation. In February 1985, for example, we examined the story of Christ's 40-day fast in the Judaean wilderness and asked ourselves, since fasting involves sharing with the needy, what should we do this Lent in response to the famine in Africa? One million lives had already been lost.

In time every issue confronting the church and community was addressed: abortion, homosexuality, homophobia, prejudice, conflict, mixed marriage, Orange marches and the clash of cultural identities. The year 1994 was typical. In November we discussed the role of women in the church with the help of Rev Ruth Patterson of an interdenominational prayer group, Restoration Ministries, and Sr Roisin Hannaway, leader of the Columbanus Community of Reconciliation. While the door to ordained priesthood within the Catholic Church remained firmly closed to women, in 1976 Ruth had become the first woman to be ordained within the PCI. Sadly, resistance to the trend has remained and less than five per cent of the PCI's 600 ministers are women. We also devoted four meetings to the booklet *What the Bible Says about Sectarianism*. A photograph on the front shows a four-year-old child wandering into a smoke-filled street of terraced houses engulfed in flames. These discussions brought to the surface painful experiences of insult and injury rarely expressed even within a mixed setting. The nineteenth-century County Tyrone novelist William Carleton once observed:

> If you hate a man for an obvious and palpable injury, it is likely when he cancels that injury by an act of subsequent kindness, accompanied by an exhibition of sincere sorrow, you will cease to look upon him as your enemy; but where the hatred is such that, while feeling it, you cannot, on a sober examination of your heart, account for it, there is little hope that you will ever be able to stifle the enmity which you entertain against him.

Our annual weekend retreats also contributed greatly to the development of our faith. Two of our favourite locations were the Corrymeela Centre for Reconciliation on the north Antrim coast and the Dromantine Conference Centre in south Down, set in 320 acres of colourful woodland. Long walks, unrushed conversations, stimulating lectures, periods of quietness and laughter galore at our Saturday-night parties reinforced our friendships. But there were also awkward moments too. Fr Gerry would usually conduct Mass on Saturday evenings and I would celebrate the Lord's Supper on Sunday morning. All 40 or 50 of us would attend both, but the unresolved differences between our traditions divided us at what Christ intended to be the sacrament of unity. Despite this, we tried to make each service as inclusive as possible. At the Lord's Supper I would invite Fr Gerry to preach and fellowship members would read the Scriptures and offer prayers. At the Catholic Eucharist, a similar pattern prevailed. But it was bizarre to hear the accustomed words of Christ inviting us all to the Lord's table while ecclesiastical legislation was blocking the path for some of us. Our Clonard friends found this embarrassing; it was less so for the Presbyterians, because when we celebrate Communion the minister declares:

> The table of our Lord Jesus Christ is open to all who are in communion with the Church Universal. We therefore invite members of any branch thereof who love the Lord Jesus in sincerity and truth to join with us in this holy fellowship.

For me, this rubric of grace remains one of the jewels of our Reformed tradition.

Most of the Clonard members would have loved to participate in our Presbyterian form of Communion and occasionally some did. Loyalty to their church's directives, however, kept tugging at their consciences. In truth, we all felt pulled in two directions. The practice we adopted, therefore, was that at the Presbyterian Communion the Clonard members would come forward in the same line as ourselves and place their hands across their chests, to receive not the elements but, instead, a blessing or short prayer from me or one of Fitzroy's elders. In similar fashion, when our Clonard friends went forward to receive Communion from Fr Gerry, we would join them. Despite our disappointment at being unable to receive the tokens of Christ's love, the placing of Fr Gerry's hands on our heads never failed to move us. The weight of the restrictions they felt they had to abide by often reduced him and the other Clonard members to tears. In a stunningly honest homily in 1999, Fr Gerry expressed his anguish:

> Since coming to Belfast in 1983 I have pondered the question, "What happens when my Church of Ireland, Presbyterian and Methodist friends gather for Communion in obedience to Jesus' command, 'Do this in memory of me'?" Does our Father give to them the bread from heaven he gives to us in the Eucharist, or does he give them something less? Does our crucified and Risen Saviour become really present to give them the fruits of his passion, or do they have to settle for something less? Is the Holy Spirit poured out

upon the bread they break and the wine they drink to hallow them as the body and blood of Christ for their spiritual nourishment or do they invoke the Spirit in vain?

If we simply pose the questions, the inadequacy of the traditional answers stands exposed. For me, if the Berlin Wall can come down in 1989, if apartheid can be dismantled in South Africa in 1994, and if the Good Friday Agreement can be signed in Belfast in 1998, surely it is not beyond the ingenuity of our finest Christian leaders and theologians to construct a path to Holy Communion for all the followers of Christ.

### Creating Space

There never seemed to be an auspicious time in the 1980s to launch any public initiative aimed at bringing people together. The temptation to stay tucked up safe in the anchorage of our own communities was easy to succumb to. But, in the summer of 1985, Myles Wilson, a Campus Crusade for Christ worker, asked me to join a committee planning an innovative evangelistic campaign entitled Project Hope. Campus Crusade for Christ had been founded in Los Angeles by Bill Bright in 1951 and over the years had developed an evangelical openness that was comfortable cooperating with Catholics. Three hundred Protestant churches and some Catholic parishes across Northern Ireland decided to link into the project. One major thrust of the outreach was a colourful magazine on whose cover was a photograph of Dana, the singer from Derry who became a superstar at the age of 19, in 1970, when she won the Eurovision Song Contest. The magazine, which featured an interview with Dana about fame, family and her Christian faith, was posted to each of the 600,000 homes in the province. It was widely read, but unsurprisingly drew a modicum of criticism from evangelical quarters because Dana was a devout Catholic.

Project Hope encouraged churches to promote some aspect of the campaign locally. As a result, I approached the Kirk Session on behalf of the Clonard–Fitzroy Fellowship to seek permission to invite the Presbyterian moderator, Dr Robert Dickinson and the Catholic bishop of Down and Connor, Cahal Daly, to speak together on Tuesday, 22 April 1986 on the theme, "There is Hope in Christ". Courageously, the elders gave us the green light and the two church leaders accepted our invitation, but for different reasons. It was the first time in Northern Ireland that leaders of the two largest Christian traditions had spoken together at such a public event. Dr Dickinson, a leading anti-ecumenical figure, was keen to preach the Gospel to a mixed audience; Dr Daly was eager to build relationships with Christians from the other churches. Our purpose was to provide a platform for them to speak of hope in a time of intense anger, confusion and despair. It was not going to be easy for them: the Anglo-Irish Agreement, signed six months earlier, had unleashed a storm within unionism, much of it whipped up by Ian Paisley.

In March we released publicity about the event and made 600 tickets available to the public. They were snapped up with such speed that I suspected that some sort of opposition was being orchestrated, especially when several letters arrived requesting blocks of up to 50 tickets. Then, as the event came closer, the phone in our manse began ringing in the middle of the night. When we answered we were treated either to heavy sustained breathing or the raucous strains of "Kick the Pope" bands. Dr Dickinson came under pressure to pull out and Bishop Daly received a bullet through the post, warning him not to appear. Eventually I discovered that some Free Presbyterians and assorted fundamentalists were indeed rallying their supporters to protest against the occasion. I began privately to fear that a loyalist madman might some night petrol-bomb our historic church, a catastrophe from which my conscience would never let me recover if I made the wrong choice. When I turned to Val for advice, her words not only calmed me down but also reinforced the clarity of my own convictions – sometimes you have to face down those who would take great delight in putting you down. "If we don't do it now, Ken," she said, "we'll never do it."

This strengthened my determination not to give in to the bullying. Finally, at Martyrs Memorial Church, just two days before the meeting, Dr Paisley preached a sermon against what we were doing, entitled, "Why Bible-Believing Protestants Cannot Dialogue with Priests of Rome". It was delivered with the usual apocalyptic fervour:

> This is a day of surprises both in the political and in the religious world in which we live … The Bible tells us that in the last days perilous times shall come. The Lord Jesus Christ also said, that so dark will be the apostasy, so terrible will be the compromise, so tremendous will be the satanic influence, that in the last days, if it were possible, the very elect of God would be deceived. We are living in that day.

On Tuesday evening, Dr Paisley and a posse of 100 protesters surrounded the front gates of Fitzroy. Dozens of policemen and army personnel struggled to hold open paths into the church for the 600 people who had decided to attend. They had to walk, often one by one, through the ranks of aggressive hecklers. As the service itself got underway, I introduced our speakers and led the congregation in the singing of "Rejoice, the Lord is King". The volume of praise drowned out the drone of the protesters outside, and inside looked deceptively calm. Then the storm broke. As Dr Dickinson was delivering his talk, protestors strategically sited throughout the church sprang their feet at intervals and hurled at him the customary Ulster catcall, "Judas!" When Bishop Daly started to speak, one protester ran up the aisle, grabbed hold of the Communion table in front of the pulpit and screamed "Antichrist!" Our ushers escorted 12 protestors out the door, and those refusing to budge were quickly persuaded to change their minds by the firm grip of plain-clothes policemen, who had also taken up strategic positions within the congregation. With the descent of decorum, those who came to listen were treated to two excellent addresses.

Some of those who decided to sit through the talks were unquestionably sympathetic to Dr Paisley's views, but were infuriated at the disruptive antics of the protestors. When the service was over and people began to leave, I watched as rows broke out on the steps of the church between those who had respectfully remained inside and those who had been removed. One of the former vented his anger at the ejected protestors and said, "You are a disgrace to Protestantism!" The ugly images of confrontation before and after the event and the sight of the police and the army attempting to hold open a corridor of access to people wanting to get into a church were captured by the media and screened across the British Isles. They generated such negative publicity for the protestors that the practice of disrupting a religious service was eventually dropped as a tactic of fundamentalist dissent. Thankfully, none of Dr Paisley's fulminations had the effect they threatened. The lightning of divine judgment seemed to ricochet off our evening of hope and strike some unsuspecting agitators. I concluded that the protestors felt endangered – not by the modest numbers of people attending the event, but by the capacity of our witness to spread more widely throughout a province where every inch of the space available to meet, listen, learn, change and hopefully embrace each other is vigorously contested. This collision was inevitable; others lay ahead.

In the days leading up to the service, I had a strong feeling that some people would be positively affected just by being there. I was not surprised, therefore, to receive a letter a few days later from a Presbyterian ministerial student living in Union Theological College. He confessed to being angry that a Catholic bishop was speaking in a Presbyterian church and came to support the protest. But someone in the melee slipped a ticket into his hand and he decided to go into the church and observe the unfolding scandal. During the evening he noticed himself changing, as he was caught up in the fervour of the hymns and the quiet sincerity of the prayers. "When it came to the speakers," he wrote, "I was prepared to give them a fair hearing." By the time they had finished, he realised he had been carrying a considerable amount of personal prejudice. "Since then," he continued, "I've been thinking about my attitudes and I realise I need to change. Last Tuesday was a start, but I've still some way to go."

The positive media coverage of the Daly–Dickinson evening and the negative reaction to the Paisley protest surrounding it catapulted Fitzroy's links with Clonard into the public eye as never before. In some quarters our witness was seen as a sign of hope in a seemingly bleak landscape, but in others it was viewed as a betrayal and threat. In an environment of conflict such threats can spark sinister reactions, which are clearly intended to send out a threatening message. Many of those determined to protect and strengthen their communities learned to live with such threats, including those in the security forces, business, the media, politics, and reconciliation initiatives. They learned to keep their eyes and ears open, check under their cars for explosives and, while courageously pressing ahead with their lives, cast an occasional glance over their shoulders.

One evening, shortly after our Project Hope initiative, my mother phoned in tears to tell me that her front living-room window had just been smashed with a brick. She lived alone as a widow on the Shore Road. She was shocked, terrified and certain that it was because of the contentious publicity surrounding my association with Clonard and Catholics. I rushed across town to see what had happened and found her in a terrible state. She was angry with me for landing her in this situation. I felt heartbroken and just listened to the distress flowing from her. For over 40 years she had lived peacefully and securely among neighbours whose friendship she valued and whose children had all grown up together. Nothing remotely like this had ever happened before and she now felt unsafe in her own home. She was convinced that somebody from outside the area who knew about me had targetted her. Sectarian intimidation of this nature was not uncommon in Belfast, particularly at times of heightened social and political tension. I sensed that the horrible childhood memories of the incident in Belmullet were being rekindled within her.

Privately, however, I wondered if it had just been a random act of antisocial behaviour. If someone had wanted to frighten her to get at me, then perhaps all of her windows would have been smashed. That was not how she interpreted it, and she may have been right. I apologised for being the source of her distress, made a cup of tea, boarded up the window and organised a glazier to come the next morning to replace the glass. When I offered to say the night she insisted that I should be at home with my own wife and children. Thankfully, in the years that followed, there were no more attacks. I was taught two salutary lessons: one, to size up carefully the situations into which I was stepping in a way that protected my wider family circle; and two, not to underestimate the darker side of Ulster sectarianism and the levels to which those who resented what I was doing might stoop.

While the pressures I was under toughened my resolve to bring people together, the fears I harboured for my family as well as the security of Fitzroy made me carefully weigh up the wisdom of the risks we were taking. I confess, however, that I did not always give adequate attention to the strain I was unconsciously putting on our children, Tim and Jennie. From the beginning, Val and I had decided to keep the details of our working lives to ourselves, so as to preserve a relaxed environment at home and not awaken unnecessary anxiety. Despite our best efforts, though, it was not always possible to dodge their questions. Val was now working full time as an English teacher in Belfast's Crumlin Road Gaol, a foreboding Victorian building dating back to 1845, which was connected to the courthouse by a tunnel running under the main road. Originally designed to house 550 inmates, it had reached a capacity of 900 as the Troubles escalated in the early 1970s. Most occupants were dedicated republican and loyalist remand prisoners who were at war on the streets outside. As a consequence, the gaol constituted an explosive environment. Fights and riots were commonplace and prison officers would often be sent into the middle of the chaos to restore peace. Those working in it as administrators, staff and prison officers were urged to exercise extreme caution when arriving at and leaving the premises. Although Val was a teacher and mixed well with the inmates, I often worried about her when she set off for work each morning and was always relieved when she returned safely late in the afternoon. Although our children knew generally what was going on in Northern Ireland through television and conversations with their friends at school, we rarely discussed these matters in front of them.

As Tim and Jennie entered their teenage years, they became more aware of the activities we were involved in and the relationships we enjoyed, particularly that with Fr Gerry Reynolds, who became a firm family friend. As their flow of questions naturally increased, we always sought to answer them honestly and sensitively, but there were times when the strain we were under seeped out at home. They wondered why some people insisted on phoning in the middle of the night and waking up the whole house. Jennie tended to be more fearful than Tim; it was only much later that she divulged her inner thoughts and occasional dreams of someone coming to our front door to shoot me, as well as Val, Tim and herself. Despite all this, our family life was surprisingly normal, relaxed and enjoyable, and we looked forward to our summer holidays in England, France and Spain.

Two long-term consequences developed from the Project Hope initiative. Firstly, it added grit to the fellowship's determination to continue creating space. In November 1995 our moderator, Dr John Ross, spoke at a reconciliation service in Fitzroy with Cardinal Cahal Daly. During the service, a huge scroll containing the names of the 1,768 civilians and 1,007 security personnel killed in the Troubles to date was slowly and prayerfully unfurled across the tops of the pews in Fitzroy. It stretched almost from wall to wall. Then, in 1997, a large congregation welcomed the former moderator, Dr John Dunlop, and the new Catholic archbishop of Armagh, Dr Seán Brady.

"The coming down of the Berlin Wall in 1989," noted Dr Dunlop, "is instructive for those living in Northern Ireland. The once brash barriers of Europe are now just rubble. We cannot trap God inside our denominations. He is always breaking out and breaking down our divisions. Dialogue is the only way to achieve reconciliation."

All of these events continued to be widely publicised, but now there was not a protester to be seen. Coming together in this way was, in some parts of the city, becoming normal.

The second consequence of Project Hope was to convince the fellowship that we needed to open up dialogue – not only between church leaders but also between our best theologians. Religious reasons continued to be trotted out to justify the historic distance between the Protestant and Catholic churches and thereby maintain a form of social and spiritual apartheid in our cities, towns and villages. With the support of fellowship members, Fr Gerry and I initiated biannual evangelical and Roman Catholic conferences in Fitzroy and in St Clement's Conference Centre on Belfast's Antrim Road. They were designed primarily for ministers and priests and took their inspiration from the Evangelical–Roman Catholic Dialogue on Mission (1977–84), co-chaired by Dr Basil Meeking and Rev John Stott, one of the most respected leaders of the worldwide evangelical movement. Many Catholic priests rarely had an opportunity to listen to our best evangelical theologians, while many evangelicals considered dialogue suspect and unbiblical. In contrast, influential sectors of world evangelicalism were moving in the direction as the Evangelical–Roman Catholic Dialogue on Mission. We adopted for our conferences, therefore, its classic rationale for dialogue:

> We see no compromise in a frank and serious conversation in which each side is prepared to listen respectfully to the other. On the contrary – it is essentially Christian to meet one another face to face. In this process our caricatures of one another become corrected. Honest and charitable dialogue enriches our faith, deepens our understanding, clarifies our convictions, testifies to a desire for reconciliation and expresses a love which encompasses even those who disagree.

The conferences regularly attracted around 100 clergy and many of those went on to develop influential reconciliation initiatives in their parishes. Sacred space was being cleared in Ulster's narrow ground. It always came at a price, but it was worth paying for.

### Drawing Close to the Afflicted

It was only after the IRA and loyalist ceasefires of 1994 that something approaching normality began to return to the province. As the community embraced a nervous peace, the scars of three decades of conflict became more noticeable. A World Health Organisation survey into post-traumatic stress disorder in 28 conflict-affected countries revealed that the incidence in Northern Ireland was, per head of the population, three times higher than in Israel, South Africa or Lebanon. Its symptoms were widespread: nightmares, flashbacks, isolation, irritability, guilt, numbness and depression.

This was not surprising. Out of a small population of 1.6 million, 3,200 had been killed and 40,000 injured. "If this was England," some critics of British security measures would stress, "the death toll would be 150,000 and the number of injured 2,000,000." But statistics do not tell the whole story. Behind each tragedy was a circle of anguished family members, friends, neighbours, colleagues and often the congregations to which they belonged.

One week in July 1990 provides a window into this reality. On Tuesday, 24 July 1990, a 1,000-pound IRA landmine hidden under the Armagh–Killylea road was detonated as a Royal Ulster Constabulary (RUC) patrol car was passing. The car was hurled into the air, instantly killing three officers, Joshua Willis (35), David Sterritt (34) and James Hanson (37). A second vehicle was caught in the blast and Sister Catherine Dunne (37) became the first and only nun to die in the Troubles. The heartlessness of the killers was branded a "total blasphemy" by the Church of Ireland primate, Dr Robin Eames.

When news reports revealed that James Hanson had been a youth leader in Redrock Presbyterian Church, I felt strongly that I should attend his funeral and asked Fr Gerry if he would come with me. As we walked towards the church through the ranks of the RUC guard of honour, I noticed the eyes of several officers following us. Gerry's collar unmistakably identified him as a Catholic priest, and in 1990 priests were rarely seen at such funerals. It was equally uncommon to see a Presbyterian minister and Catholic priest walking side by side to pay their respects. We hoped that they could detect our concern for them and their families. We squeezed into the gallery of the small church and surveyed a congregation silently drawing comfort from its faith. In the front pews sat Constable Hanson's widow, their four young children, their parents and their brothers and sisters. The minister of Redrock, Rev Howard Gilpin, was a close friend of the deceased and spoke movingly of his commitment to Christ, to his family, to his career and to helping the young people of Redrock. He also questioned the UK government's resolve to defeat violence: "Why," he asked, "are we here burying the 273rd RUC officer to be murdered and the 2,806th member of the community to be killed?" Afterwards I introduced Fr Gerry to my fellow ministers who had taken part in the service.

A week later, on Tuesday, 31 July, another vicious murder took place just off Belfast's Springfield Road. It was part of a sequence of loyalist murders carried out by "Top Gun", a UDA commander from the Shankill area. The victim was a Catholic, John Judge, a 34-year-old married man with three young children. Around 11.00 pm he was enjoying a beer at his front door with three friends, having spent the day celebrating the fifth birthday of one of his children. A hijacked taxi sped into the street and two masked men leapt out and opened fire with handguns. As everyone ran for cover and John attempted to shield his two sons, the killers shot him five times before the taxi screeched out of the street. The Belfast city coroner later described him as "a completely innocent family man".

The family was part of the Clonard congregation and Fr Gerry knew them well. He was deeply distressed and asked them if he could hold a prayer vigil in the house along with Rev Sam Burch, the Methodist leader of the nearby Cornerstone Community, and some Presbyterian friends. Fifteen of us from Fitzroy travelled across town to attend, including some parents and children. Some of us were fortunate to be able to squeeze into the room where the immediate family was sitting close to the coffin. Every space in the house was taken up and many had to stand outside. During the prayers that Fr Gerry offered, we felt a deep emotional connection with the devastated family. The roles that Gerry and I had played were now reversed. I had brought him into the heart of the Presbyterian community in Redrock; he had brought us into the heart of the local Catholic community. The grief coursing through the mourners in both situations was identical.

Then, something totally unexpected happened. During the prayers one of the Fitzroy children, a boy of seven manoeuvred his way across the room towards an elderly woman who, I assumed, was a grandmother. She had been sobbing quietly and inconsolably. Like the rest of us, the child could not take his eyes off her. Without saying a word, he put his arm over her shoulder and she slipped her arm around his waist. It was a moment of unifying grace I will never forget.

These visits convinced me that if our two communities were only more prepared to journey into each other's sorrow rather than to grieve in isolation, they could release a river of healing into a deeply wounded community. They also tipped my equivocating mind towards saying yes to an invitation from Fr Alec Reid to participate in a private dialogue with Sinn Féin. I was now convinced that what is not befriended is not redeemed.

### Integrating into Each Other's Congregations

A major temptation faced by peace groups, noted Peter McLachlan, director the Belfast Voluntary Welfare Association, is to "become cut off and frozen out from the rest of their community". As the fellowship took root in Fitzroy and Clonard, I could see what he meant. While our strength was the unshakable loyalty of 50 people, our weakness was that we were small islands in two large congregations. My dream for Fitzroy was that peacemaking would become one of its central mission priorities and the choice facing us was stark: integrate or disintegrate. Following my first meeting with Fr Gerry in 1984, he and some Clonard members began to turn up at regular intervals to our Sunday-morning services in Fitzroy. I had the joy of publicly welcoming them and at the end more and more members of the congregation would encircle them with smiling faces and outstretched hands. Gradually I got them to take part by offering prayers or reading the Scriptures, and by 1988 this had created enough confidence to enable Fr Gerry and me to preach together. Little by little, even fringe members of Fitzroy began to feel at ease with the new reality.

Into this increasingly inclusive atmosphere were drawn young couples who had fallen in love across the religious divide and were seeking a Christian marriage that honoured both faith traditions equally. Some had grown up in Fitzroy, but others sought us out because their home congregations refused to let a priest participate. In the 1990s I was conducting ten weddings a year in Fitzroy, of which three were mixed marriages – or, as we preferred to call them, inter-church weddings. A decade later this had risen to one in two.

With the advent of peace in 1994, mixed marriages in Northern Ireland had inched upwards towards ten per cent of all marriages, but many couples were still frustrated with trying to accommodate the aspirations of family members vying over the venue or threatening not to attend. Some of the parents I spent time with feared negative comments from their co-religionists at church. These were legitimate concerns. A 1989 survey revealed that one-third of Ulster people would "mind a lot" if relatives married outside their religious grouping. Thankfully I was able to persuade most perplexed parents to attend the weddings that Fr Gerry and I were conducting by giving them my word that nothing in the service would offend their sensitivities. By 1998 the numbers of those "minding a lot" had fallen to 16 per cent. "Couples," declared the Northern Ireland Mixed Marriage Association, "are putting love before traditional allegiances and tribal loyalties." Over the years, thousands of visitors and hundreds of our own members were guests at these fully inclusive weddings in Fitzroy. The feedback Fr Gerry and I got was overwhelmingly positive. Lingering clouds of suspicion and hesitation were dispersing in the authenticity and joy of the celebrations. Exactly the same response was experienced when similar weddings were held in Catholic parishes. It has been my experience that, while theological dialogue can slowly transform attitudes, these romantic occasions have defrosted far more Ulster people than anyone could ever have imagined.

Another catalyst towards integration took place when some of these couples later asked me to baptise their children. For several years I had conducted inter-church baptisms on Sunday afternoons in a large room at Fitzroy. Fr Gerry would preach the homily, and Denis Boyd, our clerk of session, would present a copy of the Children's Bible to the parents. I did not consider this arrangement unusual until one young couple asked me, "Ken, could we have our baby baptised on Sunday morning just like everyone else?" I quickly realised that this was a much healthier spiritual setting than a small private family affair in the afternoon. After receiving permission from the elders, we celebrated our first inter-church baptism at a full Sunday-morning service in the presence of the whole congregation. Fr Gerry took part in the prayers, and grandparents from both sides of the family did the readings from Scripture.

Attendance was always swollen on these occasions, with a large number of family guests and friends attending. The moment in the service that consistently affected those present was after the act of baptism, when I carried the baby up one of the aisles as the congregation sang,

> Welcome to the family; we're glad that you have come
> To share your life with us as we grow in love and
> May we always be to you what God would have us be,
> A family always there, to be strong and to lean on.

So many of those present, from toddlers to pensioners, would reach out to touch the baby's fingers or lay their hands on the child's head in a gentle gesture of blessing. When I returned to the baptismal font, I would transfer the baby to Fr Gerry, who would carry the child up the other aisle to the same deeply moving response. A child who could not speak was conveying an appeal for unity far more eloquent than either Gerry or I could compose.

The process of integrating more fully into the wider life of each other's congregations evolved along similar lines and I became a frequent guest at lunch with the other Redemptorist priests at Clonard. The first time I ever preached in Clonard was at the Week of Prayer for Christian Unity in January 1989. The Clonard chronicler noted: "As an indication of the influence of the Clonard–Fitzroy Fellowship, the church was 80 per cent full."

But the event in Clonard that dwarfs all others is the Great Novena held every June. It attracts around nine thousand people to ten services per day for the full nine days and has a special focus on the Virgin Mary. When Gerry asked me to preach on Mary at three of the services on Thursday, 24 June 1999, I replied "Get me a chair!" He knew that I did not accept some of the traditional Marian dogmas such as the Immaculate Conception. On the other hand, I identified with a stream of opinion that lamented the lack of consideration given to Mary within Protestantism. An evangelical article I had read some time previously began with the plea, "Give Mary a chance!" I suggested to Gerry that, if it was acceptable, I would preach on the theme "Jesus and His Mother in the Gospels". He was happy with that.

When I stood up to speak later at the Novena I was welcomed by a sea of devout and attentive faces. I offered three observations about how Mary is presented in the Gospels. She is a loving daughter of God, her heavenly Father, a faithful follower of Jesus, her son, and a receptive dwelling-place for the Holy Spirit. When she is invited to become the mother of the Messiah, she says yes and conceives Jesus in her heart before she conceives him in her womb.

"Our mission," I concluded, "is to learn from Mary how God can transform our lives into expressions of his love towards each other here in Ulster."

With that, I asked everyone to join with me in a prayer of commitment, repeated three times. Each time I said, "Father, make me an expression of your love," the congregation would reply "Make me a channel of your peace." With each refrain I increased the volume of my voice and back from the pews came the resounding response. A momentum for peace was quietly working its way through the Novena, undergirding the shakier peace process going on at Stormont. Thousands in Clonard now recognised my face, appreciated my ministry and increasingly valued the witness of the fellowship. Integration into the wider life of Clonard and Fitzroy continued steadily, but the pace at which it happened was never forced. Ours was the experience of the American poet Eve Merriam (1916–92):

> There go the grownups
> To the office,
> To the store.

Subway rush,
Traffic crush;
Hurry, scurry,
Worry, flurry.
No wonder
Grownups
Don't grow up
Any more.
It takes a lot
Of slow
To grow.

## Connecting with the Loyal Orders

Belfast is like a patchwork quilt of communities, often clearly distinguished from each other by religion, politics and culture. Graffiti, menacing murals and kerbstones painted with the colours of the flags flying proudly from lampposts mark out territories in high definition. When I was appointed to Fitzroy in 1976, the parish area assigned to me was divided by the Ormeau Road into the Holyland and the Lower Ormeau. It was changing rapidly. The Protestant community was growing old, developers were busy converting family homes into flats for students, and Catholic families had begun to move from the nearby Markets area into larger homes. Fifty per cent of those living in the parish were Protestant, but within 20 years they had declined to 30 per cent and were clustered around the Holyland. The Lower Ormeau side of the road was 95-per-cent Catholic. Older residents repeatedly complained of the antisocial behaviour of an increasing number of students who at weekends and on special occasions would binge and party late into the night.

But as the area changed in its religio-political profile, it found itself targetted by paramilitary organisations operating out of the nearby loyalist communities. In 1974, six Catholic civilians were killed when a bomb planted by the Ulster Volunteer Force (UVF) exploded at the Rose and Crown Bar. In addition, the Ormeau Road was becoming a flashpoint for confrontations over Orange parades. Since 1887 the Ballynafeigh lodges of the Orange Order, the Royal Black Preceptory and the Apprentice Boys of Derry had paraded down the road into the city centre during the marching season. They would march behind their bands, wearing sashes and carrying banners and Union Jacks to display their loyalty to king and country. Local Protestants would flock down to the road to welcome them and on average seven parades passed through the area each year. In the 1980s the number of Protestants standing at the roadside gradually diminished, while angry nationalists began to crowd the footpaths, objecting to the marches as "sectarian and triumphalist". In 1987, the Lower Ormeau Residents Action Group (LORAG) was formed to enhance the quality of community life for the growing nationalist community. Its leadership was predominantly republican. Other, more moderate, groups were also socially active: St Malachy's Catholic Church, the Mornington Project, the Lower Ormeau and Botanic Environmental Association, and the Community Forum.

With tension over the parades building, the situation rapidly deteriorated in 1992. At 2.00 pm on Wednesday, 5 February, two loyalists wearing boiler suits and balaclavas strode into Sean Graham's bookmaker's shop on the Ormeau Road and opened fire with an AK-47 assault rifle and a 9 mm pistol, killing five Catholic men from the area. This attack had absolutely nothing to do with the Ballynafeigh Orangemen; it was carried out by a UDA unit operating from the nearly Annadale estate. However, during an Orange parade six months later, some lodge members were caught on camera shouting pro-UDA slogans and holding aloft five fingers to taunt local residents. "The actions of the marchers," declared Sir Patrick Mayhew, secretary of state for Northern Ireland, "would have disgraced a tribe of cannibals." The incident sparked the formation of the Lower Ormeau Concerned Community (LOCC), whose chief spokesman was Gerard Rice. They campaigned against marches being forced through the area by the police without the consent of the local community. This, they insisted, would only be given if the orders entered into direct dialogue with the residents.

During the 1993 marching season I decided to accompany one of the Orange parades as it returned from the city centre through the Holyland *en route* to Ballynafeigh. The supporters among whom I mingled were mostly excitable teenagers, holding aloft their beer cans and roaring out their raucous songs to the strains of the flutes and the thump of the drums. They walked on the pavements alongside the bands and were on edge, with patriotic fervour stoked to dangerous levels by too much alcohol. When the parade reached the nationalist side of the Ormeau Road and the crowds of marchers and residents came face to face, the place erupted. The police had cordoned off the streets leading to the bridge with their Landrovers and crowds of infuriated young republicans were jammed in behind them. They screamed their resentment at the lodges while the supporters let rip with equally aggressive obscenities. If the police had not held both sides apart, blood would have flowed.

The extreme hatred on display was reminiscent of Sir Walter Scott's observations on his 1825 *Tour in Ireland*. He wrote:

> I never saw a richer country or ... a finer people; the worst of them is the bitter and envenomed dislike they have to each other. Their factions have been so long envenomed, and they have such narrow ground to do battle in, that they are like people fighting with daggers in a hogshead.

The term "envenomed" may seem an exaggerated one but, as I stood on the brink of an all-out riot on the Ormeau Road, I could see the aptness of Scott's description. My regret was that so little had changed since 1825.

Over the next six years, my office in Fitzroy became a venue for discussions with Gerard Rice and members of the LOCC as well as the Ballynafeigh Orangemen and their district master, Noel Liggett. My goal was to encourage them into long-term dialogue, but attitudes had hardened and I suspected that the LOCC's bottom line was the complete removal of Orange marches from that stretch of the road. The Orangemen of Ballynafeigh were prepared to take risks for dialogue despite the Grand Lodge of Ireland's insistence that no conversations be held with republicans. Both sides were rumoured to have met on 12 different occasions, but I was not confident that there would ever be a meeting of minds.

Into this vortex of antipathy the Clonard–Fitzroy Fellowship decided to step. In August 1993 the *Belfast Telegraph* carried a hard-hitting and candid article written by Professor Marianne Elliott of Liverpool University, entitled "How Little They Know About Us!". She wrote:

> Catholics are baffled and offended by the kind of Protestant attitudes outlined in yesterday's paper ... They find Protestant rejection of things Irish and general ignorance of what Catholics believe puzzling ... [There is] a general Catholic belief in a continuing Protestant tendency to see them as an inferior breed ... Protestants, they believe, cling to the Union with Britain from fear of losing their "ascendency".

In an attempt to redress this ignorance, we invited the Orange Order to send two representatives to Fitzroy on Wednesday, 30 October to discuss the question "What has the Orange Order Got against the Catholic Church?" They designated a chaplain well regarded in evangelical circles to attend, along with the county grand master.

The room was crammed to capacity for their visit and the front-row seats were occupied mainly by Catholic women from Clonard. There was a strange, convivial mood in the room. Fr Gerry chaired the event and gave everyone a warm welcome. As the chaplain expressed his appreciation for being invited, he came across as a genuinely kind man; but then he devoted the next 30 minutes to listing for us "the fatal errors of the Church of Rome": the infallibility of the Pope, the heresies of the Mass, the worship of Mary, indulgences, baptismal regeneration, purgatory, and so on. In fairness, he never raised his voice in anger, but the more he continued in this exclusively negative vein, the more the threatening the manner in which the phalanx of Clonard women in front of him folded their arms across their chests. When he had finished, the floor was thrown open for questions and comments.

Then the fireworks began. These females were fuming and told him in no uncertain terms how hurt and humiliated they felt at the battering to which their beliefs and their church had been subjected. The chaplain looked embarrassed at the strength of the reaction and rightly defended himself: "I was simply following the brief you gave me!" The questions then came thick and fast. Towards the end of the evening I was keen to rectify what I considered to be the imbalance in his presentation and asked him, "Are there any fundamental points of agreement between the Protestant and Catholic churches?" He looked hesitant for a moment and then replied, "God, I suppose." I pressed him a little further. "Is there anything else?"

"Jesus," he answered.

"Can I ask just one more question?" I continued. "Are there any other key areas of faith we share?"

"Yes," he responded, "prayer."

As I drew him out on the areas of Christian belief, spirituality and morality that we all held in common he began to notice just how substantial they were and, with his comments becoming more positive, some semblance of ease returned. But it was Fr Gerry's intuitive genius that redeemed what could have turned out to be a disaster. He thanked the chaplain for his honesty and invited him to bring the evening to an end by leading us all in the Lord's

Prayer. He happily agreed. We all stood and linked hands across the room – the chaplain, the grand master and the rest of us – and, with eyes wide open to see each other's faces, we prayed: "Our Father, who art in heaven ..." Four days later, Fr Gerry wrote a pastoral letter to the somewhat traumatised Clonard members:

> Peacemaking is no joy-ride. Last Wednesday I came back home wounded but not crushed. I learnt that reconciliation involves a sharing in the pain of Calvary. So let us pray every day for the two representatives who came to be with us. Come, Holy Spirit, empower us all – Catholic, Presbyterian and Orange – for the further journey.

The meeting confirmed to me the truth of Professor Elliott's exclamation, "How Little They Know About Us!" Many good men and honourable chaplains in the Orange Order have had little or no experience of learning directly from Catholic theologians about how their church understands and communicates the Christian faith. Furthermore, when we fail to criticise honestly the flaws in our own religious tradition, what comes across to others is a harsh dogmatism formed from standing at a prejudicial distance.

On 5 July 1999, the Parades Commission ruled that the Ballynafeigh Orange parade would not be allowed to cross the Ormeau Bridge. Since then, no Orange parade has passed through the Lower Ormeau and another layer of resentment has been added to the unionist psyche. Aware of this disappointment, I wrote to the Ballynafeigh Orangemen and asked if our fellowship could visit them and learn directly from the leaders more about the order. We got a very positive response and on Wednesday, 19 January 2000, 40 of us turned up at the hall. Half of us were from Clonard, including three priests. It was my first time across the threshold of an Orange hall since leaving the order in 1967.

Noel Liggett and two other office-bearers were there to meet us and brought us inside to the lodge room. Soon we were gawking at the colourful banners, pictures of the Queen and King Billy, a Union Jack leaning against the wall and a large chair behind the table where the worshipful master would sit to convene meetings. For two hours we discussed parades, the Bible, the anti-Catholic aspects of the "Qualifications of an Orangeman", residents' groups and the Grand Lodge of Ireland. When some Orange sashes were passed around so that we could examine the emblems on them, Fr Gerry slipped one over his head and round his shoulders. We erupted in laughter. Even funnier was the response of a more sober-minded Falls woman sitting beside him. She nudged him firmly in the ribs and said, "Father, you don't have to go that far!"

Our conversation drew to a close with prayer and we then proceeded to enjoy some light refreshments and food, which our hosts had kindly laid on for us. Realising they had gone to considerable expense to entertain us, we took up a collection among the fellowship members for the Orange Widows Fund. Fr Gerry and I went around the room with empty Jacob's biscuit tins and soon they were well filled with coins and notes.

That was the last of many encounters with the Loyal Orders. The Ormeau Road marching issue died a slow death. I became convinced that the people of Northern Ireland are more than capable of resolving the complex issues they face, but only if they reach out to each other with the generosity of esteem presented so clearly to us in the life and teaching of Jesus Christ. Our divergent narratives of history give us little hope of success, but our shared faith opens up new possibilities.

### Not Unnoticed: Pax Christi

Most of the people I know who have invested time in reconciliation work have had more than their fair share of disparaging letters. Over the years I have kept mine in a folder marked "Hotmail.com"! This one is not untypical:

> Dear Rev Newell, I wouldn't like to be in your shoes on that Day of Judgement. To even associate with Rome is an abomination in the sight of God. Darkness and light just don't mix. Do you ever tell these heretical friends of yours that they need to be saved?

The names, addresses and phone numbers of the senders are usually not included.

It is a welcome relief, therefore, when some encouragement comes knocking on your door. In the summer of 1999, a letter arrived from the secretariat of Pax Christi International in Brussels. It informed me that the Clonard–Fitzroy Fellowship had been nominated to receive its twelfth peace prize for its work in "building the kingdom of the Prince of Peace in the traumatised community of Northern Ireland where it has been a shining example and a beacon of hope". Fr Gerry and I were quite astonished, and when we broke the news to our congregations there was immense joy. It was the first time that the award had been made to any group in Ireland, or indeed conferred on a Protestant congregation. They planned to present it to us at a ceremony in the Gresham Hotel, Dublin on Tuesday, 30 November, and the president of Pax Christi, the archbishop and Latin patriarch of Jerusalem, Dr Michel Sabbah, was flying in from Israel to preside at the occasion.

Pax Christi (Latin for "the Peace of Christ") is an international Catholic peace movement and was founded in France at the end of the Second World War. It draws its inspiration from Christ's teaching in the Sermon on the Mount, recorded in the Gospel of Matthew. By 1999 it had established branches in 60 countries and was working closely with the United Nations in conflict zones across the world. The purpose of the prize was to "bring global attention to those who daily go forth in their pursuit of peace and justice". Previous recipients had been from Brazil, Uruguay, Czechoslovakia, Angola, the Congo, Poland, Yugoslavia, Rwanda and East Timor. Dozens of our friends and family descended on Dublin to join the fellowship members and 300 other guests, who included politicians, church leaders and ambassadors. Letters of congratulation were received from President Mary McAleese, Taoiseach Bertie Ahern and the Ulster Unionist leader, David Trimble.

There was a touch of surrealism about the ceremony in the Gresham. Fr Gerry and I sat on the platform in front of a huge white banner emblazoned with the Pax Christi logo: a large red rose growing through barbed wire. Across it was written "Violence ends when love begins." We felt honoured to be sitting on either side of Dr Sabbah, an extraordinarily courageous Middle Eastern Christian. He was born in Nazareth in 1933 and appointed in 1987 by Pope John Paul II to be the Latin patriarch of Jerusalem. He was the first native Palestinian to hold the post for centuries. In the face of considerable opposition he consistently championed the rights of Palestinian refugees to return home from exile and advocated a two-state solution to the Arab-Israeli conflict. His keynote address, "The Challenge of Peace for the Twenty-First Century", set the tone for the evening:

It is with profound sorrow, we have to admit that in the twentieth century tens and tens of millions of people lost their lives in war; much [more] than all the deaths from wars in previous centuries put together. And it continues relentlessly in an unprecedented manner in the so-called post-Cold War period. East Timor, Kosovo, Serbia, Bosnia, Haiti, Congo, Rwanda, Burundi, Somalia, Mozambique, Iraq, Afghanistan, Cambodia, Sri Lanka, Northern Ireland, and ... my region – the Middle East. These are just some of the regions of the world where hopes for growth and prosperity have been stifled by chronic conflicts.

Despite the undoubted advance of civilisation as a whole, acts of barbarism in our time have sunk to new levels. Exterminations, genocide, mass killings, deportation, torture in the extreme have scarred the memory of this century. Distinctions between soldiers and civilians have disappeared; human-rights violations against women and children occur in an unabated manner ... God's peace is broken in our world today ... In the past decade alone, 2,000,000 children have been killed in armed conflict, 6,000,000 disabled and 12,000,000 left homeless ...

The conflict in Northern Ireland is one of the longest ongoing conflicts in Europe in this century ... For lasting peace in Northern Ireland it is essential for the two communities to talk to one another and hear one another's point of view. It is important to devise ways in which people from both sides, including young people, can meet and talk to one another. There can be no lasting peace without mutual understanding. The vast majority of the people in Ireland voted for the Good Friday Agreement. It is essential that all the provisions of that agreement be wholeheartedly implemented, including those related to economic, social and cultural issues.

Pax Christi was born out of a commitment to work for peaceful methods of resolving the most intractable of problems ... and it is pledged to proclaim that the peace of Christ has been victorious over division and hatred through his death and resurrection. Our movement ... is working for a peace that is not an optional extra, a curious hobby that some people take up, but is an essential feature of the Gospel mission because it bears witness to the effects of the Gospel in renewing lives, building a new heaven and a new earth (2 Peter 2:13).

Repeatedly, Pax Christi International has been appealing to Israelis and Palestinians, Jews, Christians, and Muslims to allow peace to be born. As we approach the new millennium, I deeply hope that both regions, Northern Ireland and the Middle East, will become "zones of peace" in which all religious traditions can live and work together in a peaceful way. One must dream that one day ... people from around the world would flock to learn the art of peacemaking. Today we have the pleasure of granting this award to the Clonard–Fitzroy Fellowship, to honour their work for the kingdom of peace.

With that, Patriarch Sabbah resumed his seat and the Nobel laureate Mairéad Corrigan was invited to introduce the story of the fellowship more fully. I felt as if my life had come full circle. After all, it was Mairéad's personal courage as co-founder of the Northern Ireland Peace Movement in 1976 that first sparked a passion for peacemaking in me. I was also delighted that her tribute concentrated on the role of the lay members of the fellowship:

It took courage ... to break out of the security and cosiness of familiar surroundings, and begin to share and learn from others of a different tradition. They have shown that by ... listening and truthfully sharing what we feel and believe, [we] can bring about deep and lasting friendships which are capable of not only accepting but celebrating diversity ... Sometimes what we do seems small and unimportant, but when we do it from a motive of love then it is work of the heart and it is a big work ... We must make Northern Ireland work, and become best friends. Thank you for your example – you give us all Hope. Blessed are the peacemakers of the Fitzroy–Clonard Fellowship.

With that, Patriarch Sabbah presented the 1999 International Peace Prize to Fr Gerry and me and gave us each a cut-glass vase engraved with the logo of Pax Christi. We had decided beforehand that Fr Gerry should make the acceptance speech – and it was masterful:

I stand in awe at the fact that the simple friendships which have developed between the Presbyterians of Fitzroy and the Catholic people associated with Clonard Monastery should be recognised by Pax Christi. I accept this award not just on behalf of the fellowship, but on behalf of all those who have striven over the years to develop the dialogue of faith and the search for reconciliation in Ireland. We share with them the hope that one day the nations will finally hammer swords into ploughshares and their spears into pruning hooks (Isaiah 2:1–5).

The fellowship is primarily about witnessing to a different God in our sectarian society – not one who divides but one who unites us through Jesus Christ for the task of transforming our history. This God is seen in every human face. He sets no bounds to his love and compels us to set none to ours. We are learning that the church must be Catholic or it will not be the church at all; the believer must be Protestant or he or she will not be a believer at all. A divided church appears the same as other human organisations; a reconciled church is made from above. The destiny of Christians in Northern Ireland is to help make an end of the Reformation conflict, to recognise that those we used to call outsiders are truly brothers and sisters in Christ and that we hold our traditions not against but for one another.

We are being called to cast off the sectarian religion we have inherited and to become a community of friends, who have no excuse for passing on a divided church to the first generation of the new millennium. It will be a long and difficult haul and it is not for the faint hearted, but this evening we look back with immense gratitude to all those who have inspired us to keep walking the path.

As I watched Gerry delivering his speech I was reminded of a phrase that once described Paul Couturier: "a man who came out of the future".

At the end of the ceremony, Patriarch Sabbah invited Gerry and me to stand on either side of him and shake hands one final time. I noticed him looking down at the firmness of our grip with a soft smile on his face, as if anointing our handshake with the oil of a divine blessing. The silver cross he was wearing around his neck rested above our fingers, and underneath our hands his placed his own, gently supporting ours. Perhaps some day, I thought, we might get the opportunity to support him in facing the monumental problems of the Middle East.

It may seem strange, but during the joy of the formal proceedings I felt a deep sadness steal over my spirit. I would have given anything to share this occasion with my father, who had died suddenly in 1981, and with my sister Margaret, who had passed away in December 1996 after a prolonged illness. In addition, my mother was now in poor health and unable to travel down with us. Margaret would often have brought my mother along to Fitzroy for Sunday-morning worship and it was encouraging for me to see the old lady enjoying the music and feeling the warmth of welcome extended to her. She also began to meet Fr Gerry and some of the Clonard people who joined with us for services on various occasions. I would have loved to have shared this Pax Christi celebration with them as a way of saying thank you for all that they had put into my life so freely and generously. Indeed, my parents instilled in their three children a sense of prayerfulness, confidence and well-being. They sacrificed many of their own needs in favour of ours, and in their own quiet way practised the selfless truths of the Gospel.

With that, the evening turned to music, fun and food. The combined Fitzroy/Clonard choir, under the direction of Chris Blake, led the assembled gathering in the rousing Israeli-style song "Jesus Put This Song into Our Hearts". Some of the ambassadors, bishops, politicians and journalists looked surprised at our departure from the formality of the ceremonial protocols. But within a few minutes they also started to relax, as those around them, accustomed to the exuberance of our worship, clapped their hands to the rhythm of the music and poured their souls into lyrics that had become the anthem of the fellowship:

Jesus put this song into our hearts,
Jesus put this song into our hearts;
It's a song of joy no one can take away
Jesus put this song into our hearts.
Jesus taught us how to live in harmony,
Jesus taught us how to live in harmony;
Different faces, different races, he made us one,
Jesus taught us how to live in harmony.

During the long drive back up to Belfast with Val, my thoughts drifted towards the last four weeks of the year, of the century and of the millennium. With this trinity of endings, culminating on 31 December 1999, the excitement of the Pax Christi presentation felt a bit like a retirement celebration. Was my work over? Was my future heading towards sitting in front of the fire, admiring the cut-glass vase on the mantelpiece and rummaging through the memories of past days? Or did I need time out to relocate my soul and step away from the ceaseless activity of people driven by an inner compulsion? On the motorway back to Belfast I realised how blessed I had been on my life's journey. Many stretches of the road had been pleasant, but others had definitely turned out rough and confusing. But most of all, in my family, in Fitzroy and in the fellowship, I had been enriched beyond measure by companions who had left their footprints in my heart.

## CHAPTER FIVE

# Days Like This: Engaging Politics

The driver barely noticed me as I climbed aboard Bus Éireann 222 in the seaside village of Fountainstown, just south of Cork. With a cursory glance in my direction, he punched out a return ticket, took my money and disappeared back into the sports page of the *Southern Star*. I was his only passenger. With the engine idling and the local radio station playing in the background, I eased into my seat and cleared the mist away from my window. It was not far off 6.00 pm on Good Friday, 10 April 1998. I was heading into Cork to meet up with Rev John Faris, for whom I was conducting a Holy Week mission in Trinity Presbyterian Church.

A few minutes later the music was abruptly interrupted by the excited voice of a newsreader. She reported that US Senator George Mitchell, chairperson of the peace negotiations at Stormont, had just announced that the Northern Ireland political parties had agreed to set up a power-sharing assembly. The Irish and British prime ministers, Bertie Ahern and Tony Blair, had worked through the night with the parties to clinch the deal. A weary and triumphant Blair declared: "Today I hope that the burden of history can at long last start to be lifted from our shoulders." After two years of talks, the elusive agreement had been finally nailed down. The DJ hosting the show realised that something momentous was unfolding and, following the news, played Belfast-born Van Morrison's song "Days Like This". In the empty bus I clenched my fist, punched the air in a victory gesture and sang along:

> When it's not always raining, there'll be days like this.
> When there's no one complaining, there'll be days like this.
> When everything falls into place like the flick of a switch,
> Well, my mama told me, there'll be days like this.

When another passenger clambered on board as the bus was about to leave, I put my voice on silent but sang into myself all the way into Cork. John remembers me arriving at Trinity feeling elated. But why had a political event stirred up such emotion in me? That is a long story.

I cannot remember a time when faith and politics were not in some form interwoven in my psyche. In this I was typical of most children growing up in a predominantly Protestant and staunchly unionist community. By the age of 18 these twin loyalties propelled me towards the Orange Order, and it was not until my mid-twenties that I began to question the religio-political mix I had absorbed. The experience of working in the multicultural environment of Indonesia crystallised for me the more inclusive kind of lifestyle I wanted to adopt when I returned to Ireland. At the age of 32 I found myself back in Belfast ready to live it out in Fitzroy Presbyterian Church, but it was God's job, I believed, to show me how to do that. Throughout the intervening 14 years of personal change, I never lost my respect for the noble vocation of politics. It was nurtured in me by Christ's Nazareth Manifesto (Luke 4), by the teaching of St Paul (Romans 13) and by the example and practice of the reformer John Calvin in the city of Geneva. Calvin described those called to civic responsibility as "ministers of God whose chief concern should be to guide the life of their community by good laws and to promote the welfare and tranquillity of their people". I knew, of course, that politicians, like everyone else, could fall victim to the ambition of their egos or the lure of lining their own pockets. But at their best, I believed, they could become channels for a political form of grace that nourishes greater social integration and well-being.

As the newly installed minister of Fitzroy in 1976, I was determined not to identify with any local political party. The conflict murals celebrating battles against each other were no longer painted on the gables of my mind, having been replaced with images of the Gospel, which clashed with the estrangements around me. I longed for an alternative Ulster, one furnished with generosity, friendship and respect, but it seemed like a far-off fantasy. At the start of my ministry in Belfast, however, I was ready to pursue it.

## On the Streets
I have already recounted how deeply I was affected by the death of Anne Maguire's three young children on Tuesday, 10 August 1976 – a stolen car driven by an IRA volunteer and pursued by a British Army patrol veered off the road and plunged into them. Finaghy Road North in west Belfast, where

Anne was walking with her children, was less than a mile from where Val and I lived with our own children, Tim, then aged five, and Jennie, then aged one. That evening Anne Maguire's sister, Mairéad Corrigan, made an impassioned plea on television for the violence to end and the Northern Ireland Peace Movement was born. A few days later, the sight of Anne's husband Jackie carrying three small white coffins out of his house seared itself into my soul. I knew that this was God's moment for me to start marching for a peace that would not come easily. In the weeks that followed, Protestants and Catholics turned out in their tens of thousands across Northern Ireland, singing the anthem "We Shall Overcome".

The most personally threatening of the four marches I attended in Belfast was in the republican stronghold of Belfast's Falls Road. A middle-aged woman of substantial proportions and with sleeves rolled up screamed at me from a crowd of onlookers gathered at the door of a pub, "Go home, you Orange bastard!" She had obviously spotted my clerical collar. A few minutes later the marchers came under a barrage of bricks and bottles from young people also armed with clubs and iron bars. It was frightening. A few weeks later, in a strongly loyalist part of east Belfast, although none of us was physically attacked as we processed through the area, the glares of hostility were brutally intense. Thankfully, the only things we were showered with on that occasion were water-bombs and bags of flour.

This reaction removed any doubt in my mind that the Peace Movement, with its stand against violence and for the sanctity of life, was seen as a serious political threat in a community coiled up with rage. Peace would have to be struggled for and won; it would not fall softly from the sky, even in response to many devout prayers offered in churches that shunned contact with neighbouring churches well within sight of each other but across the religious divide. The Peace Movement also bore witness to a new phenomenon that most people had never seen in their lifetime: Protestants and Catholics marching together in common cause and declaring that no one-sided dominance was desirable or capable of establishing justice. Many of those I marched with were deeply committed Christians, but I was surprised that ministers and priests were not there in larger numbers, particularly some prominent evangelicals I looked up to. What more than three small white coffins, I wondered, would it take to get them to advocate for peace?

I was, however, still very new to Fitzroy and faced the task of bringing the congregation with me. I decided to move slowly, a centimetre a year. During my first ten years I preached through the life and teaching of Jesus Christ so that Fitzroy could see that he was the supreme peacemaker and the spiritual impulse behind our own vocation to be reconcilers. But it was linked-up preaching, connected to what was happening in the community. When 11 members of the loyalist murder squad known as the Shankill Butchers were sent to prison in 1979, a journalist covering the trial wrote, "They killed innocent people savagely, without mercy or pity, simply because they were of the 'wrong' religion." In his summing up the judge observed, "The butcher-gang killings are a lasting monument to blind bigotry." I was so distressed by the harrowing details of their savagery that I kept asking myself how the virus of prejudice in Northern Ireland was transmitted from generation to generation. How does a child born without bitterness grow up to hate? What influences are children exposed to at home and in the community that darkens their view of the "other"? Have the churches contributed to this toxic atmosphere by promoting a version of the Christian faith that puts others down? I shared my rather anguished self-questioning with Fitzroy in a pastoral letter:

> There any many people who would never lift a gun or plant a bomb, yet if you listen to the way they speak about others it is obvious just how hostile and bitter they can be. Mental and emotional violence within us towards others who differ religiously or politically is another way of describing hate. The Bible is clear: I cannot share the life of God and despise those whom he loves.

Peering into the soul of the Shankill Butchers convinced me that elements of the Ulster mindset on both sides of the community needed to be substantially changed. By 1980 the Peace Movement had largely faded out and with it the short-lived and naive belief that "feet on the street" would bring change. Then, months later, a door of opportunity opened up for me quite unexpectedly to create a connection between Fitzroy and Clonard Monastery in west Belfast.

### Targetting the Gunmen

In November 1982, Patrick Murphy (aged 63) went to work as usual in his grocery store in the Rosetta district of south Belfast. As he stood behind the counter, a UVF gunman walked in and shot him in cold blood. When his daughters, who were in the back of the shop, heard the shooting they rushed out, only to find him slumped on the floor.

For over a year the atmosphere of confrontation had been intensifying throughout the province. A hunger strike had begun in March 1981 when Bobby Sands, the officer commanding the IRA in the Maze Prison, refused food. After 66 days he died and 100,000 people lined the streets of west Belfast for his funeral. By August nine others had followed his example. When the strike ended the IRA unleashed a ferocious assault on the RUC. To add insult to injury, Sinn Féin made its first foray into politics and achieved alarming success with a policy characterised as "the ballot box in one hand and the Armalite in the other". Loyalist fury reached boiling point. Anyone from the Catholic community was now considered a legitimate target.

I felt so outraged by Mr Murphy's murder that, with the help of some Anglican and Methodist colleagues, we invited ministers of our own denominations to attend his requiem Mass in St Bernadette's Catholic Church. Forty of us turned up in clerical attire, including four former Presbyterian moderators. Fr O'Hanlon, the parish priest, reserved seats for us behind Mr Murphy's widow, Barbara, and her family.

After the service, journalists swarmed around us to ask why we had come in such large numbers, and the following day the initiative was featured on the front pages of our local newspapers. The *Belfast Telegraph* commented:

> It isn't enough to feel sympathy, in front of the TV screen; a presence, at the funeral service, is proof of a ready desire to provide comfort, as well as to confront the divisions in society.
>
> For as much as some Churchmen would like to deny it, there is a religious basis, however twisted, behind a lot of the violence. The church establishments have kept each other apart ... and out of this has grown division and prejudice.
>
> The Protestant clergy, going from funeral to funeral, are accepting that there must be greater dialogue between the Churches, and between the two communities, to attempt to break down some of the barriers.
>
> After 13 years of funerals, it is time to say "sorry".

The nationalist-inclined *Irish News* underlined the limitations of our approach:

> We trust that we shall not be misunderstood if we point out that implicit in [the call of the Protestant ministers] is the dreadful recognition that these tragedies will continue ... political instability is the fundamental cause of these tragedies.
>
> Surely it is relevant to say that we are being most perfectly Christian and human when we exercise our intellect searchingly on the root causes of the violence in our midst. Let us honour [God] by using it vigorously and honestly to tackle our problems. Let us begin by recognising and eradicating from our culture the false idols we have inherited on all sides from history.

We already knew this, of course, and were active in tackling the problems raised. But our problem was this: how does one discover a pathway into the paramilitary organisations carrying out these crimes?

Did our corporate presence at Mr Murphy's funeral send out any other signals? I believe it did. It demonstrated that a community of people was emerging who were determined to bond with each other in grief and hope rather than to go on observing the sanctified theological taboos that were designed to stop Christians worshipping together. Furthermore, there was a message for the death-squads in our action: loyalist blood-lust would not safeguard the union but erode it; republican violence would not unite Ireland but intensify the antipathies that keep it divided.

We were repeatedly told that the paramilitaries were deaf to the words of moral denunciation from the churches, and this would unquestionably have been true – if words had been our only weapon. But what got through to some of the leaders of the loyalist paramilitary organisations, and what angered them most, was not our words but our action of standing shoulder to shoulder with the families of the innocent victims of their hatred. Real change, however, is never effected by denunciation from a distance; it is only possible through with a dialogue of sustained closeness. To my surprise, I soon found myself in that situation and mixing freely with paramilitaries.

**Strange Friends**

In the early 1980s I began to form friendships with former paramilitaries through the Charismatic Movement and the work of Prison Fellowship Northern Ireland. I was a frequent visitor to their headquarters close to Fitzroy and this afforded me the opportunity to meet a broad range of ex-prisoners, most of whom had recently been released. Occasionally I would lead a Bible study and a time of prayer for those who were seeking a deeper source of strength to help them rebuild their lives. As time passed, Val and I would invite some of them to the manse or, if they wanted to talk over their situations with me, we would go for a walk along the River Lagan. In this social environment Val's years of experience of working in prison proved invaluable and many strong friendships were developed. In fact, a small stream of ex-prisoners began to integrate into Fitzroy and slowly discover the kind of family support network and warmth of friendship that they had either lost over the years or never really experienced growing up. Often their biggest need was to get a job or a chance at further education. In these circumstances I would introduce them to some members of the Fitzroy congregation who had contacts and could open doors.

On one occasion I found myself as a guest speaker at a large Charismatic gathering of Protestants and Catholics in the centre of Belfast. I sat on the platform, listening spellbound while a south-Armagh IRA man and a north-Belfast UVF weapons instructor told how Christ had turned their lives around and given them a love for "the other side". When the meeting was over I invited them to speak at a morning service at Fitzroy and the impact it had on the congregation was profoundly significant. It paved the way for more progressive attitudes to develop. Some of our members said to me, "If God can bring those two guys together, there really is hope for our province." Many more were privately thinking the same thoughts and beginning to wish to be part of that process of reconciliation.

In June 1985 I travelled to Perth to speak at a Church of Scotland youth conference with Liam McCloskey, a 29-year-old former volunteer of the Irish National Liberation Army (INLA). The four days we spent together gave us time to hear more about each other's journey of faith. I noticed that when Liam was speaking publicly he did so in a soft voice, but his flow of thought was slow and his speech slightly slurred. I wondered why.

Like many other young people growing up in the Sperrin Mountains, he had felt alienated from the state of Northern Ireland and had joined the INLA with his friend Kevin Lynch. Both of them ended up serving ten years in the Maze Prison for a string of offences. When Kevin Lynch died on hunger strike in 1981, Liam took his place and, after 55 days without food, began to drift in and out of consciousness. On the frontier between life and death, he became increasingly aware of a divine presence embracing him and he began to pray: "God, you are so real, but how can I come before you with nothing but a self-centered life and so much bitterness in me?" His mother, afraid that his starvation-induced blindness could become permanent, told him in no uncertain terms that if he went into a coma she would have him fed intravenously. Her determination eventually won through and he signalled his readiness to take food.

As Liam's health improved, so did his relationship with Christ. It also forced him to face a decision he could not dodge – his membership of the INLA. Given the vows that volunteers take and the knowledge of the command structure they possess, it is almost impossible to leave. Amazing though it may seem, conversion is one of the few routes out, but its genuineness is tested by comrades skilled in ferreting out informers. Regarding his choice, Liam was clear: "I took the way of Jesus. I realised that God loved me and I had begun to love him." In contrast to many stories of religious conversion in Northern Ireland, Liam's conversion birthed in him a resolve to work for reconciliation. His first step in that direction was to join Protestant inmates in the prison dining room, breaking a pattern of segregation considered essential for personal survival. There he met Jimmy Gibson, a loyalist inmate who, by his own confession, loathed republicans. Through Liam's witness, Jimmy turned over his own tangled life to Christ and joined an integrated Bible-study group composed of former enemies.

Following their release in 1982, Liam and Jimmy spoke at numerous events, including the first international conference of Prison Fellowship (a prayer and support organisation for prisoners), held at Queen's University in 1983. An audience of 800 people listened as they shared the story of their friendship and their decision to live a reconciled life. When they had finished speaking, Liam put his emaciated arm over Jimmy's muscular shoulders and said, "God is changing the hearts of men like us and it is the only hope for peace. Before, if I had seen Jimmy on the street, I would have shot him. Now he's my brother in Christ. I would die for him." The crowd rose from their seats and started clapping and cheering.

In those days I prayed a lot for more Jimmys and Liams to surface within our fractured community, but I also longed that those who rose to their feet to applaud would also rise to the Christian challenge confronting them – the challenge of cutting themselves loose from relationship choices that perpetuate the social and spiritual estrangement prevailing within the churches. Interacting over the years with former paramilitaries enabled me to learn the social factors and the group fears that conditioned them as young people and led to their being sucked into these organisations. In fact, the more I was involved with them, the more I felt at home in their company. I realised that my role was to accept rather than judge, to challenge rather than to sweet-talk them. But it was obvious to me that not everyone was going to become a Christian before the violence was brought to an end and a much-needed political transformation could take place. I was convinced that God's Spirit was not confined to the cloisters of the church, but worked unceasingly and universally in a wounded and conflicted world, raising up individuals and organisations with a passion for healing and reconciliation. An ancient chant declares "Ubi caritas et amor, Deus ibi est" – "Where kindness and love are found, God is present."

## The Anglo-Irish Agreement: A Body-Blow for Unionism

The summer of 1985 saw the social divisions widen as the marching season of the Loyal Orders reached its peak. The vast majority of the 2,000 annual parades would pass off peacefully, but when conflict did erupt it was frequently bitter and intense. On 12 and 13 July, when the RUC decided to reroute an Orange Order march away from the Catholic Obins Street district of Portadown, loyalists fought a running battle with the police for two days. It left 52 policemen injured. The orders claimed it was their right to march their traditional routes, but nationalists argued that the parades were sectarian and supremacist. The police not only acted as a buffer between opposing factions, but found themselves in a kind of war zone, shelled by the incompatible aspirations and animosities of both sides. The winter months confirmed the growing sense of insecurity and frustration among unionists: not only was the RUC now prepared to resist Orange demands, but the British and Irish governments were finalising an initiative designed to erode Sinn Féin's growing electoral fortunes and draw Ulster unionists into a power-sharing arrangement with the majority nationalist party, the Social Democratic and Labour Party (SDLP). Also driving the initiative were the spiralling cost of keeping an army in Ulster and the rising human cost in the lives of young British soldiers.

On 15 November 1985, Prime Minister Margaret Thatcher and Taoiseach Garret FitzGerald signed the Anglo-Irish Agreement at Hillsborough Castle. For the first time it conceded to the Irish government a modest consultative role in the affairs of Northern Ireland, but balanced this by affirming that there would be no change in Northern Ireland's constitutional position. Conditions were also laid down for the formation of a devolved power-sharing government at Stormont. The agreement won massive backing when presented to the Westminster parliament: 473 MPs voted for it and only 47 against – the biggest majority of Thatcher's premiership. For unionists it was a humiliating disaster; they felt like they had been abandoned by "the mother of all parliaments". Paisley castigated Mrs Thatcher:

> Having failed to defeat the IRA you ... have set in motion machinery which will achieve their goal ... a united Ireland ... Ulster unionists ... are to be sacrificial lambs to appease the Dublin wolves.

In truth, the unionist case had been steadily losing support at the heart of British democracy for many years.

The unionist community's fury at the agreement focussed on three major grievances. Firstly, they claimed, conceding any role to Dublin meant that Northern Ireland's position within the UK was no longer on the same basis as that of England, Scotland and Wales. Secondly, democracy was denied – all the local democratic parties had been excluded from the negotiations. Thirdly, coercion had replaced persuasion – unionists were being bludgeoned into accepting power-sharing. These indeed were strong arguments.

To add further weight to their opposition, James Molyneaux of the UUP and Ian Paisley of the Democratic Unionist Party (DUP) mobilised an "Ulster Says No" campaign, which saw unionist MPs at Westminster resign their seats and 400,000 people sign a petition opposing the agreement. In some places rioters went on the rampage against Catholic homes and 400 attacks were recorded against police families. Half a million people crowded into the centre of Belfast to protest at a rally in front of the City Hall on 23 November. Ian Paisley's was the most rousing of the speeches:

> Where do the terrorists operate from? From the Irish Republic! That's where they come from! Where do the terrorists return to for sanctuary? To the Irish Republic! And yet Mrs Thatcher tells us that that republic must have some say in our province. We say never, never, never, never!

While I recognised the legitimacy and force of the unionist argument, I could not help but notice some serious blind spots in the speeches. No references were made to the equally legitimate aspirations of the 42 per cent of the province that was Catholic and nationalist. A more accurate slogan would have been "Fifty-eight per cent of Ulster Says No!" I also wondered, given the presence of some Protestant clergymen on the podium, why Christ's supreme commandment, to "love your neighbour as yourself" had been consciously or unconsciously screened out of their pronouncements.

But it was not only unionists who reacted against the Anglo-Irish Agreement. Sinn Féin's president, Gerry Adams, rejected it on the grounds that it copper-fastened Northern Ireland's position within the UK. The same agreement was capable of being interpreted in two completely different ways: as strengthening the union and as weakening it. The nationalist SDLP and the cross-community Alliance Party were the only groups to support it.

The day after the City Hall rally, an opinion poll revealed that, if a referendum on the Anglo-Irish Agreement was held, 75 per cent of Protestants would vote no and 65 per cent of Catholics would vote yes. Surprisingly, a considerable Protestant minority was willing to give it a chance. I was one of them. Despite its flaws, I valued the agreement's emphasis on inclusiveness and partnership, and the opportunity it offered Ulster people to get rid of the patronising policy of direct rule from Westminster. With 32 other Presbyterian ministers, I signed a statement asking the public to evaluate it in the light of four faith propositions:

1. Loyalty: our primary loyalty is to … Jesus Christ. If we are in Christ, no secondary allegiance, whether to Loyalism or Nationalism, can separate us from Him or should separate us from each other.

2. Rights: we believe that the Rights and Freedoms of all the people of Ireland, minorities and majorities alike, are given by God and are to be honoured in obedience to Jesus Christ. It is … foreign to the mind of Christ for the Churches of this island to become the advocates of the rights of one Community to the exclusion of the other.

3. Reconciliation: Christ demands reconciliation, and reconciliation demands repentance from self-centredness…The identification of the Kingdom of God with any political ideology

is Idolatry and an affront to Almighty God … It is a perversion of the Gospel of our Lord and Saviour, Jesus Christ.

4. Choice: Whatever our political choice will be, if it is not founded on the Christian principles of forgiveness, peace, justice and reconciliation, the alternative will be increasing misery and chaos.

The consequences of life under the Anglo-Irish Agreement were mixed. For Margaret Thatcher it meant presiding over the worst polarisation in Northern Ireland for a decade. But for unionists it was a reality check. Never again would Westminster back a one-sided majority-rule solution in Ulster. The culture of "No!", "Never!" and "Not an inch!" had lost its power to persuade the citizens of the United Kingdom. At the City Hall on the third anniversary of the "Ulster Says No" rally, I mingled with only 300 supporters who turned up to reaffirm their opposition. They looked leaderless and demoralised.

The first signs of a movement away from the mentality of reactive unionism towards something more inclusive surfaced, surprisingly, among the ranks of the UDA. In 1987 its political think-tank, the Ulster Political Research Group, published its vision of the way forward in a document entitled *Common Sense: Northern Ireland – An Agreed Process*. While upholding the union, it advocated power-sharing with nationalists, as well as a new constitution and a bill of rights guaranteeing fair treatment for everyone. Its proposals met with a frosty reception from a mainstream unionism still in no mood to think outside its traditional patterns. The continuing armed struggle of the IRA also crushed any prospect of moving in a new direction.

**Poppy Day Massacre, 1987**

Remembrance Sunday, the second Sunday of November, holds a revered place in the observance of the Protestant-unionist community in Northern Ireland. It recalls Armistice Day, 11 November 1918, when the Allies and Germany brought hostilities to an end on the Western Front. Religious services are held at war memorials across the UK and throughout the British Commonwealth, to which civic dignitaries, ex-servicemen and servicewomen and serving members the police and armed forces parade together. Poppy wreaths are laid and a two-minute silence is observed at 11.00 am.

I was leaving Fitzroy after our remembrance service on Sunday morning,

8 November 1987, when a member of the congregation rushed up to me and informed me that there had been an explosion in Enniskillen. When Val and I got home and turned on the TV, the full horror hit us. As hundreds gathered at the town's cenotaph, a 40-pound IRA time-bomb exploded at 10.43 am, claiming 12 lives and injuring 63 others. Soldiers in ceremonial uniform clambered over the debris, frantically trying to rescue those trapped underneath. All the victims except one were civilians and Protestants; most of them were devout Christians. The youngest to lose her life was a 20-year-old nurse, Marie Wilson, home from Belfast to spend the weekend with her parents. She had been standing beside her father, Gordon, when the bomb had gone off and buried them both under mounds of rubble. In the darkness they had felt around for each other's hands and, when they found them, they had held on tight. In an interview a few hours later, Gordon described his last conversation with Marie.

"Daddy," she said, "I love you very much." Then she fell silent.

When asked by the media what he thought of the killers, Gordon replied: "I bear them no ill. That sort of talk is not going to bring Marie back. She is in heaven now and we shall meet again. I will pray for these men tonight and every night. Please don't ask me for a purpose, but there has to be a greater plan. If I didn't think that, I would commit suicide."

The interview was screened across the world and, in my opinion, in 25 years of violence, no words made such a powerful impact. In Gordon Wilson I felt as if Christ himself had returned to Enniskillen. Some survivors, however, found it hard to think thoughts of forgiveness. I wondered how I would have reacted if one of my family had been killed. Prime Minister Margaret Thatcher described the massacre as "a desecration of the dead", and Queen Elizabeth sent her heartfelt sympathy to the people of the town. The incident presented me with a problem: the following Sunday, Fitzroy was due to broadcast morning worship on Radio Ulster and I had already submitted to the BBC most of the content of the service. When I contacted the producer we agreed that I should rewrite everything with Enniskillen in mind. For a week I agonised over what this tragedy was saying to us about what was most flawed in our province as well as what we most valued. Prior to Enniskillen I had devoted considerable time to bringing church leaders and politicians together in the hope that they would articulate a common pathway to peace. Now, I decided, it was time for me to give full expression to my own convictions.

On Sunday morning, Fitzroy was crowded and distressed. At the beginning of the service, I conveyed to the people of Enniskillen the sympathy of our congregation. Later in the worship, one of our members led us in prayer for the town, the families of those who had lost loved ones and all who were caring for the injured at home or in hospital. Then in my sermon I turned to what I believed Christ was saying to us as a province through the heartbreak of Enniskillen:

> It is easy to condemn violence when it comes from the other side, but when it issues from those whose political aspirations we have sympathy with, it's amazing how in the back of our minds we find ways of condoning it. Enniskillen must surely now have destroyed all such mental manoeuvrings. It has changed me. I am a Protestant, but with no desire to see a Protestant ascendency. I am British, but with the highest regard for the richness of our Irish heritage. I am a Presbyterian, but I enjoy the closest of relationships with my Catholic brothers and sisters in Christ. The only ascendency I am interested in is that of Christ's love and his reverence for life.
>
> All week I've been thinking about those who primed the bomb. "How, Lord," I asked, "did they develop such destructive attitudes? Did they pick them up from slanted views expressed by friends or handed down by religion? Or were their young minds primed at home to explode with bitterness later in life?" I will never forget what happened within seconds of the explosion. People from all walks of life bonded together into one team to rescue the injured. This, I believe, is Christ's model for our country's future. To walk this path together would be the greatest tribute we can pay to those who died or were injured at the cenotaph last week.

The Poppy Day Massacre was later seen to be a turning point for Northern Ireland. When the remembrance service in Enniskillen was restaged two weeks later, 5,000 people attended, including a large number of local Catholics, as a public gesture of solidarity against violence. Indeed, Catholic representation at such civic events accelerated significantly in the years that followed. For the first time the IRA admitted it had made a mistake and the Fermanagh Brigade was stood down. The truth is that the IRA had made a chilling judgment: civilian deaths were the acceptable collateral of war. As a result of the bombing, Sinn Féin's electoral support plummeted and, two years later, in local government elections, it lost 16 of its 59 councillors. Regrettably, Margaret Thatcher's promise to bring the bombers before the courts was not fulfilled and no one was ever convicted of the crimes. Nevertheless, after Enniskillen, a momentum towards peace began to build up across the province. However, this was not without its setbacks.

## Glimmer of Hope

Following the Poppy Day Massacre, the violence escalated. In March 1988, loyalist Michael Stone launched a gun and grenade attack on a large funeral for three IRA volunteers in west Belfast's Milltown Cemetery. Seventy mourners were wounded and three killed. Three days later, when two British Army corporals accidentally drove into the funeral of those killed in the cemetery, they were pulled from their car, shoved into another vehicle and driven off. The crowds assumed that they were loyalists about to launch another attack. In the crowd was a well-known priest from Clonard Monastery, Fr Alec Reid; he followed the direction of the vehicle on foot and found the two men 200 yards away, close to Casement Park. They were stretched, face downwards, on the ground. Noticing how still they were lying, it suddenly dawned on him that they might be British soldiers. He lay down between them and covered them with his arms. Out of the corners of their eyes they looked at him and realised he was a priest. No words were exchanged, but he sensed that they saw him as someone who might be able to save them. Then one of their captors came up behind Alec, grabbed him by the back of his coat and shouted, "If you don't get out of here now, we shoot you as well." They pushed him away, bundled the soldiers into their car and drove off towards a derelict site a short distance away. Minutes later shots rang out and Fr Alec ran to where he thought the sound had come from. It was a horrific sight – the two soldiers lay dead, face upwards and arms outstretched, like Christ on the cross. He knelt down beside them and attempted to give them mouth-to-mouth resuscitation, but when this failed he began to pray into their ears the words of the Last Rites. As he knelt over their semi-naked and blood-spattered bodies, a photographer captured the scene. It became one of the most harrowing images of the conflict and one of the most iconic expressions of Christian compassion.

That evening Belfast was gripped in a vice of communal tension. As darkness fell over the city, a sense of foreboding for some kind of reckless revenge mounted. I had never before witnessed such intensity of fear. When I shared with Val my concerns for the safety of the Clonard–Fitzroy Fellowship members preparing to attend our planned meeting, her response was swift and clear: "We can't let the men of violence to intimidate us and wreck what we believe is the right thing to do." Still unsure, I rang Fr Gerry and asked if he thought it would be wiser under the circumstance to cancel our meeting. "No one," I insisted, "should be out on the streets after dark."

Like Val, he felt that we should let it all unfold, go ahead as usual and see if anyone turns up. Thirty of us from Fitzroy waited at the doors of the church to see what would happen. At 7.30 pm Fr Gerry and several carloads of Clonard members arrived from west Belfast. Their courage left us speechless. We had an inspiring evening together and bit by bit it began to dawn on us that the bonds between us were much stronger and deeper than any of us could ever have imagined.

No one was aware that Fr Alec had been attempting to persuade John Hume (SDLP) and Gerry Adams (Sinn Féin) to meet each other privately in Clonard for discussions on how to bring the violence to an end. The rift between the moderate nationalism of Hume and the hard-line republicanism of Adams was acute and the bitter political rivalry split the Catholic community. In fact, as Fr Reid knelt over the soldiers, he had inside his black jacket, under his right arm, a brown envelope containing a letter from Adams setting out Sinn Féin's position and an agenda for any possible dialogue. On returning to Clonard, Reid noticed that the envelope was stained with blood. He replaced it with a new envelope, got into his car and drove to Derry to deliver its contents to John Hume. Shortly afterwards the two leaders began meeting secretly in the monastery, Hume entering by the front door and Adams by the back. In the quietness and privacy of this sacred site, a peace process was birthed.

Born in County Tipperary, Alec Reid was named after his Presbyterian grandfather. He was ordained as a Redemptorist priest in 1957 and assigned to Clonard in 1961. In August 1969 the monastery found itself on the frontline as loyalists stormed the streets around it and burned down houses. The conflagration made Alec aware of his vocation to peacemaking. In 1975 he mediated a ceasefire between republican factions in west Belfast and became well known to the families of emerging Sinn Féin leaders such as 19-year-old Gerry Adams. In the monastery's private diary for 11 January 1988, the chronicler noted:

1994: Ken, Fr Gerry and Rev Sam Burch en route to a meeting with the Ulster Democratic Party (UDP) in Lisburn just prior to Loyalist Ceasefire on 13 October 1994.

1995: Sir Patrick Mayhew (Secretary of State for NI 1992–1997) and his wife Jean speak at Morning Worship in Fitzroy.

1995 Fitzroy Advent Reconciliation Service: Presbyterian Moderator Dr John Ross *(third left)* and Archbishop Cahal Daly *(third right)*, Rev Ruth Patterson *(second right)* and Denis Boyd (Clerk of Session) *(extreme right)*.

1998 Mayoral Visit: The Lord Mayor Dr David Alderdice and his wife Fiona and their three children at Fitzroy with Joan and Harlan Rector (USA).

1998: The world renowned evangelical scholar, Dr James I Packer *(centre)* speaking at Fitzroy's launch of *Evangelicals and Catholics Together in Ireland*, along with Fr Pat Collins (All Hallows College, Dublin).

1999: Ken and Fr Gerry with the Latin Patriarch of Jerusalem, Dr Michel Sabbah, on the occasion of the presentation of the Pax Christi International Peace Prize to the Clonard–Fitzroy Fellowship.

Sabbatical 2001 in the Presbyterian Church of Old Greenwich, Connecticut: Ken with the extended family of Bob and Ginnie Masson *(second and third left)* at the dual baptism of the two grandchildren of their son Rob and his wife Cameron *(right and left of Ken)*.

Sabbatical 2001 in the Presbyterian Church of Old Greenwich, Connecticut: Ken preaching on the Sunday after the September 11th attacks on the World Trade Centre, New York.

2001: 25th Anniversary of Ken's ministry in Fitzroy with Jennie, Renee, Siobhan (daughter in law), Val, Ken and Tim.

2002: Clonard/Fitzroy evening in Clonard with Lord Mayor Alex Maskey *(third left)* and David Ervine (Progressive Unionist Party) *(third right)* and Frances Livingstone (Chairperson) *(centre)*. Also included *(l-r)* Ken, Fr Peter Burns, Rev Norman Hamilton (PCI) and Fr Aidan Troy.

2004: Return to Timor. Ken and Val visit a church based orphanage and women's centre near Kupang.

2001: Return to Timor. Val with mothers and children at the health clinic in Soe, Central Timor.

Moderatorial Year 2004–2005: Getting ready for the General Assembly in June 2004. My theme was 'Live a Life of Love'.

Moderatorial Year 2004–2005: Getting used to the Moderator's Chair.

Moderatorial Year 2004–2005: Addressing the congregation at the Opening Night at the General Assembly, Church House, Fisherwick Place, Belfast.

Moderatorial Year 2004–2005: Reception for invited guests and family after the opening service of the General Assembly in June 2004: *(l-r)* My sister Audrey Kerr, Ken, Jennie, Tim and Val.

Moderatorial Year 2004–2005: Interview time at the Youth Night Assembly celebration.

Moderatorial Year 2004–2005: The inauguration of President Mary McAleese in November 2004, St Patrick's Hall, Dublin Castle. The Chief Rabbi of Ireland offers a prayer.

Moderatorial Year 2004–2005: Meeting with President Mary McAleese in Aras an Uachtarain, Phoenix Park, Dublin with Rev Lesley Carroll and Rev David Moore.

Moderatorial Year 2004–2005: Clash with Alex Maskey (Sinn Féin) on BBC Northern Ireland's 'Hearts and Minds' programme following the Northern Bank Robbery, 20 December 2004.

Moderatorial Year 2004–2005: Visiting First Lisburn Presbyterian Church as a guest of the Minister, Rev John Brackenridge *(third right)* and other church leaders before Christmas.

Moderatorial Year 2004–2005: Four Church leaders preparing for an Ulster Television broadcast service at Christmas: (l-r) Rev Brian Fletcher (Methodist), Cardinal Sean Brady (Catholic), Dr Robin Eames (Church of Ireland) and Ken.

Moderatorial Year 2004–2005: My first Baptism of one the 'new Irish' African families in Waterford Presbyterian/Methodist Church with the Rev Dr John Parkin *(second left)*.

Moderatorial Year 2004–2005: Opening new halls at Helen's Bay Presbyterian Church with Rev Colin Megaw, his wife Margaret and members of the congregation.

Moderatorial Year 2004–2005: Rev Mairisine Stanfield of First Ballynahinch Presbyterian Church with some of the Men's Mission heading to Africa from George Best Belfast City Airport.

Moderatorial Year 2004–2005: Ken with the Rev Ivan Hull (Ulsterville Presbyterian Church) and Val at the Synod of the French Reformed Church in Aix-en-Provence with Rev Gordon Campbell, his wife Sandra and their children.

Moderatorial Year 2004–2005: Ken and Val visit the staff and some of the children in an Irish Language pre-school in Derry.

Moderatorial Year 2004–2005: Visit to the ravaged Tamil Nadu region of India to see reconstruction work funded by the Tsunami Appeal of the Presbyterian Church in Ireland.

Moderatorial Year 2004–2005: A meeting with Cardinal Edward Cassidy in the home of Rev David Campbell, St Andrew's Presbyterian Church, Newcastle, New South Wales, Australia.

Moderatorial Year 2004–2005: A visit in the company of the Rev David Montgomery (*fourth left*), Knock Presbyterian Church, to Crusaders Football Club to meet the manager Stephen Baxter (*second left*) and some key members of the club.

Moderatorial Year 2004–2005: With the Rev Liz Hughes, the minister of Whitehouse Presbyterian Church, and Fr Dan Whyte at the official reopening of the church following a serious arson attack in 2002.

Moderatorial Year 2004–2005: Ken chatting with Dean John Bond at Church of Ireland Synod in Armagh.

John Hume and Gerry Adams are having secret talks in Clonard.
Fr Reid seems to have brought them together.

By the time the dialogue tapered off in August 1988, both leaders recognised that an "agreed Ireland" could never be achieved by coercion. It would necessitate the involvement of the UK and Irish governments and the elected representatives of both jurisdictions, north and south. If such an agreement was to be achieved by the politicians, it would require the democratic endorsement of all the people of Ireland. To create this possibility, Westminster and Dublin needed to affirm in the clearest terms the legitimacy of the Irishness of northern nationalists and the Britishness of unionists.

A few months later, in January 1989, I preached for the first time in Clonard and was overwhelmed by the reception I got. More people than ever came up to welcome me as word about the links between Fitzroy and the monastery spread steadily on the west-Belfast grapevine. There was no question in my mind that large numbers of west-Belfast people were longing for peace; they were eager to build bridges with the Protestant community, which was in some way represented by my presence among them and by my affection for them. I was heartened, therefore, when Gerry Adams made it known publicly in March that he desired "a non-armed political movement working for self-determination". This significant declaration of intent was reciprocated by another: in November the Northern Ireland secretary of state, Peter Brooke, admitted that "the IRA cannot be defeated militarily". Like many others, I sensed that talks were happening somewhere behind the scenes; but I did not realise they were being hosted in Clonard, in the same room where I would regularly meet with Fr Gerry.

## Secluded Conversations

Early in 1990, Fr Alec and Fr Gerry approached me about participating in a small inter-church dialogue in the monastery with Gerry Adams. It would be kept strictly private and confidential. Sinn Féin, I was informed, was keen to connect with the Protestant churches and, hopefully, through them, with the unionist community. I was not immediately receptive to the idea, for various reasons. My biggest fear was for my family. If it was leaked to the press that I was talking with Adams and other republican leaders of the political wing of the IRA, I knew that my wife and children could find themselves targetted by loyalist paramilitaries. I also knew that within the same shadowy circles

I could be seen as a collaborator with the enemy, and I was fully aware of what this might mean. Moreover, I would almost certainly find myself so demonised by some extreme unionist politicians that my position in Fitzroy could be undermined. There was now wide support within the congregation for our work with Clonard, but talking directly to the top representatives of the IRA's killing machine might be a bridge too far, especially for members of Fitzroy who had suffered at the hands of the IRA. Once again, I took time in deciding what to do and talked over all the likely consequences with Val. We both viewed Fr Reid's invitation as a God-given opportunity to talk directly with those who, however they were justifiably judged by others, held the future of the people of Northern Ireland in their hands. Moreover, we trusted the assessment of Fr Alec and Fr Gerry that the desire of these influential republicans who wanted to engage with us contained seeds of hope, although there was absolutely no guarantee that the seeds would germinate. Internally I also wrestled with the clear and simple teaching of Jesus. If we are commanded to "love [our] enemies" (Matthew 5:43–8), this must include talking with them.

As with all big decisions, part of me preferred to evade the invitation and to quell my conscience with wholly reasonable excuses; but in terms of my commitment to Christ I felt that I had little option but to take a leap of faith and go ahead. Val steadied my resolve and encouraged me to press on. I also asked Denis Boyd, Fitzroy's clerk of session, if he would be willing to join me. If news of what we were attempting to do was leaked to the press, his standing in Fitzroy might be enough to rescue me and interpret honestly the motives behind our involvement. Eventually I explained to Fr Alec the nature of my reservations and that we would be willing to take part only if secrecy was guaranteed. He gave his word that it would be.

As Denis and I drove across town, I felt distinctly uneasy at the prospect of meeting the man I considered to be the public face of the IRA. At the monastery, Fr Gerry accompanied us to a room where we joined four other church ministers and three Sinn Féin representatives. On being introduced to Adams, I shook his hand and he greeted me with a courteous smile – which, at that time, I was incapable of returning. Fr Gerry opened the meeting with a reading from Psalm 85 (8–10):

> Let me hear what God the Lord will speak,
> for he will speak peace to his people,

to his faithful, to those who turn to him in their hearts …

Surely his salvation is at hand for those who fear him,
that his glory may dwell in our land.

Steadfast love and faithfulness will meet;
righteousness and peace will kiss each other.

Fr Alec chaired the meetings, which took place every 6–8 weeks. Apart from Adams, the other Sinn Féin leaders were usually Tish Holland, a community activist from Andersonstown, and Aidan McAteer, an advisor to Adams. In addition to Denis and me, our group consisted of Rev Sam Burch, leader of the Cornerstone Community of Reconciliation, Rev John Dunlop of Rosemary Presbyterian Church, Rev Desmond Maxwell of Belfast Bible College and a local Methodist minister.

Our early conversations centred on our experiences of growing up in Northern Ireland and being moulded by its religious, cultural and political influences. From time to time, anger and accusation would boil up between us as Sinn Féin spoke of the aggression of the police and security forces, or we vented our fury against the continuing activity of the IRA. On one occasion I almost lost control of myself. Earlier in the week I had attended the funeral of a much-loved Presbyterian youth leader and member of the RUC, murdered by the IRA. I was so angry that I wondered what I was doing sitting down to talk with the Sinn Féin justifiers of the armed struggle.

Eventually an atmosphere of greater calm was restored and this allowed us to move into the sensitive domain of identity formation – how we had come to view ourselves as unionist, nationalist and republican, Protestant and Catholic, Irish and British. We discovered that sometimes identity is complex and elusive; it does not fit easily into the simplistic categories to which others want to reduce it. For example, my mother's family were from County Mayo in the west of Ireland and often as children we visited our relatives there. Not surprisingly, I have always had a love of things Irish and had already integrated this aspect of my background into the understanding of my deepest self. I now interpreted and expressed my identity inclusively, like a three-leafed shamrock: I was British, Ulster and Irish. Furthermore, I was not unique. Six million British citizens have an Irish grandparent – ten per cent of the UK population.

As we swapped these personal insights with each other, the common ground between us grew. We discovered that we had enough emotional space within us where those from the "other side" could come and feel comfortable. Furthermore, those of us from a working-class background identified with familiar patterns of family life and socio-economic struggles that were similar, irrespective of the flag we waved. As time passed, we inched our way into the beginnings of friendship, helped along by the irrepressible Irish instinct for humour. If we could laugh together, I thought, why could we not build peace together?

In time we were ready to venture into the more contentious terrain of the cherished and divergent political aspirations of a divided community. We were asked to give our honest opinion of Sinn Féin's key position papers, as well as speeches delivered by Adams at the party's national conventions in Dublin. A typical example was the May 1992 document, *Towards a Lasting Peace in Ireland*. It argued forcefully that a peace process must address the causes of the conflict and proceed on the principles of democracy and national self-determination. The British government, it claimed, had consistently denied these rights to the Irish people. Through military and political coercion it had partitioned the island, manufactured an artificial unionist majority and underwritten the unionist veto over partition. For nationalists in Northern Ireland, this translated into a daily experience of having to live with a sense of alienation, inequality, injustice and instability. The onus, therefore, was on London to admit that partition had failed and to persuade unionists that they had nothing to fear from a united Ireland. In our Clonard conversations, this analysis was repeatedly driven home to us by the Sinn Féin representatives with a kind of evangelical dogmatism. Nevertheless, we admired their courage in letting a group of churchmen comment on it with the best intellectual rigour and moral passion we could muster.

The critique we offered generally revolved around five observations. Firstly, there was much truth in what Sinn Féin affirmed about the consequences of partition for the nationalist community. In our view it was not an ideal solution, but it had perhaps been the only feasible option to avoid all-out civil war. Secondly, we had little enthusiasm for propping up the "majority rule" principle so beloved of unionists and so doggedly used to keep themselves in power. The future would require everyone agreeing to a just, equal and inclusive form of government that did not perpetuate the pattern of winners and losers. Thirdly, the principle of national self-determination was a two-sided coin. If it is justly asserted by Irish nationalists, then why should it be denied to unionists whose identity is British? Fourthly, the republican grievance that UK policy in Ireland has been implemented through "political and military coercion" sounds like a perfect description of the IRA armed struggle. Republicans cannot, therefore, condemn in others what they themselves are practising. Morally, we argued, you don't have a leg to stand on. Finally, *Towards a Lasting Peace in Ireland* highlighted the gruesome fact that "ninety percent of deaths caused by Loyalists and fifty-five percent of those killed by the British Army have been civilians". But why, we asked, had Sinn Féin chosen to present only a selective slice of such horrendous statistics? Civilian casualties at the hands of the IRA had just recently risen to 900.

The conclusion of *Towards a Lasting Peace in Ireland* was stark and seemingly uncompromising: "Armed struggle is an option of last resort, a legitimate part of a people's resistance to foreign oppression." Despite the challenges we presented in the dialogue to what seemed like the creation of a politically fundamentalist mindset, it remained rock solid. This started us questioning, therefore, Sinn Féin's sincerity when they spoke about "lasting peace". It was a noble sentiment, but the rattle of IRA AK-47 assault rifles at night around the hills of Belfast tended to drown it out.

Some onlookers might have thought that we were a soft touch and seriously naïve in hoping for change. Far from it! Our exchanges were respectful and mature, but equally confrontational on key issues. The whole process of the dialogue proved highly informative and a steep learning curve for us all.

In November 1990 the secretary of state for Northern Ireland, Peter Brooke, delivered another speech in London, this time one that revealed a distinct shift in the thinking of the Thatcher government. It strengthened my hunch that some new initiative was underway, well out of public view. Brooke declared that Britain had "no strategic or economic interest" in the province and would facilitate the unification of Ireland if the people of Northern Ireland desired it. His comments went further than his statement of the previous year that the IRA "could not be defeated militarily". Taken together, I concluded that the British government was repositioning itself in an attempt to become an honest broker to a fair deal for both sides rather than the traditional ally of one. Alternatives to armed struggle were now being dangled before the eyes of Sinn Féin. However, nothing I had gathered from Adams in the Clonard dialogue indicated that the IRA would end its campaign without first achieving its goal of a British declaration of political and military withdrawal from Northern Ireland.

Our conversations with Sinn Féin throughout 1991 continued to explore the landscape of republican thinking and, as we came towards the end of the summer 1992, I felt we were just going around in circles. All of us from the church side could have delivered lectures on the nuances of the republican mindset to a unionist audience as accurately as any Sinn Féin devotee. Our objective, however, remained firmly on resolving the conflict, whereas Sinn Féin's focus seemed to be simply on justifying the armed struggle. We had reached out to each other in good faith and learned a great deal, but we could not get beyond the roundabout to a route that would take us into a completely new situation. I thanked everyone for what I had gained, but felt that the time had come for me to pull out. The other church representatives had reached a similar conclusion. We were weary of words while lives were still being lost.

Fr Alec and Fr Gerry were naturally disappointed and afterwards stressed to Adams that, if Sinn Féin could not sustain its relationship with the Protestants they had been talking with for 18 months, there was no way they would ever build a bridge to the larger unionist community. For a credible dialogue to continue, it would require a major shift of direction towards sketching together the outline of a strategy that might bring the conflict to an end. As the summer drew to a close, I was pleasantly surprised when Fr Reid informed us that Adams had agreed to undertake this challenge with us. When we gathered together again in Clonard in October I sensed a definite change of mood. But how do you begin a serious exploration of alternatives to armed struggle in the cauldron of Northern Irish politics?

Efforts by the secretary of state for Northern Ireland, Peter Brooke, to engage our democratic parties in forging some new political way forward were running into difficulty and the prospects of agreement looked bleak. Meanwhile, the unexpected arrival of an extra battalion of British troops over the Christmas season heightened community fears that the intelligence agencies had been alerted to IRA plans to unleash a new wave of attacks on the general public. When the violence did erupt early in 1993, most of it was directed at London – incendiary bombs exploded in four stores in Oxford Street. The purpose of the assault on the capital was to wring more concessions out of the government of Prime Minister John Major.

As events outside Clonard spun out of control, our conversations inside took on a new urgency. As Protestants, we attempted to put ourselves in the shoes of republicans who were serious about initiating a peace process. We suggested that Sinn Féin first mend the rift with the SDLP, then construct together with them a nationalist peace agenda that both Dublin and Washington could buy into. If successful, this pathway to peace should be presented for consideration to Prime Minister John Major, who was keen to make progress in the province. Through him it should be offered for consultation to unionist politicians, among whom the desire for a peaceful political settlement was growing. The central proposal of this whole initiative would be the establishment of all-party negotiations aimed at setting up a new power-sharing administration at Stormont.

Adams welcomed our suggestions, well aware that we were not skilled in the ways of politics. It was much more important for him to realise that, if we could think our way into such an inclusive pathway to peace, there might be some hope of the wider unionist community doing the same. He admitted, however, that it would be no easy matter to draw such diverse political groupings into the common task of seeking a solution. From our perspective, it would be an even bigger undertaking for the Sinn Féin president to convince the IRA to deliver a permanent ceasefire in order to create the confidence and stability for a peaceful and democratic resolution of the conflict.

As I strongly suspected, other private dialogues had indeed been going on in parallel with ours. In April 1993, Adams and Hume took a risk in temporarily switching the venue for their meetings from the seclusion of Clonard to Derry. A member of the public spotted Adams coming out of John Hume's house and within hours their cover was blown. It triggered an avalanche of media speculation and unionist criticism. To explain to a puzzled province what they had been talking about, both leaders released a joint statement on 23 April, which inspired some hope:

> [T]he most pressing issue facing the people of Ireland and Britain today is the question of lasting peace and how it can best be achieved. Everyone has a solemn duty to change the political climate away from conflict and towards a process of national reconciliation which sees the peaceful accommodation of the differences between the people of Britain and Ireland and the Irish people themselves … a new agreement is only achievable and viable if it can earn and enjoy the allegiance of the different traditions[.]

Rumours started circulating that the IRA was considering a ceasefire if the

Hume-Adams proposals were welcomed by the UK and Irish governments. Unionists closed ranks to oppose them, primarily because they did not deal with the republic's offensive territorial claim to Northern Ireland.

Towards the end of April 1993 the Clonard Inter-Church Group realised that its work was coming to an end, as others much more centrally placed and politically gifted began to move in the direction we had long hoped for. We were convinced that Adams was genuine in his intention to pursue a peace process, but he would need a lot of support. Fr Gerry and I promised that in the event of a credible ceasefire being declared by the IRA, we would go public and commend it to a sceptical community. Then, as we prepared to break up, Adams said something that caught my attention: "I regret the death of every young soldier who is returned to Britain in a box." I later discovered that he carried away a comment of mine that took him by surprise:

> As a Presbyterian minister I would have no difficulty living in a democratically chosen united Ireland; it wouldn't threaten my faith or weaken the value I place on the Britishness of my heritage. For Presbyterians, Ireland is our home; we aren't British implants, nor have we any plans to go home to England or Scotland. We're here for good.

As we all looked back over the three years we had spent together and reflected on the personal benefits that time had brought us, Adams asked us to recruit some other Protestant ministers to engage in a similar dialogue with a broader circle of republican activists. I was happy to do so and asked one of my closest friends, Rev Ivan Hull of Ulsterville Presbyterian Church, Belfast, to participate. On 4 May 1993, the "Clonard Two" dialogue got underway, with around nine members: four Protestant clergy; Fr Alec and Fr Gerry; and three prominent figures in Belfast republicanism: Alex Maskey, Tom Hartley and Denis Donaldson. As we ourselves had found, the interchange yielded valuable insights into each other's worlds, kindled a spirit of honest and mutual challenge, generated hope and stimulated the beginnings of genuine friendship.

## Barbarism Makes a Comeback

After a restful summer holiday with my family, I launched myself once again into the joyful and challenging routines of being the minister of Fitzroy. But, despite significant moves towards reconciliation on the larger national stage, Belfast was still an unhappy city. On 27 May Mary Robinson, the first female president of Ireland, travelled to London to visit the Queen at Buckingham Palace, the first ever official contact between an Irish president and a British monarch. Then, on 18 June, President Robinson came north to Belfast and during her visit shook hands with Adams, a gesture which unionists found offensive.

Then, in brutal contrast to these fragile hints of hope, came one of the most savage assaults on the citizens of Belfast going about their ordinary every day activities. On Saturday, 23 October, a unit of the IRA placed a bomb in Frizzell's fish shop on the Shankill Road. Allegedly the intended target was a meeting of loyalist paramilitary leaders in a flat above the shop, but it had been cancelled. At 1.00 pm, two junior IRA operatives dressed as delivery men carried a plastic tray of cod into the shop, which was crowded with women and children. Underneath the fish was a five-pound time-bomb. It exploded prematurely, killing one of the bombers and nine other civilians, including the owner, his recently married daughter and two young girls.

The incident sent shock waves through the whole community and on Sunday morning prayers were offered in both Protestant and Catholic churches for the victims. In Fitzroy I invited the congregation to come with me to the Shankill in the afternoon and place the display of flowers adorning the front of our sanctuary at the site of the explosion. Thirty of us later travelled across to the Shankill, placed the flowers among the sea of bouquets brought by people from all over the city, and prayed silently for the families now engulfed in grief. As I stood quietly with hundreds of others looking into the blackened shell of the shop, I started to question whether our investment of time and energy in the conversations with Sinn Féin in Clonard had achieved anything. I also feared there would be retaliation attacks by loyalist paramilitaries on ordinary Catholic civilians. Later that day the Ulster Freedom Fighters (UFF) issued a chilling statement: "John Hume, Gerry Adams and the Nationalist electorate will pay a heavy, heavy price for today's atrocity." A week later seven customers of the Rising Sun Bar in Greysteel, County Londonderry, were shot dead in cold blood. Six were Catholic and one Protestant.

My doubts intensified a few days later, when Gerry Adams acted as one of the four pallbearers carrying the tricolour-draped coffin of the Shankill bomber Thomas Begley. The "Walk of Shame", as it was dubbed, fuelled

Protestant anger and made me wonder again if our dialogue group had been deliberately deceived. The only explanation I found even slightly plausible was that the Sinn Féin leader, if he was to carry the IRA's armed struggle to its final resting place, had to be seen carrying the coffin of those who had lost their lives promoting its goals. I really did not know what to think.

## Downing Street Declaration: 15 December 1993

The final months of 1993 were filled with foreboding. The secret Hume–Adams talks made people suspicious of what was going on. That suspicion turned into major distrust in November, when London finally admitted that they had been in covert contact with the IRA for years. Furthermore, Sir Patrick Mayhew, secretary of state for Northern Ireland, acknowledged that the back-door channels remained open, but that no direct talks with Sinn Féin would begin until a convincing ceasefire had been in place for ten weeks. Nobody knew whom to trust and the need for transparency was crucial. The signing of the Downing Street Declaration by Prime Minister John Major and Taoiseach Albert Reynolds on 15 December provided it.

Both governments unveiled proposals to frame a peace process that would address all the relationships that were sustaining the conflict and aim for a comprehensive settlement. It affirmed the right of the people of Ireland alone, on both parts of the island, to "exercise their right of self-determination on the basis of consent, freely and concurrently given, North and South, to bring about a united Ireland, if that is their wish". These sentiments clearly heartened Irish nationalists. But the declaration equally insisted that the UK would "uphold the democratic wish of the greater number of the people of Northern Ireland on the issue of whether they prefer to support the Union or a sovereign united Ireland". This was reassuring for unionists, as was the revelation that the Irish government would be willing to remove its constitutional claim to Northern Ireland. Finally, London and Dublin invited Sinn Féin and the loyalist paramilitary parties into the talks, provided they ended their support for violence.

The aspiration at the heart of the Downing Street Declaration was essentially the same as the Christian vision of peace and reconciliation that had been my motivation for almost 20 years. The stage was now set for inclusive talks and the time had come for our local parties to step up to the plate. It was disappointing, therefore, when Dr Ian Paisley branded the whole exercise a sell-out to Dublin and a moral cop-out because more had not been demanded from Sinn Féin than an IRA ceasefire – specifically, the destruction of their arsenals of illegal weapons. The UUP leader, James Molyneaux, criticised the "tortuously worded statement" of the declaration but accepted that it posed no threat to the union. Sinn Féin complained that it would be hard to sell the proposals to the IRA without further clarification, but they would attempt to do so. Reading between the lines, I was sure that Adams would welcome the declaration but, because the stakes were high, it would require a lengthy process of consultation within the party and the IRA Army Council. In May 1994 the Northern Ireland Office published a 21-page booklet clarifying the outstanding issues raised by the parties. In the meantime, gestures were made towards Sinn Féin to nudge its internal discussion in the right direction: Dublin lifted its broadcasting ban against Sinn Féin so that republicans could once again use their own voices in media interviews. Shortly afterwards, President Bill Clinton issued Adams with a visa to enter the USA to address a conference on peace. A momentum of hope was building.

## Listening to Loyalists

In parallel with our conversations with republicans in Clonard, Fr Alec, Fr Gerry, Rev Sam Burch and I were also locked in discussions for a year with the political representatives of loyalism. We met at the Columbanus Community of Reconciliation in north Belfast with Ray Smallwoods, chairperson of the Ulster Democratic Party (UDP) and two of his younger associates, Gary McMichael and David Adams. The UDP was the political voice of the UDA, the largest of the loyalist paramilitary groups formed in 1971 to protect Protestant areas from IRA attacks and to combat Irish republicanism in all its forms. Its military campaign was now in its twenty-third year and most of its victims were innocent Catholic civilians.

Smallwoods was in his early forties and, though strong in his loyalist convictions, was of a pragmatic rather than a dogmatic disposition. He grew up in Lisburn and was a close friend and ally of John McMichael, the UDA brigadier who headed up the UDP until his death in 1987. In 1981 Smallwoods had been sentenced to 15 years in jail. While incarcerated, he had slowly come to the conclusion that politics might serve loyalism better than armed conflict. On release he was quickly recruited into the Inner Council of the UDA as a political advisor. Through the influence of Rev Roy Magee, the Presbyterian minister who had cultivated contacts with the UDA since the 1970s, Smallwoods continued to moderate his views. Magee opened up for him doors of access to the Church of Ireland Archbishop Robin Eames and the former Presbyterian moderators Dr Jack Weir and Dr Godfrey Brown. A new chapter in his development occurred in 1993, when the UDA gave him permission to initiate a dialogue with Catholic clergy. He was the first high-ranking loyalist to do so. This was the background to our meetings with him.

His purpose in talking with us was to find out what was happening within Sinn Féin. Were they really genuine about a peace process? How close were they to a ceasefire? Our goal was to ascertain how the UDA Inner Council would respond if Sinn Féin moved in the right direction. But more was happening in the conversations than simply the transmission of insights. I looked on as a friendship developed between Ray and the Clonard priests, which started him shedding some of his inherited anti-Catholicism. We concluded that he was becoming a key advocate within the UDA Inner Council for the need to bring the violence to an end. But would the hard men of the council believe the positive reports he was conveying back from us? There was only one way to make sure. He persuaded them to meet us face to face. In April 1994 we were invited to the UDA headquarters in east Belfast.

As the day approached I became increasingly fearful for my family and myself. The RUC had uncovered loyalist hit-lists of Protestants, including some ministers, considered "suspect" because they were too close to the enemy. I wondered if my name might be on one of the lists. I felt no fear when moving among republicans, but sitting down with UDA commanders who might view me as a traitor was altogether another matter. When Fr Gerry, Rev Sam and Fr Alec arrived at Fitzroy to pick me up for the meeting I told them I had decided not to go. They were surprised but kept coaxing me and reminding me how close we might be to a breakthrough. "Come on, Ken," they insisted. "In for a penny, in for a pound!"

Eventually they persuaded me to get into the car, but I said nothing on the short drive across the city – which was unusual for me (as everyone remarked). When we pulled into the car park behind the headquarters I noticed the cage-like staircase and security cameras. Soon we were in a large room surrounded by 15 seated men, only a few of whom I recognised. We sat opposite them as if in a business interview. The chairperson welcomed us and then the council members introduced themselves – not by name, but by the areas of Northern Ireland they represented. We, then, introduced ourselves. Fr Alec took the lead and, with a calmness born of seeing the best in others, expressed our thanks for the invitation. He spoke frankly about our motives. We were not emissaries of Sinn Féin, but ordinary Christians concerned with seeing an end to violence. When they realised we had no hidden agenda, they relaxed and questions began to flow. What was the leadership of Sinn Féin up to? Was it true that the IRA was contemplating an end to its armed struggle? For half an hour I was loath to express an opinion about anything, but when some native humour broke out among us I managed a smile. Fr Alec and Fr Gerry noticed on the wall behind the UDA leader chairing the meeting a large map of Ulster's six counties, totally detached from the rest of the island. He teased them by innocently enquiring if the other 26 counties had floated off somewhere into the middle of the Atlantic. A ripple of laughter went round the room. Only a priest from Tipperary and one from Limerick could get away with that kind of naïve impudence inches away from Ulster's primary paramilitary leaders. When they enquired if we had any questions for them, we asked how they would respond if the IRA called a permanent ceasefire. Also, would they accept the government's invitation to inclusive talks?

The questions I was keen to put to them related more to the underlying anti-Catholicism frequently associated with loyalism and often identified in court as a motive in the murders of Catholic civilians. "Why do you dislike the Catholic Church so much?" I asked them. "What would you say to its leaders if you had a chance to explain to them face to face the beliefs you hold?" It turned out to be like peeling an onion. My questions exposed layers of inherited prejudice worth getting out into the open in the presence of two Catholic priests. By the time the meeting drew to a close we were well on the way to viewing each other in a healthier light. We concluded that they would indeed buy into a peace process if the IRA committed itself first. The internal advocacy of Ray Smallwoods was bearing fruit. They invited us to come back any time we wanted but on the way out of the parking area I still checked under our car for explosives.

## Brutal Summer

Our hopes for loyalism were temporarily raised, only to be quickly dashed by more UVF killings on Saturday, 18 June. Two days earlier the INLA had assassinated three UVF members on the Shankill Road and the secluded County Down village of Loughinisland was selected for a revenge attack. In the Heights Bar, customers had crowded around the large TV to cheer on Ireland in a World Cup soccer match against Italy. Just after 10.00 pm, two UVF gunmen wearing boiler suits and balaclavas burst into the pub and fired into the crowd. Six people lay dead and five others wounded as the gunmen ran back to their getaway car, reportedly laughing. On Sunday morning I led Fitzroy in prayer for the families involved but I felt strongly that something more than prayer was needed. Once again I shared my thoughts with the congregation. I would be leaving the side door of the church at 3.00 pm to drive the 21 miles down to Loughinisland to pray at the pub and lay some flowers from our church. If anyone wanted to join me they would be most welcome. I was humbled when 20 of our members turned up, including some young parents with their children. At the pub we formed a circle of prayer and remembered the families in the houses nearby. The following Sunday, Robert Robinson, one of our Bible-class leaders, who had come down to Loughinisland with us, shared with the teenagers how deeply the incident and the visit had affected him. When they asked what they could do to demonstrate their concern, he suggested that all seven of them write individual letters to the bar owner and send them off together. A month later I received this reply:

> The Heights Bar, Loughinisland, Co. Down
> 01.08.94
>
> Dear Matthew, Alan, Andrew, Peter, Naomi, Justin and Emma,
>
> Thank you so much for your kind letters of sympathy. Just reading the thoughts of all you young people shows how much you care and how much you and everyone else want this violence to stop. Maybe you can grow up to be adults in a peaceful country. Your prayers for us at that time were really appreciated. Some of you asked us to somehow forgive the men who carried out this evil deed in my pub. Well I do. These men need so many prayers because they like us have to meet God someday. God forgave us, so we have to bring ourselves to forgive others. Please keep praying for peace in this beautiful country and I pray that God will bless you and keep you safe.
>
> Yours sincerely,
> Hugh and Frances O'Toole and family

Following Loughinisland, there was an upsurge in tit-for-tat killings, the most high-profile of which was the assassination of our dialogue partner Ray Smallwoods. On 11 July 1994, as he was leaving his house at Donard Drive, Lisburn, at 9.00 am, an IRA gunman ran down the street and fired several gunshots at him from close range. He died on the way to the Lagan Valley Hospital. It was a bitter blow for his family and friends, but also for Fr Alec, Fr Gerry, Rev Sam and me. We had grown to like him and respect him. Fr Alec and Fr Gerry were dejected by the murder and made known the strength of their feelings to local republicans. But they went further – they visited his wife Linda and her family in Lisburn to convey their deepest sympathy. The following day, along with Rev Sam, they walked through the loyalist estate as part of the funeral procession. A journalist covering the event commented that two clerically attired Catholic priests walking among so many prominent paramilitaries was a sight that loyalists had never witnessed before. Their presence, he hoped, softened the intense anger simmering under the surface. The gesture may also have contributed to a statement released shortly afterwards by the Combined Loyalist Military Command: there would be no retaliation for Ray's death and they would go on ceasefire if the IRA did the same. The second part of the statement had apparently been drafted by Ray shortly before his death. Once again, I found it extremely difficult to figure out what was going on within loyalism and republicanism. Were we on the edge of a breakthrough or another brutal backlash?

A few weeks later our group decided to reconnect with the UDP, now that the leadership mantle of Ray Smallwoods had been passed to Gary McMichael. We wanted to gauge the level of support among loyalist paramilitary groups for the proposed ceasefire. At the party's office in Lisburn, Fr Alec, Fr Gerry, Rev Sam Burch and I met up again with Gary McMichael, David Adams and three other leaders. On the way to the meeting I had suggested to my colleagues in the car that we should not go straight into discussion but rather ask our UDP friends if we could stand together with them in silent remembrance of Ray while Fr Gerry offered some prayers for his family. They agreed. When I asked Gary and his colleagues if this might be appropriate, they were quite moved and welcomed the suggestion. As we stood silently around the table I realised that this was another of those special moments that convinced me that God was present in what we were doing. In my wildest dreams I would never have imagined a group of grieving loyalist leaders bowing their heads as a Catholic priest prayed for them. We had moved to a deeper level of openness and trust.

When we moved from prayer to the business in hand we offered them our analysis that, despite appearances, Sinn Féin was still guiding the IRA towards a ceasefire. If it arrived, we had to push for the creation of inclusive all-party talks. They reassured us that, despite instincts towards retaliation, the Combined Loyalist Military Command had made up its mind to call a ceasefire if the IRA called one first. We all believed that these initiatives could transform life in Northern Ireland. We headed home, holding our breath.

### We've Got a Pulse

Then at 11.00 am on Wednesday, 31 August 1994, the seemingly impossible happened. The IRA announced "a complete cessation of military operations". The statement read:

> We believe that an opportunity to secure a just and lasting settlement has been created ... A solution will only be found as a result of inclusive negotiations ... It is our desire to significantly contribute to the creation of a climate which will encourage this.

Within an hour, celebrations broke out in Catholic areas across the province. In Belfast a cavalcade of cars drove past the heavily fortified Anderstonstown Police Station, honking their horns in celebration and waving Irish tricolours. On the Falls Road, Gerry Adams and Martin McGuinness were swamped by crowds, who cheered when Adams declared, "We remain undefeated by the British."

Unionist reaction varied from outright scepticism to cautious optimism. Speculation was rife about what London may have conceded to Sinn Féin to get the ceasefire. Paisley dismissed it all as a sham: the IRA had expressed no regret for their slaughter of innocent people and offered no assurances that they would "surrender all the weapons of their killing machine". Ulster Unionist leader James Molyneaux underscored the absence of the word "permanent" from the ceasefire declaration and insisted there would be no moves towards talks until this omission was credibly corrected. While these were legitimate reservations, I had learned that intractable situations of conflict inch towards a resolution rather than take instant, giant strides.

Outside the arena of unionism, responses were more positive. Irish nationalists north and south were delighted and even the British prime minister, John Major, was upbeat: "We are beyond the beginning but we are not yet in sight of the end." The most relieved people of all, however, were RUC police officers and their families, as well as young British soldiers, who had daily been exposed to the threat of IRA attacks. I was optimistic and hoped that the new and fragile peace would not be killed off by old, die-hard attitudes.

However, the ceasefire created an awkward predicament for me. While the general public now knew about the secret meetings between the London and Sinn Féin as well as those between Hume and Adams, journalists were still busy trying to ferret out information about the details of what had been discussed and who else might had been involved. Attention now focussed on Clonard, where Hume and Adams had met, and speculation was rife that other clandestine conversations may have been taking place there. Fr Gerry and I felt certain that at some point a journalist might ask us if we knew anything about other private discussions. I therefore phoned our clerk of session, Denis Boyd, and suggested that we should inform Fitzroy's elders as soon as possible of our involvement in the Clonard dialogue, before anything appeared in the press. He agreed. Four days later, on Sunday morning, 4 September, as ten of our elders gathered with us for prayer before the Communion service, Denis revealed to them the extent of our engagement with Sinn Féin and our reasons for getting involved. I was unsure how they would react. But, one by one, they congratulated us on the initiative we had taken and on the outcome of our discussions. I felt a huge sense of relief and gratitude.

That evening in Clonard, Fr Gerry and I gave the first of a series of joint interviews to the media about the IRA ceasefire and spoke openly about the extent of our talks with Sinn Féin and the loyalists. A senior English journalist from ITN interrogated us about whether we believed the ceasefire was genuine and would last. He then quizzed us about how long we had been involved with Adams and what we really thought about him as leader of Sinn Féin and the public face of militant republicanism. I got the distinct impression that he privately dismissed us as typical naïve men of the cloth, easily taken in and used by the anti-British propaganda machine. His last question confirmed my hunch. In an attempt to destroy our credibility he asked, "Do you believe Gerry Adams will go to heaven?"

"That's not a question I could answer," I replied. "I leave such judgments to God, who created us, knows us inside out, confronts us honestly about our sins, offers us forgiveness and loves us unconditionally. As for myself, I look to Christ and his grace alone." Surprisingly, none of the interview was ever screened – probably because our cautiously optimistic assessment of the ceasefire did not match that of ITN's news editors. Shortly afterwards, at an evangelical conference in Coleraine, I presented a similar assessment to a more generally sympathetic audience. But one of those present forthrightly rejected my point of view and voiced what many unionists were thinking: "The ceasefire won't last three months! You can't trust anything Sinn Féin say because their only objective is a 32-county socialistic republic." I was about to reply, "I bet you're wrong!" when I remembered where I was. Instead, I drew attention to the fact that a few months earlier unionists had been adamant that the IRA would never call a ceasefire unless the British government first declared its intention to withdraw from Northern Ireland.

Within days of the ceasefire, Dublin and London followed through on pre-planned gestures of encouragement to Sinn Féin. The smiling triumvirate of Taoiseach Albert Reynolds, John Hume and Gerry Adams shook hands outside government buildings in Dublin. Shortly afterwards, the British prime minister, John Major, lifted the six-year broadcasting ban on proscribed organisations and an army of actors employed to mimic the accents of leading republicans on radio and TV lost their jobs. On a more practical level, the British Army reopened ten secondary cross-border roads which had long been sealed for security reasons.

Six weeks later, on 13 October, the Combined Loyalist Military Command announced their ceasefire. At a press conference in the Shankill area of Belfast, former UVF commander Gusty Spence, flanked by six loyalist political leaders including David Ervine of the Progressive Unionist Party (PUP) and Gary McMichael and David Adams of the UDP, read out a statement. It contained one feature noticeably absent from the IRA declaration – an apology to the victims of violence: "In all sincerity," Spence read, "we offer to the loved ones of all innocent victims over the past twenty years, abject and true remorse."

I wondered if their contacts with Fr Alec and Fr Gerry may have been behind this important apology. The final sentences of the statement also embodied a hope that had been growing among Protestants for some time:

> We are on the threshold of a new and exciting beginning with
> our battles in future being political battles, fought on the side

of honesty, decency and democracy against the negativity of mistrust, misunderstanding and malevolence, so that, together, we can bring forth a wholesome society in which our children, and their children, will know the meaning of true peace.

The loyalist ceasefire was widely welcomed but, sadly, in the following months it was dogged by serious breaches in its implementation. Violence did not stop either immediately or completely and lucrative loyalist criminal enterprises were not shut down. It came as no surprise therefore that sentiments about "honesty and decency", as well as the internal integrity of the ceasefire itself, were highly questionable. Moreover, progress towards the goal of all-inclusive negotiations slowed to a snail's pace because both the IRA and loyalist groups refused even to discuss the dismantling of their large arsenals of illegal military hardware. The issue of decommissioning was shaping up to become a real impediment to peace.

# CHAPTER SIX

# The Drama of High-Stakes Politics

With the two ceasefires now in place – officially, at least – new channels of communication started to open up across Ireland. In late November 1994, Fr Gerry, Fr Alec, Rev Sam and I travelled to Dublin by train at the invitation of the American Embassy. We were part of a consultative group that included 20 others: businessmen, peace activists, community workers and leaders of the Loyal Orders. The invitation had been issued by Jean Kennedy Smith, the newly appointed American ambassador to Ireland and sister of John F. Kennedy, the thirty-fifth president of the United States. President Clinton had chosen her specifically to contribute to the peace process and she was keen to meet a wide range of people from Northern Ireland. She questioned us primarily about the stability of the ceasefires and was heartened to discover that most of us remained confident that they would hold, provided that all-party talks got underway soon. The analysis of the Loyal Orders, however, was much less optimistic.

When she steered the conversation towards US policy in Northern Ireland, a lot of straight talking ensued. The decision by President Clinton to grant Gerry Adams a visa to enter the USA was cited as one of a list of evidences that American interventions in Northern Ireland were too "green" (that is, pro-Irish). She was politely reminded that 17 out of the 44 US presidents had an Ulster-Scots lineage. When she asked what America could do to change this image, many suggestions were offered and noted down carefully by her aides. The recommendation I put forward advocated a genuine policy shift towards greater political balance. The US should become the partner and friend of both sides, not the ally of one. When she asked us to be specific and practical about ways to implement such a process, I offered one example: "Why not invite unionist politicians to the White House for the annual St Patrick's Day celebrations as well as the usual nationalist contingent?" She asked why they would come. "Try them and see," I answered. She must have been getting similar nudges from other quarters, because in March 1996 David Trimble, the new leader of the UUP, was invited to Washington for St Patrick's Day. Unionists have been regular visitors since then and American policy towards Northern Ireland has been noticeably more balanced and supportive of a shared future.

### "Not a Bullet and Not an Ounce of Semtex"

The celebratory mood among republicans following the ceasefire continued to be bolstered by encouragements flowing in their direction. John Major revoked the exclusion order against Gerry Adams and Martin McGuinness travelling within the UK and promised talks with Sinn Féin before Christmas. But the noise of celebration within the jubilant republican community dulled their capacity to hear what unionists were saying about the decommissioning of weapons as an essential ingredient in the building of trust. Every time the issue was broached, the answer appeared in big letters on gable walls in republican areas: "Not a Bullet, Not an Ounce". The IRA would not countenance what it considered to be the surrender of its weapons, the gesture of a defeated army in the face of conquering British forces. But the legitimate questions of the general public refused to go away: "Why do democratic parties need private armies?" "If Sinn Féin doesn't get what it wants from political negotiations, will the IRA go back to doing what it does best?" "Why should Sinn Féin be surprised when it chants 'Not a Bullet' and unionism responds antiphonally, 'Not an Inch'?"

With the optimism generated by the ceasefires steadily evaporating in the heat of the decommissioning controversy, Fr Gerry and I organised a consultation in Fitzroy in May 1995 between 30 representatives of civic society and 10 republican activists. Following a standard presentation from a leading republican spokesperson, I presented a paper entitled *Decommissioning of Paramilitary Weapons with Special Reference to the IRA*. I decided not to build my case for decommissioning on the morality of the issue, which various church bodies had already been articulating clearly and forcefully. The line I adopted was to convey to the republican movement the potential benefits of moving decisively towards decommissioning:

If commitment to lasting peace is now a central tenet of the republican movement, as has been declared, then the logic of peace is clear: a democratic resolution of conflict erodes any necessity to retain weapons or sustain organisations created for armed struggle. Furthermore, the ceasefire has attracted an international sympathy-shift towards republican ideals. Even at home, some in the nationalist community are now considering voting for SF for the first time. Decommissioning would undoubtedly enhance these trends. But if you drag your feet on the issue, it will intensify the suspicion that SF is only begrudgingly committed to a peace-process; world-respect will diminish and your political influence [will] wane. A positive and speedy response is the only thing that will eventually create space within unionism for direct interaction with republicans in order to reach a just settlement based on self-determination and consent.

Beyond this appeal, I acknowledged that decommissioning would not be easy and would carry certain complications. The memory of fallen comrades would haunt the republican mind because the goals for which they died had not been realised; the hands of informers would be more ready to stretch out for the financial inducements proffered by British intelligence agencies eager to identify the IRA's core arsenals of 200,000 tons of weapons. Those weapons, forensically examined, could put certain individuals behind bars for decades. Despite these risks, however, I asserted that the rewards of peace were a thousand times greater than the cost of war.

Finally, I made a suggestion: that decommissioning should be overseen by a specialised professional body assisted by a few respected church representatives, so that the process could carry a moral transparency in the eyes of the public and not be manipulated by outside political influences. In addition, I argued, rather than waiting for the decommissioning process to be completed, London should set up a parallel process of inclusive inter-party discussions to design a road-map to a new democratic political agreement.

My call for decommissioning went down like a lead balloon. The republicans present dismissed it in four strong words, just in case anyone of us did not understand what they had been saying: "It will never happen!" I was not surprised, but at least the issue had been opened up with the only people who could make it happen. It certainly was not going to disappear.

## Icebreaker in Conway Mill

Despite the republican rebuff regarding decommissioning, Sinn Féin remained committed to building bridges with the unionist and Protestant community, partly in order to accelerate movement towards all-party talks. That goal was now top of its political agenda, as the organisers of the West Belfast Festival were fully aware. Two months later, an invitation was sent to me to take part in a public debate in Conway Mill on the Falls Road on Wednesday, 9 August 1995. The other participants included the Derry-based republican leader Martin McGuinness, reputed to be one of the seven-man IRA Army Council, Mark Durkan, chairperson of the SDLP, and a former taoiseach, Albert Reynolds. The only person prepared to break the unionist embargo on talking with anyone from Sinn Féin was Roy Garland, press officer of the UUP's Lisburn branch. His decision to take part drew a blast of criticism from the DUP and a stinging rebuke of silence from his own party. I phoned Roy to express how much I appreciated his courage and would value his moral support at the event.

When I arrived at the hospitality lounge at Conway Mill early on Wednesday evening, Gerry Adams came over to welcome me and introduce me to his friend Martin McGuinness, whose relaxed demeanour and smile impressed me. His rather fearsome reputation, however, was cycling around in the back of my mind. A capacity crowd of 600 squeezed into the hall, with the result that many had to sit on the floor, including the Sinn Féin president. As the evening unfolded it was evident that the vast majority of those present were ardent republicans; I suspected that some might be high-ranking IRA commanders. It turned out to be one of the toughest and most exhilarating debates I have ever been involved in. "Warm applause for unionists in the lions' den" was how one reporter described it.

Loud cheers greeted Albert Reynolds when he lambasted London for dragging its feet on all-party talks. He gave us the line of the night: "I would never have signed the Downing Street Declaration with John Major if decommissioning had been a prerequisite for all-party talks." Roy Garland countered the bias in Reynolds's rhetoric by insisting that "unionists need to be reassured that the IRA has renounced violence for good". Mark Durkan pressed home his opinions more calmly and cogently than Reynolds did. There should be no preconditions to all-party talks and no delay in getting them up and running. The loudest applause, though, was reserved for Martin McGuinness, a hero in the eyes of most of those in the audience. He pulled no punches: "The British government and the unionists need to understand that we have lived with the gun to our head since the foundation of this state and we have resisted like the people of South Africa. The greatest responsibility for the mess we have lived in for 70 years lies with London." The roar of approval for this uncompromising claim almost took the roof off. When the cheering had settled down, I asked a question: "Putting a gun to anybody's head is sickening, but isn't this exactly what the IRA has been doing? That's precisely why unionists are demanding that the guns pointed at our heads for 25 years should be dumped in the Irish Sea." Thankfully there were no boos, just disapproving looks and a stern silence.

When the questions turned to all-party talks, I confessed that I could not at the moment see any unionist leaders willing to champion power-sharing with republicans. They had resisted even modest moves towards sharing power for so long that unionism was in danger of turning into a graveyard for creative thinking. After devoting so much energy to trying to smash Sinn Féin, it was not surprising that few were now willing to accommodate it.

"I don't at the moment see a unionist de Klerk figure emerging as in South Africa," I commented, "one who would be willing to strike an historic deal with nationalists. It may take three or four years before the Protestant community has fully thought through its future."

When the highly emotive issue of prisoner releases was broached, McGuinness launched into another tirade, this time against the British Army: "If there was any justice in Northern Ireland there would be 400 members of the British Army now serving life sentences for murder." I challenged him on this assertion and pointed out the glaring contradiction in his argument: "How can you call for soldiers who have not had a legal trial to be jailed for life while those whom the courts declared to be guilty of murder should be set free? People who have taken life and devastated families cannot expect to simply get up and walk out of jail free." This was greeted, again, with a restrained silence. I sensed that the crowd were genuinely trying to hear where Roy and I were coming from, because they knew we had no animosity in us towards them but were in Conway Mill with our own agenda – to forge a new future with them based on friendship, justice and peace.

The Conway Mill evening was a strange mix of bluntness and hope. The loudest cheers thundered out for McGuinness, but the warmest applause was reserved for Roy and me. They had hissed early on in the discussion when I mentioned that my father had been in the B-Specials; but later, when I paid tribute to "those who had joined the Royal Ulster Constabulary to serve both communities and had paid the ultimate sacrifice", they strangely applauded at some length. My parting contribution to a remarkable evening was an appeal: "I've been conscious of anger towards me as well as a welcome. It's a funny feeling. We need to talk with each other much more because a lot of bad feeling has built up on both sides. At the moment we haven't got the emotional bonding we need if we are going to build a community that is worth living in. There's no future if we can't become friends."

This was reciprocated with such strong applause that it sounded to me like a west Belfast choral "Amen". One journalist summarised the evening precisely:

> The years of violence and isolation have left these people with a deep feeling of having been treated unfairly and unjustly by Unionism and by Britain. But on Wednesday night they also displayed other characteristics: tremendous hospitality and good humour, toleration and goodwill, and a palpable eagerness to reach out and enter dialogue with old foes.

## Decommissioning and Disillusionment

Unionist reservations about the IRA ceasefire, however, were reinforced a few days after Conway Mill, when Adams addressed a large republican rally at the front of the City Hall. Someone in the crowd shouted "Bring back the IRA!" and in an off-the-cuff remark he responded, "They haven't gone away, you know!" His comment was greeted with cheers, but it sent shock waves through Belfast, London and Dublin and cemented suspicions about Sinn Féin's intentions. Were the modest social gains of the ceasefires about to disintegrate and hope take flight again from a suffering community? Storm clouds started to gather and the country felt a desperate need for decisive political leadership. It came in November, when John Major and the new Taoiseach, John Bruton, issued a joint communiqué outlining a twin-track approach to decommissioning and inclusive talks. They appointed US Senator George Mitchell and two other eminent persons to assess the difficulties around the removal of illegal weapons. Preparatory talks on establishing all-party negotiations would begin early in 1996.

## Presidential Persuasion

Two days after the Major–Bruton communiqué, on Thursday, 30 November 1995, President Bill Clinton and his wife, Hillary, flew into Belfast in an attempt to stabilise the peace process. On their way in from the International Airport, the motorcade stopped at their request on the Shankill Road, ostensibly to pick up some fruit and vegetables at a grocery store. It was a short distance from the scene of the 1993 Shankill bombing. The presidential limo again came to a halt at a bakery on the Falls Road, where the couple just happened to bump into Gerry Adams. At both locations they were mobbed by well-wishers and they were given a rapturous reception everywhere they went. The choreography of the visit reminded me of our conversations in the US Embassy a year earlier, when we had advocated greater American balance regarding Northern Ireland. It was working.

Clinton's speech a few hours later to an audience of 500 at the Mackie Metal Plant on west Belfast's peace-line was inspirational:

A big part of peace is children growing up safely, learning together and growing together ... Here in Northern Ireland you are making a miracle ... In the land of the harp and the fiddle, the fife and the Lambeg drum, two proud traditions are coming together in the harmonies of peace ... Among many others, David Trimble and John Hume have laboured to realise the promise of peace. And Gerry Adams, along with loyalist leaders such as David Ervine and Gary McMichael, have helped to silence the guns. Engaging in honest dialogue is not an act of surrender but one of strength and common sense. The greatest struggle you face now is not between opposing ideas or interests. It is between those who, deep down inside, are inclined to be peacemakers, and those who, deep down inside, cannot yet embrace the cause of peace. You must say to those who would still use violence, your day is over. But also say to those who renounce violence that they are entitled to be full participants in the democratic process.

Clinton's speech was, in my opinion, the most astute and socially healing ever delivered in Northern Ireland. But even he was outshone by nine-year-old Catherine Hamill, one of two children chosen to read a message to the president. She told how her father, Patrick, had been shot by the UFF in 1987 when she was two. She said:

> My first daddy died in the Troubles. It was the saddest day of my life. I still think of him. Now it's nice and peaceful. I like having peace and quiet for a change instead of people shooting and killing. My Christmas wish is that peace and love will last in Ireland forever.

Bill and Hillary, like the rest of us, were reduced to tears. That evening Val and I joined tens of thousands at the front of Belfast's City Hall to bring to a rousing end an emotional day. In front of a giant Christmas tree shipped over from Nashville, Tennessee, President Clinton switched on the festive lights and closed a memorable visit with a blessing:

> May the Christmas spirit of peace and goodwill flourish and grow in you … We celebrate the world in a new way because of the birth of Immanuel … When God was with us, he said no words more important than these: "Blessed are the peacemakers, for they shall inherit the earth."

What Jesus actually said about peacemakers in the Sermon on the Mount was "they shall be called the children of God". Few noticed the *faux pas*; we were too excited by what was happening, too thankful that he had rekindled the hopes of the whole community.

### Return to Bombing

The British, Irish and US governments were making valiant efforts to get an inclusive political process off the ground, but they were constantly hampered by evidence that the IRA was still active. It had stopped targetting the security forces but had begun to confront head-on the legion of drug dealers who were now brazenly operating in republican areas and taking advantage of the IRA's cessation of violence. In January 1996, Senator George Mitchell published his report on how to remove all illegal weapons and move towards inclusive talks. Like Major and Bruton, he recommended a twin-track process: decommissioning would take place during all-party talks. In order to participate in the talks, each party had in advance to commit itself unreservedly to what came to be known as the Mitchell Principles. There were six:

1. The use of exclusively peaceful means in resolving issues
2. The disarmament of all paramilitary organisations
3. Cooperation with an independent commission appointed to verify disarmament
4. The abandonment of force or threats of force to influence negotiations
5. A willingness to abide by any agreement reached
6. Effective action to prevent and end killings and beatings

The SDLP and Alliance Party welcomed the report; Sinn Féin and the UDP viewed it as a potential way forward; the Ulster Unionists expressed reservations; but the DUP under the leadership of Ian Paisley rejected it outright.

When the twin-track talks commenced a few days later, the two major unionist parties refused to turn up and the process died in the water. Its funeral followed a week later. On Friday, 9 February, the IRA detonated a lorry bomb at Canary Wharf in London, killing two people, injuring 40 others and causing wreckage estimated to be in the region of £150 million. The 17-month-long ceasefire that had generated so much hope was over. Darkness again stalked our streets and despair returned to our hearts. On Sunday morning, Fitzroy joined churches across the UK in praying for those caught up in the blast. On behalf of the congregation I wrote to Rev John Weir, vicar of St Peter's Church in Bethnal Green, who was coordinating the churches' pastoral response to the bombing. To my surprise, he wrote back: "The local clergy would like to be better trained for this kind of emergency and have asked me to set up a training day. From your experience in Northern Ireland, could you recommend anyone skilled enough to help us?" I was happy to put him in touch with some of my friends.

Then the blame game started. The following day, the IRA released a statement that pointed the finger squarely at John Major:

> Instead of embracing the peace process, the British government acted in bad faith with Mr Major and the Unionist leaders squandering this unprecedented opportunity to resolve the conflict.

Over the 18 months of the ceasefire, the prime minister had refused to open up direct negotiations with the leaders of Sinn Féin. The reasons were easy to understand. He had lost his majority in parliament and needed the help of unionists to stay in power. In addition, he knew that if republicans were allowed into political negotiations without decommissioning, unionists would walk out. His hands were tied. But the fine-sounding intentions of the IRA seemed hypocritical: they refused to admit to themselves that it was their own intransigence over decommissioning that had aborted the process. The long-suffering people of Northern Ireland would have to wait for another 18 months before the IRA ceasefire was reinstated. Many feared that we were slipping back into the dark old days of the past and political opinion hardened as people shifted their support towards the more hard-line perspectives of the DUP and Sinn Féin. We were sitting on a powder keg.

**On a Knife-Edge**
The collapse of the IRA ceasefire with the Canary Wharf bombing in 1996 sparked a major media debate in Northern Ireland and London about how to create the conditions for a new and more convincing ceasefire. I got involved in some of the public debates, which were characterised by bitter exchanges and tough questions. Gerry Adams articulated the IRA's key question to John Major: "Would you treat another ceasefire in the same way as the last one? In the 18 months of the IRA ceasefire there were no armed actions and no negotiations. This bad faith has created a gap of mistrust which the British must move to close." Unionists hit back furiously at republicans with questions of their own: "We want a real and permanent ceasefire, the decommissioning of weapons and the dismantling of the structure of the IRA. Why won't Sinn Féin abide by an exclusively democratic process like everyone else?"

The position I sought to get across was that Prime Minister John Major should respond to the IRA's question by unequivocally affirming his government's commitment to creating a universally acceptable solution to Ulster's problems and back it up by immediately establishing talks with Sinn Féin in Downing Street. It had been leaked to the press that Major had in fact been planning to do this for the first time on the day of the Canary Wharf bomb. Taking advantage of my involvement with some in the leadership of the republican movement, I pressed them publicly to give unionists a straight answer to a straight question: "Will the IRA accept the democratic outcome of all-party talks if Sinn Féin doesn't get all the demands they are making?" If the answer was a clear yes, then the IRA should act on it without delay by engaging with those officially tasked with overseeing the decommissioning process. This, I argued, would quickly get us to the point where each party could come to the negotiation table on the same basis – no guns behind backs, no guns under the table.

As the bitter media debate around these matters intensified and community relations plummeted, Fr Gerry and I organised another private peace consultation in Fitzroy on 29 October 1996 between 15 Sinn Féin representatives and 40 members of civic society. Our subject was posed as another question: "Is it possible to reach an agreement between all our parties that is fair to everyone?" The speakers were Jim Gibney (Sinn Féin) and Alex Attwood (SDLP). Gibney, a member of Sinn Féin's Executive Committee, warned us that the situation on the ground in republican areas could easily slip back into conflict. But it was not irredeemable; Sinn Féin was ready to engage sincerely with every grouping without any preconditions. We took that to mean that decommissioning was still not possible. Alex Attwood, a practising solicitor who represented Upper Falls on Belfast City Council, alerted us to the fact that the destiny of the nationalist community was on a knife-edge. The IRA stood ready to continue their bombing campaign, he claimed, while the British Army and loyalists were making their own plans to respond in an equally vigorous manner. He informed the delegates, "We've only got a few weeks to sort it out." Many of us left Fitzroy depressed at the renewed danger hanging over the community if the deadlock was not broken.

## A Major Moment

I received a letter a few days later from Lady Jean Mayhew, wife of Sir Patrick Mayhew, the secretary of state for Northern Ireland. She had a deep concern for reconciliation and had previously invited Fr Gerry and me to Hillsborough Castle for some private discussions. The letter was an invitation to a buffet lunch at the Ulster Folk and Transport Museum at Cultra, just outside Belfast, on 19 December 1996. Correspondence of this kind usually identified the name of the VIP in whose honour the event was being organised, but on this occasion it was absent for security reasons. Like all who received it, I surmised that it could be Prime Minister John Major. In a parliamentary debate the previous week on the critical situation unfolding in Northern Ireland, he had blasted Sinn Féin, denouncing it as a "pariah". As I listened to his speech on TV, I winced at his words and wondered if anyone had briefed him about how volatile the situation was within republicanism.

However, other, more personal, considerations were occupying the thoughts of our whole family circle. My eldest sister, Margaret, died on Tuesday, 10 December after a prolonged illness and with my sister, Audrey, we had not only to plan her funeral but also to comfort our mother. For most of her life, Margaret had poured her considerable spiritual energies and musical talents into the life and witness of our home church, Seaview Presbyterian, but over the last eight years she had worshipped at Fitzroy. It was a fitting, therefore, that at the thanksgiving service in Fitzroy we were able to combine the choirs of our two congregations. Seaview's minister, Rev John Dickinson, led the worship and I paid tribute to Margaret's strong faith, teaching skills, musical talents and love of her friends. For weeks I felt numb with sorrow and shrouded in an emotional silence that disconnected me from normal life. I had little appetite for mixing with the crowds at Cultra.

At the museum the 150 guests were shepherded into small groups of 6 or 7. When John Major walked in, few were surprised, but they gave him a courteous welcome. As he made his way slowly towards the podium, surrounded by aides, he stopped to talk briefly with some of those present. Our group was taken by surprise when he came across, smiled and asked each of us in turn what we made of the present situation. Most of our responses gave very little away but were politely pessimistic. When he looked at me for a comment, I thanked him for his concern for the province but asked if I could make a somewhat negative comment. "Of course," he replied, as his aides pressed in a little closer. I began.

"As a Christian minister I have been encouraging republicans for years to come into the political process and abandon violence. At the moment our situation is on a knife-edge and in the last few weeks I've been urging them to reinstate the ceasefire. But they carry so much anger and mistrust towards Britain. That's why I felt your recent 'pariah' comments were counter-productive, like throwing petrol on a fire. Is it not possible to be critical of them without being scornful?"

Before he could reply his aides whisked him away and, for the rest of event, I was consumed with guilt and self-doubt. Should I have kept my mouth shut and just smiled? I did not take in a word of his speech, but when the applause died down I wanted out. When Major stepped down from the podium and was escorted towards the exit, I froze when he headed back towards our group. When he arrived he smiled again and, in a lowered voice, said to me, "I'll think about what you said." I was humbled by his own humility.

The following day I talked the incident over with Fr Gerry and concluded that I should write to him on behalf of both of us and explain what lay behind my comments. I wrote him the following letter:

20th December 1996

Dear Prime Minister,

I was delighted to meet you at the Transport Museum at Cultra yesterday. Following our conversation about the fragile peace process, which is close to both our hearts, I was deeply touched by your parting comment that you would remember what I said. Because our exchange of views focussed on the basic distrust that exists between your government and Sinn Féin, I did not get sufficient opportunity to express to you how much I appreciate the time, thought and energy you have put into helping the people of Northern Ireland find each other in an inclusive peace process leading to a new and historic political accommodation. I believe that God has given you this inner sense of commitment to the people of Northern Ireland and that he has used you to open for us the possibility of a better future politically, socially and economically.

For 21 years I have been working in the sphere of reconciliation between the communities, political groupings and Churches in NI and I recognise in you the same concern as is within myself. I am conscious that we are on the same team. This morning Fr Gerry Reynolds and I were interviewed in Clonard Monastery about the current tense situation in NI for BBC Breakfast News. Because we have been close friends and allies in reconciliation for 13 years I discussed with him afterwards the nature of our conversation at Cultra and your very genuine concern about the republican movement's present attitudes and activities. Two words recurred in our analysis of the present situation: "opportunity" and "danger". It is our firm belief from talking with SF leaders from various parts of NI and at different levels that there is a real desire to enter into a credible and inclusive peace process based on the Mitchell Principles. On the other hand, we are very worried that the military build-up in west Belfast on both sides could easily explode through one incident into open and widespread violence such as was part of the nightmare of our lives for 25 years.

At this Christmas season, as we celebrate the risk God took in befriending a hostile world through sending his Son, Jesus Christ, to make peace, we believe that there is a huge need for your government to find ways of befriending those who belong to the republican community and their elected representatives. We recognise that this is extremely difficult for you and we would not presume to tell you how to go about this. We trust and pray that in seeking you will find. For our part we will never give up our efforts to encourage nationalists and unionists, Protestants and Catholics to befriend each other in order to create an atmosphere in which peace can develop. This includes continuing to persuade republicans that the only way forward is through a process of dialogue that is exclusively democratic. Fr Gerry and I joining in wishing you and Mrs Major a peaceful and happy family Christmas and thank you for visiting our people once again.

Early in the new year, I was pleasantly surprised to get a response from 10 Downing Street:

8th January 1997

Dear Reverend Newell,

The Prime Minister was most touched to receive your kind letter. He much enjoyed his brief talk with you, and will continue to think about what you told him, although the difficulties at every turn do not need spelling out. The essential point now is for all concerned to continue to engage actively in the peace process, and avoid creating a vacuum which the men of violence will be all too ready to fill. For his part, the Prime Minister will continue to strain every nerve to secure progress in the talks towards the lasting and peaceful settlement that the people of Northern Ireland deserve. I am sending a copy of this letter to Father Gerry Reynolds.

Yours sincerely,
Edward Oakden, Private Secretary

We learned shortly afterwards that the Irish Department of Foreign Affairs had heard of our letter; it was referred to in conversations between the prime minister's advisors and their counterparts in Dublin. But the days of Major's government were now numbered as all the parties prepared to contest a general election set for 1 May 1997.

## Towards Another Ceasefire

If anyone underestimated just how close the province was to a return to all-out violence, the private consultation we held in Fitzroy in February 1997 between the loyalist political parties, members of civic society and the churches would have dispelled their illusions. UDP and PUP representatives gave us a gloomy insight into the current thinking of the three main loyalist paramilitary groupings, the UDA, the UVF and the Red Hand Commando. David Adams (UDP) laid it on the line:

> Why is it that all we have achieved since the 1994 IRA and loyalist ceasefires is agreement on rules and procedures? The reason is that there are wreckers inside the negotiations process; they want to collapse it because they have no alternatives. And there are wreckers outside the process, including elements of the republican movement; they are not prepared to face political realities. But how are loyalists different from IRA? The IRA ended their ceasefire because they could not sign up to the principle of consent. We can. But let me warn you in no uncertain terms: the loyalist ceasefire will collapse if the IRA does not renew its ceasefire soon.

Billy Mitchell (PUP) pleaded with us, like an evangelist, to support his party's "fresh approach":

> We are fast returning to the same old crisis-producing attitudes of the past. We desperately need a language that is not about confrontation but accommodation, relationships that are not based on unionist privilege and supremacy, but on a pluralistic morality that recognises each other's humanity.

The first hint that the tide was turning towards conditions favourable to a new IRA ceasefire came with the UK general election in May. Tony Blair's

Labour Party swept to power in a landslide victory. In Northern Ireland, Sinn Féin, with 16 per cent of the vote, surged past a disappointed DUP, with 13 per cent, to become the third-largest party, while the UUP, with 32 per cent, and the SDLP, with 24 per cent, consolidated their leadership of moderate unionism and nationalism. Blair moved quickly to reaffirm Northern Ireland's valued place within the UK, and urged Dublin to enhance the peace process by removing its offensive constitutional claim over the province. He also ordered his officials to set up talks immediately with Sinn Féin in order to clarify all outstanding issues. The final piece in his new, energetic initiative was to invite Sinn Féin into all-party talks provided that the IRA reinstated their ceasefire within five weeks. If not, the peace train would move off without them.

By mid-July 1997 Adams and Hume were in a position to issue a joint statement paving the way for a reinstatement of the ceasefire:

> At our meeting last night we reviewed progress in removing the obstacles, erected by the previous British government, to an inclusive and meaningful negotiations process ... We welcome the moves that have been made to remove these obstacles ... A just and lasting settlement will only be achieved if it is based on the principles of democracy and equality and has the allegiance of both traditions ... It is for the Irish and British governments ... to bring this about in the shortest time possible ... Our objective is agreement and reconciliation ...
>
> There is a heavy onus on both governments, and particularly on the British government, to respond positively ... in terms of the demilitarisation of the situation ... in dealing with the issue of prisoners ... and in assisting the search for agreement among the people of this island.

Everyone knew that, before issuing this statement, Adams had already persuaded the IRA Army Council to back it. The following day the IRA announced the renewal of its 1994 ceasefire and Northern Ireland breathed a communal sigh of relief. Most unionists welcomed it but remained wary about the ultimate destination of the peace process. However, Peter Robinson, deputy leader of the DUP, was enraged: "Sinn Féin/IRA have got everything they wanted and can now enter talks without giving up their weapons."

In contrast, the UUP leader, David Trimble, welcomed the ceasefire but remained adamant that it must be accompanied by disarmament and the disbandment of all paramilitary organisations. To gauge support for his party's risky position of negotiating with Sinn Féin without the prerequisite of decommissioning, the UUP conducted a public consultation during August and September 1997 with the business, voluntary and church sectors of the community. The Clonard–Fitzroy Fellowship seized the opportunity and presented a well-reasoned paper. We commended the party for "its determination to continue participating in the Stormont talks despite intense criticism from the DUP. We do not consider an immediate start to decommissioning to be so important that the UUP should regard it as a pre-condition for negotiation with Sinn Féin." When the final report of the consultation was published, the finding was clear: almost all the groups urged the UUP to engage with republicans. "Sinn Féin cannot be marginalised," it noted, "and talking does not jeopardise one's principles. Unionism has a good case and should be confident." We were encouraged when the report referred to our contribution: "One Church forwarded a letter signed by over sixty members of its congregation."

I personally believed that the fears of most unionists about the direction of the all-party talks would ease with the passage of time; but I was equally convinced that the process being embarked upon by Sinn Féin's president, Gerry Adams, and its chief negotiator, Martin McGuinness, would not work without decommissioning. Hard-headed negotiations would require compromise – unionists embracing power-sharing and republicans putting their desire for a united Ireland on the long finger. Creative and courageous leadership would be necessary. When the IRA renewed its ceasefire in July 1997, London and Dublin announced the setting up of the Independent International Commission on Decommissioning (IICD). Three days later the new secretary of state for Northern Ireland, Marjorie "Mo" Mowlam, accepted that the IRA ceasefire was genuine. Sinn Féin could enter multi-party talks providing they signed up to the Mitchell Principles.

**Defining Moment**

Tuesday, 9 September 1997 was another one of those days that left me rubbing my eyes in amazement. Adams and McGuinness led a Sinn Féin delegation up to Stormont, an institution traditionally loathed with a passion by republicans, to sign up to the Mitchell Principles. They were pledging their party to the exclusively peaceful operation of democracy and to paramilitary disarmament. So momentous was this step for republicans that I expected an internal reaction. It came shortly afterwards, when the IRA acknowledged that they had problems with sections of the Mitchell Principles. This soon became evident when 20 IRA members resigned, including a former chief of staff and the organisation's quartermaster general, who exercised control over the secret arsenals of weapons and explosives. They were convinced that Sinn Féin was embarking on a course that would lead to the tacit acceptance of partition and the deferral of a united Ireland.

For me, their conclusion was correct. But it also signalled a major and salutary shift within the party's strategy, though not every IRA volunteer could read the writing on the wall. Encouragingly, on the tenth anniversary of the Enniskillen bomb, Adams told the BBC that he was "deeply sorry about what happened. I hope there will be no more Enniskillens." We were at last moving in the right direction.

Unionists, however, viewed Sinn Féin's historic visit to Stormont as lacking any credibility: signing the Mitchell Principles was no substitute for decisive action on decommissioning. Paisley had already withdrawn the DUP from the talks process and the UUP leader, David Trimble, was under immense pressure to stay away until the guns began to be handed over. Eventually, however, the UUP, PUP and UDP re-entered the process and the thorny issue of decommissioning was wisely placed in the professional hands of the Independent International Commission, chaired by General John de Chastelain.

The negotiation process had got off to a shaky start and the spectre of past failures hovered ominously over its proceedings. In the meantime, my own life took an unexpected turn.

**History in the Making**
In June each year the 51 councillors who serve on Belfast City Council choose their new lord mayor. The contest is closely watched because it mirrors the continuous power struggle between unionism and nationalism. Remarkably, since the city's royal charter was issued in 1613, there had never been a Catholic mayor, nor indeed since partition in 1921 had a nationalist been elected as first citizen. One consequence of this traditional Protestant and unionist domination was that a large swathe of Belfast's Catholic minority, 40 per cent of its citizens, felt estranged from the architectural gem that opened its doors

to the public in 1906. With heightened speculation that Sinn Féin might be invited into all-party talks at Stormont, the possible election of a Catholic and nationalist lord mayor was followed with intense interest. The spotlight in June 1997 was focussed on the SDLP's Alban Maginness, a 47-year-old barrister who had represented the Oldpark Ward in north Belfast since 1985. It was an evening of high drama in the council chamber. With backing from Sinn Féin, the Alliance Party and one courageous independent unionist councillor, Maginness was elected by 26 votes to 22. In his acceptance speech, delivered under a portrait of Queen Victoria, he welcomed the breaking of the sectarian mould, but cautioned against nationalist triumphalism: "This is not a victory of one tradition over another, but a bold step towards creating a new partnership in this divided city, which, we hope, will lead to greater tolerance." I was glad for my friends in Clonard and also pleased that the new mayor's vision for the city merged somewhat with my own. In my spirit I wished him well.

It came as a huge surprise when, two weeks later, I received a letter from him, inviting me to become one of his two chaplains. The other would be a relative, Fr Luke McWilliams. I went down to the City Hall to talk over his request and in the calm splendour of the mayor's lounge he explained the mystery. Two years earlier, in 1995, he had turned up out of the blue at a theological conference at Fitzroy, when the speaker was Fr Bob McDougall, a 69-year-old Canadian priest who had served in the Second World War as an Air Force tailgunner. In Canada he was known as "the Billy Graham of the Catholic Church". I recalled Alban arriving slightly late for the opening of the conference, just as I was about to pray for the ministry of Fr Bob and the work of the ministers and priests who had come to hear him. In my prayer I felt I should include those who serve God in other spheres of influence, and so I prayed for Alban and "his ministry within the world of local politics". He later recalled how those words made an impression on him. He could not remember anyone ever referring to his work in politics as a "ministry", but that was exactly how he felt about his involvement in public service. He explained that he would like me to work alongside him in a dual chaplaincy with Fr McWilliams in order to commend to the wider world that Belfast was on the way to consolidating the peace and constructing new partnerships in reconciliation.

I had only just started to fulfil some of my duties as the mayor's chaplain when a tragedy of international proportions struck. In the early hours of

Sunday, 31 August 1997, Diana, Princess of Wales, was killed in a car crash in Paris. Her marriage in 1981 to Charles, the Prince of Wales and heir apparent to the throne, had been held amidst great joy in St Paul's Cathedral and was seen by a global television audience of over 750 million. However, in the intervening years the world had watched with deepening sorrow as their marriage slowly disintegrated. In August 1996 their divorce was finalised. Following Diana's sudden death, the Queen and her husband, Prince Philip, issued a statement to express their shock and distress. Given the universal love and sympathy directed towards Diana during her marriage, the whole country was plunged into displays of public grief that, at times, almost resembled religious veneration. Within hours, huge crowds began to form outside Kensington Palace, carpetting the pavements and roads with swathes of flowers, candles, cards and personal messages.

Immediately after hearing the news on Sunday morning, I phoned the mayor. Val and I had already agreed to accompany him and his wife, Carmel, to a concert that evening given by the Dallas Symphony Orchestra in Belfast's newly opened Waterfront Hall. I suggested that those attending would be coming with heavy hearts and would appreciate being led in a short act of public remembrance before the concert in order pray for Diana's family and for all grieving her loss. He agreed to make contact with the conductor, Andrew Litton, and together they decided to begin in such an appropriate manner. That evening, on the platform of a crowded Waterfront Hall, wearing his mayoral chain of office, Alban conveyed the sympathies of the city to the royal family and to Diana's extended family. He then invited Fr Luke and me to offer prayers, which culminated in a few moments of quiet personal reflection. The atmosphere among the 2,200 guests in the auditorium was deeply emotional and a solemn hush descended. The silence was only broken when we concluded this mark of respect by inviting everyone to join in the words of the Lord's Prayer. In the heart of Belfast the sharing of grief had created a sacred space where traditional divisions were not welcome.

After taking up the post, the mayor discussed with Fr Luke and me the possibility of organising a civic service in Fitzroy on Sunday, 21 September under the title "From Strangers to Friends". Each of the 51 councillors was invited to attend and, although not everyone turned up, there was not a spare seat in the church. The mayor opened the service by reading Psalm 116, from which the city's Latin motto is taken: "Pro tanto quid retribuamus?"

– "What can I offer the Lord / for all his goodness to me?" Nine-year-old Helen McGeown interviewed Alban about his plans for the year and ended by asking, "If you could have just one wish, what would it be?" He answered, "I would wish that all the people of Belfast would live in harmony and help each other."

The lady mayoress and the Ulster Unionist deputy lord mayor, Councillor Jim Rodgers, read the Scriptures. Fr Tony Curran of St Malachy's Church, Pastor Mark Houston of City Church and Fr Luke McWilliams offered prayers "for God's blessing on our city", "for the healing of wounds and the breaking down of divisions" and "for the work of the council". In my sermon I appealed to all of us to hold in our hearts the words of Paul's letter to the Ephesians (2:16–18): "By his death on the cross Christ destroyed their enmity; by means of the cross he united both races into one body and brought them back to God." Following the Benediction, the guests proceeded to a reception in the Alexander Hall, where our teenagers swarmed around the councillors whose faces they knew from television. Many animated cross-table conversations took place. One Fitzroy member commented afterwards: "I got talking to a Sinn Féin councillor about a variety of topics. We had differing perspectives but both of us left feeling it would be good to continue our discussion on another occasion." Before taking his leave, the mayor thanked everyone for making the event so memorable. "The theme 'From Strangers to Friends'," he commented, "is a perfect metaphor for the life of our city. Let us all play our part in building trust and understanding among all our people."

My year as chaplain was full of opportunities to welcome guests from all over the world to the city of my birth. At numerous official dinners I would be asked to say grace, and when US Senator Edward Kennedy visited Belfast to encourage all sides towards a political settlement, I had the pleasure of preparing a group of young people to interview him. When the year was over and I left the magnificent iconic Neo-Baroque building for the last time, I was thankful for what had been achieved: we had demonstrated the reality of partnership in a simple but highly visible way. My only regret was that the experiment did not become an established pattern for subsequent lord mayors. Some of the political parties represented in the council may have understandably decided to maintain a respectful distance between politics and religion; others may have felt that their religious constituency would not appreciate attempts to act inclusively.

## Presidential Campaign Turns Nasty

Little did I expect to find myself caught up in an increasingly spiteful election south of the border, which was in full swing to find a successor to President Mary Robinson (1990–7), the first woman to occupy the position. One of the candidates was Mary McAleese, an academic who had grown up in the largely nationalist district of Ardoyne in north Belfast, a volatile interface with the Protestant Crumlin Road. The area had gained notoriety due to an increasing number of incidents sparked by the Troubles. McAleese had studied law at Queen's University and at the tender age of 26 had been appointed as Reid Professor of Criminal Law in Trinity College, Dublin. In 1994 she had returned north to become the first female pro-vice chancellor of Queen's. As election day loomed, her emergence as one of the frontrunners unleashed a vendetta against her by some elements of the Irish press and sections of the unionist community in the north. One southern journalist, alleging that she was "a tribal time bomb", fired off an angry piece entitled "Why Mary McAleese Must Be Stopped". Rumours circulated that she was pro-Sinn Féin and her association with Clonard Monastery drew down the ill-informed wrath of one Ulster unionist, who accused her of "being closeted in Clonard with Father Alec Reid and the editor of the pro-Republican *Irish News* as part of a triumvirate pushing a Sinn Féin agenda". The 1997 presidential campaign was turning into a mud-wrestling contest. The editor of the *Irish News* countered by pointing out that he had never been involved with the monastery's peace initiatives, and that the *Irish News* had a long record of opposing republican violence. But the slur on Mary McAleese could only convincingly be countered by the Protestant ministers who had been involved directly in Clonard's peace and reconciliation ministry. As a result, Rev Sam Burch (Methodist), Rev Tim Kinahan (Church of Ireland) and I wrote to the *Irish Times*. Our letter was published shortly before voters went to the polls:

The Presidential Election

Sir, – It has been suggested in reports coming from the Republic that the Redemptorist peace and reconciliation ministry team has been promoting a Sinn Fein [*sic*] agenda.

The leader of the Redemptorist Order in Ireland has firmly rejected such allegations and we wish to underline the accuracy of his comments …

As ministers from within the mainline Protestant denominations and from the unionist community, we wish to bear witness that, in all of [our] contacts, we have never detected in our Redemptorist colleagues a desire to promote any party political agenda. We would have strenuously challenged any attempt to do so.

We want to put on record that the Redemptorist peace and reconciliation ministry, as we experienced it, was motivated solely by the Gospel of our Lord Jesus Christ and his command to speak the truth to one another in love.

Thankfully, our letter received wide coverage and the innuendos around Mary McAleese's candidature evaporated quickly. She went on to win the election, gaining 59 per cent of the vote.

As the presidential inauguration in Dublin Castle on Tuesday, 11 November 1997 drew near, speculation mounted regarding who might turn up from the north, for unionists had decided to boycott the occasion *en bloc*. Fr Alec, Fr Gerry, Rev Sam Burch and I were included on the list of invitees. On Monday afternoon, just before heading down the road to Dublin with Val, I was picking up my suit from the dry-cleaners and found myself in the queue with a well-known Belfast journalist. She asked humorously if I was going to a party. I laughed and explained I was off to something more formal – hence the suit – the inauguration of Mary McAleese in Dublin. "Enjoy yourself," she said. An hour later I was surprised to get a call from BBC, asking if they could interview me early the next morning about my apparently controversial decision to attend the inauguration. I agreed. Just after 7.00 am, the call came through and the interviewer asked why I had been invited.

"I think she identifies with the reconciliation work I have been involved with in Belfast for 20 years," I replied. "As a Presbyterian minister I am more than happy to be here." Then he cut to the chase. "You are aware of the political storm among unionists over the election of Mrs McAleese. Why, then, are you going to the ceremony in Dublin when your party leaders are insisting that no self-respecting unionist could possibly attend?"

"My party leader," I answered, "is Jesus Christ, and he has told me to go!"

When the early morning interview was over I was glad that my mind was so nimble and clear; I put it down to the help of the Holy Spirit – and a strong cup of coffee.

It was a wonderful experience to join with people from every corner of Ireland in St Patrick's Hall, Dublin Castle, for the inauguration of Ireland's eighth president. Representatives of the SDLP and the Alliance Party had come down from the north, as well as others from civic society; we were seated directly behind Gerry Adams and Martin McGuinness. The religious element in the ceremony included prayers and passages of Scripture read by Catholic, Anglican, Presbyterian and Methodist church leaders from the Dublin area. I thought it would have been much more fitting if the leaders of the four main churches, which operate on an all-Ireland basis, had been invited to participate at such an important national event. When President McAleese stood to speak, her address sparkled with insight, humour and passion. It was one of the finest I have ever heard. In it she set out the manifesto of her presidency under the theme of "Building Bridges" and prioritised justice, social equality, anti-sectarianism and reconciliation. Her vision was clothed from beginning to end with Christian content:

> I think of the late Gordon Wilson, who faced his unbearable sorrow 10 years ago at the horror that was Enniskillen. His words of love and forgiveness shocked us as if we were hearing them for the first time … His work and the work of so many peacemakers who have risen above the pain of loss to find a bridge to the other side, is work I want to help in every way I can. No side has a monopoly on pain. Each has suffered intensely.
>
> I know the distrusts go deep and the challenge is awesome. Across this island … there are people of such greatness of heart that I know with their help it can be done. I invite them to work in partnership with me to dedicate ourselves to the task of creating a wonderful millennium gift to the Child of Bethlehem, whose 2,000th birthday we will soon celebrate – the gift of an island where difference is celebrated with joyful curiosity and generous respect and where in the words of John Hewitt "each man may grasp his neighbour's hand as friend".

Sitting in St Patrick's Hall, I longed for the day when similar sentiments and passion could become common currency among the religious and political leaders of my own struggling community. Despite a few setbacks, Mary McAleese's two terms and fourteen years of presidential leadership helped to bury many ancient enmities – between north and south, and between Ireland and England. The ogre of unionist anxieties turned out to enhance their interests and charm away many of their fears. Our paths were to cross again.

## Holding Our Breath

After a stumbling start, all-party talks were convened at Stormont in September 1997 under the skilful chairmanship of Senator George Mitchell, but the prospect of reaching an agreed settlement looked bleak. Sinn Féin, the Alliance Party, UUP and the small UDP and PUP parties took their seats at the negotiating table, but the DUP, led by Ian Paisley and representing a substantial 43 per cent of the unionist population, boycotted the whole process. Could it survive without them? In a poll conducted by the *News Letter*, 69 per cent of those canvassed did not believe that a settlement could be achieved that would command the support of most unionists and nationalists. Yet when asked, "Would you support a system of power-sharing in a new Northern Ireland assembly?" 60 per cent said yes and 40 per cent no. The unionist community was split down the middle. Progress in the talks, however, kept being undermined internally by continuing loyalist and republican violence on the streets. As a result, the UDP was barred until the UFF renewed their ceasefire, and Sinn Féin was excluded for 17 days because of two IRA murders. Once again, the community was peering into an abyss and failure seemed inevitable. In the run up to Christmas, however, I was buoyed up by the words of our moderator, Dr John Dunlop, when he spoke in Fitzroy with Archbishop Seán Brady: "At the incarnation of the Son of God the frozen misery of centuries began to thaw."

Given the capacity of some Ulster politicians to argue their way into a *cul-de-sac*, on 25 March 1998, Senator Mitchell set a two-week deadline for the talks to reach agreement. A week later, I headed off to Cork by train to conduct a Holy Week teaching mission in Trinity Presbyterian Church. Even in such a southerly city, interest in the drama at Stormont was high. As the Thursday midnight deadline loomed, Jeffrey Donaldson, a member of the UUP negotiation team, walked out because he could not support his leader, David Trimble. He was opposed to Sinn Féin holding government positions without decommissioning having begun, and was against the early release of prisoners. His departure exposed again the bitter divisions within the UUP, many of whose members were now clearly in the opposition camp of Ian

Paisley. Donaldson's departure and the fact that the discussions continued beyond midnight and into Good Friday, suggested that an agreement might be on the cards. In the background, President Clinton was busy on the phone urging the party leaders to do the deal. Then, on Good Friday evening, 10 April at 5.36 pm precisely, it happened. Senator Mitchell came outside with the smile of a weary negotiator. He stepped up to the microphones of the international media and declared, "I am pleased to announce that the two governments and the political parties in Northern Ireland have reached agreement." The news was flashed around the world, and when it came through 300 miles away on Bus Éireann 222 as I sat waiting to depart for Cork, I cheered, punched the air in joy and sang along with Van the Man.

By the time the week of mission was over and I was on the train for the long journey back up north, my delight had turned to more sober reflection. A referendum that would democratically endorse the Good Friday Agreement of 10 April was set for 22 May. In a month's time Ireland, north and south, would go the polls and vote either to accept or reject it. The self-determination of the people of Ireland would be freely exercised and their consent sought in separate referenda held simultaneously. A copy of the final 65-page document was posted by the government to each household in Northern Ireland, so that everyone could examine its contents and make up their own minds. "What role, if any," I asked myself, "should Christian peace activists play in a fiercely contested public debate awaiting to erupt?"

By the time I got home I knew that we had to raise some kind of positive Christian voice and offer a balanced and sensitive contribution from within the ranks of the Yes campaign. We would not address ourselves primarily to the nationalist and republican constituency that would likely back the agreement anyway, but speak into the battle for the soul of Ulster unionism. The impression I got was that the Yes lobby of Trimble-led unionists was coming across as hesitant and lacking strong and confident conviction when presenting their case, while the No campaigners of the Paisley-led DUP and disaffected UUP supporters sounded impressively resolute.

Weighty arguments, however, were being put before the electorate by both sides. The pro-agreement case focussed on the need to make progress on resolving the conflict rather than putting up with a political deadlock that could go on forever. The time had come, it was claimed, to leave behind the intolerant bigots who trot out their weary slogans but have no solutions to offer. It was also time for the silent majority to get off their sofas and vote for change, which could bring the Troubles to an end, remove the blight of the paramilitaries and guarantee the union for the foreseeable future.

The No campaign appealed emotionally and morally to a unionist community battered by 30 years of violence and under siege from national and international forces which, it was claimed, were out to destroy the Northern Ireland state. The Belfast Agreement (as they preferred to call it, in order to remove its association with Good Friday), should be rejected because it eroded British identity, was a one-way process to a united Ireland and contained a package of immoral concessions to republicans. Terrorists, it argued, should not be released or rewarded for violence by positions in any future government. Finally, the Belfast Agreement provided no guarantee of decommissioning and, in advocating reform of the police service, threatened the future of the RUC.

Early in May I met with some Presbyterian, Anglican, Methodist and independent church colleagues to discuss what our response should be. We decided to release a statement that supported the agreement, but only invite Protestant ministers and lay leaders to sign it, because the battle was for the soul of our own unionist community. We also decided to time our input so that it came towards the end of the public debate, rather than at the beginning or in the middle. We then set ourselves to contact a wide range of leaders within our churches and in a few days had gathered over 250 signatures. We took out a large advertisement in the local newspapers, giving our statement and the names of the signatories. We also informed the newspaper editors that we would be holding a press conference in the Europa Hotel on Monday, 11 May, at which those who signed it would be present.

As it turned out, our intervention came exactly at the right time. Lord Molyneaux, the former leader of the UUP, was about to come out against David Trimble, whose position looked increasingly precarious, as did the destiny of the agreement. A poll conducted by the Northern Ireland Office showed that opposition to the deal among unionists was running at over 70 per cent and that cross-community support had still not broken through the critical 60-per-cent barrier. The timing of our input, however, proved to be crucial – a quarter of all eligible voters were still placing themselves in the "don't know" category. The statement we released was short and simple:

> We're saying "Yes". We are Christians who acknowledge the Lordship of Christ over all aspects of life, past, present and future.

Whilst there are parts of the Agreement which are unclear or even unsatisfactory, we are of the opinion that it offers an opportunity for a new beginning for our society and that it is clearly worthy of the support of Christian people. Each of us will be voting "Yes" at the Referendum and we wish to encourage others to do the same.

Our names were appended and, whatever way one looked at it, they represented a substantial section of Christian leadership in the province. We also offered three major biblical texts to substantiate our conclusions (Micah 6:8; Matthew 22:37–40; Galatians 5:22–3).

At the press conference, I introduced the statement to the media and then called on three of my colleagues from other churches to speak in support of it. I explained the reasons behind the stance we had taken:

This morning is an important moment for us, just as these days before the referendum are important for our community. After a lot of thought, study and discussion of the content of the agreement, 150 ordained ministers and 100 lay leaders from within the Protestant churches and the unionist community have decided to say "Yes". Our "Yes" is both clear and sensitive.

It is clear because some have suggested that it is a sin to vote yes. This is religious nonsense – we have enough sins in Northern Ireland without people playing God and inventing more! We should respect completely those who will vote no as well as those who vote yes. We are voting yes because that is what our minds and hearts and consciences are urging us to do. We are saying a clear "Yes".

We are also saying a sensitive "Yes", for we have found parts of the agreement hard to understand: we are not professional politicians. We have also found parts which morally and emotionally are hard to swallow – such as the early release of prisoners. Furthermore, we have found it confusing when opposing parties have taken up contradictory positions: "The union is safe"; "The union is not safe"; "The agreement copper-fastens partition"; "The agreement will lead us into a united Ireland". In this confusion, one thing is clear – they can't both be right. That is why we have gone directly to the agreement itself.

We have read and reread it; we have studied it, discussed it and finally reached our own conclusions.

Our churches have asked us to read it through Christian eyes, recalling that in a situation of conflict we should seek to love our neighbours as ourselves, and remember that the God and Father of our Lord Jesus Christ loves all the people of this island equally, and that seeing things from only one point of view is a sinful tendency.

In trying to do this, we have noticed that the core values of the agreement mirror the teaching of the Bible about how divided communities should treat each other. It speaks of learning to trust each other, of developing tolerance and of affirming each other's dignity, human rights and integrity. It stresses the need to abandon violence, cultivate a spirit of concord and desire inclusiveness, reconciliation and partnership. These are political expressions of central Christian values.

Finally, our churches have asked us to ponder two questions: 1. Does the agreement represent a reasonable accommodation between nationalists and unionists? Our answer is yes. 2. Does the agreement represent a better future for us, our children and our grandchildren? Our answer, again, is yes.

It has not been easy for us reach our conclusion about saying yes to the agreement, but we have and we now commend it to you.

The press conference at the Europa Hotel resulted in extensive publicity for our statement and considerable political reaction, but the speech that registered the biggest impact was that of Rev Bert Armstrong. The Methodist minister, who had lost his only brother, Wesley, and his sister-in-law, Bertha, in the 1987 Remembrance Day bombing in Enniskillen, urged the country to go forward:

Going backwards is not a good thing to do in Ireland. The agreement could mark the beginning of a healing process. I have great sympathy with people who find it hard to forgive, who are trying to forgive and even those who believe that it is not even Christian to forgive what some people have done. I had to sort this out for myself at Enniskillen; if I hadn't I would have found it very difficult to say the Lord's Prayer, "Forgive us as we forgive others."

His words were conveyed by radio and television to a very large audience who could not make up their minds when listening to the competing voices of campaigning politicians. Our overall contribution came as a welcome boost to those within the UUP who were commending the agreement, and an unanticipated irritant to the claim of the No campaign that there was little grass-roots support for it.

## The Results of the Referenda

Whatever side of the debate people eventually came down on, the whole country held its breath as voters across Ireland went to the polls on Friday, 22 May 1998. On their way to the polling stations, many passed huge billboard posters showing a mother and father walking hand in hand with their two young children. Across the poster was written "It's Your Decision". In Northern Ireland, voters turned out in extremely large numbers – over 80 per cent – and almost 150,000 who do not normally participate in elections decided to cast their votes, particularly in staunchly unionist areas. When the results of the referenda were declared, 95 per cent of those who voted in the republic were in favour of the agreement, while north of the border 71 per cent returned a resounding yes that sent shock waves through the ranks of the No campaign. It was unquestionably a tipping-point moment in setting the future direction of Ulster unionism: a critical mass of Protestants, estimated between 51 and 53 per cent, had declared themselves open to power-sharing. They desired a new future, one that could not be achieved by beating the traditional drums or stirring up deep-seated fears. At a soccer match a few days later, a young evangelical minister leaned across some seats to express to me his euphoria: "Ken, it's a sea-change for Ulster."

A month later, in the first elections to the Northern Ireland power-sharing assembly at Stormont with its 108 members, Trimble's UUP emerged as the largest party, with 28 seats, followed by the SDLP (24), DUP (20), Sinn Féin (18) and the Alliance Party (5). David Trimble was chosen as first minister and Seamus Mallon (SDLP) as deputy first minister. To everyone's great surprise, the assembly was up and running and the sky had not caved in. It felt like a miracle moment; I kept rubbing my eyes in amazement at the sight of Sinn Féin sitting in the council chamber, debating like everyone else, after years of trying to wreck Stormont as well as the economic and security foundation of the province.

But the historical reality in which our visions find partial fulfilment never delivers all that we long for. In some measure our dreams of transformation retreat to new horizons, which beckon us to travel ahead even further. Unsurprisingly, following the 1998 Good Friday Agreement, the divisions within unionism grew deeper and bitterer, and the large minority of unionists who were opposed to the agreement felt alienated from the whole political process. Hardly had the ink dried on the agreement than fresh problems loomed frighteningly large. If reaching agreement had been slow and gruelling, implementing it was to prove tortuous and factious. The power-sharing assembly on "the hill" of Stormont increasingly had the appearance of a house built on sand. Over the next two years, Sinn Féin failed to deliver on their commitment to decommissioning; the UK government was slow to demilitarise the province; and there was fierce resistance from the unionist parties to releasing prisoners and reforming the RUC. Almost every aspect of the agreement sparked controversy on the floor of the assembly and the province looked on, dejected at the bickering. Having lived through numerous false dawns, many expected the fragile institutions of power to slide into oblivion as they lurched from crisis to crisis and from suspension to suspension. The failure of the assembly to function properly and its consequent inability to deliver real change ultimately sealed the fate of the well-intentioned but unpopular UUP leader, David Trimble. The question on most of our minds was: could we as Ulster people ever find our way out of the morass of a malfunctioning community?

The province had to wait for another five years for the answer. The Stormont assembly would be resurrected in a format that no one would ever have imagined and the language of "miracle" was to make a comeback to the sceptical political discourse of Northern Ireland. The messiness of politics, promising more than it could ever deliver, was often frustrating and unsatisfying. But nearly all people of good will were in agreement on the eve of the new millennium that our stop/start political institutions were better than the alternative of violence and fear, a dark reality we had known all too well over the past generation.

# CHAPTER SEVEN

# An American Interlude: 11 September 2001

Belfast was ablaze with light at midnight as party fever gripped the city on Saturday, 31 December 1999. Everyone seemed to be out on the streets to herald the arrival of the third millennium. Val and I, along with a couple of friends, formed part of the 40,000 crowd that thronged the city centre and lined the banks of the River Lagan for a fireworks display. Young and old, families and friends, couples and crowds of teenagers wearing sparkly clothes and silly hats were entertained by the Abba tribute group Bjorn Again outside the Waterfront Hall – the first big regeneration project showcasing the new economic confidence of the city. When Belfast's own Big Ben, the Albert Clock, struck midnight, bottles of champagne, sparking wine and hip flasks came out, and people turned to shake hands or hug each other. Meanwhile, the singer-songwriter Brian Kennedy led the crowds in front of the City Hall in the singing of "Auld Lang Syne". With that, everyone formed up into a large procession and walked the short distance to Laganside, the best vantage point for the display. Suddenly rockets roared off into the air, exploding in a blaze of colour. Light and hope owned the sky and stirred a people's expectations.

The final months of 1999 had witnessed an easing of the logjam caused by the failure of some politicians to implement fully their responsibilities under the 1998 Good Friday Agreement. In July, London and Dublin asked the former US senator, George Mitchell, who had guided the Good Friday Agreement negotiations to a successful conclusion, to return and salvage the faltering peace process. In November he announced his rescue plan: the IRA would engage with the decommissioning body as soon as the power-sharing executive of the assembly was restored with David Trimble as first minister and Seamus Mallon as deputy first minister. When the Ulster Unionist

Council gave its backing to this plan, the assembly met and appointed ten ministers to the executive. By 1 December the laws to enable devolution to take place were rushed through both houses of parliament in Westminster. The next day, all the outstanding elements of the Mitchell plan fell into place: the Irish government removed from its constitution the territorial claim to Northern Ireland; the resented Anglo-Irish Agreement of 1985 was revoked; the new Northern Ireland Executive was convened; and the IRA appointed a representative to liaise with General de Chastelain regarding the decommissioning of weapons. We approached Christmas and the end of the twentieth century in a slightly more positive mood.

## A Welcome Sabbatical

Early in 2000, as I entered my twenty-third year in Fitzroy, I became aware that I needed to take time out to reflect more deeply on God's direction for the congregation. Fortunately, the PCI had recently established a sabbatical scheme to enable its ministers to do just that. I made enquiries and eventually received permission to take a three-month leave of absence in 2001 to study Church Growth in the United States. I would be based in the Presbyterian Church of Old Greenwich (PCOG), Connecticut, which was already reshaping its life around insights from the Church Growth Movement.

I knew the Old Greenwich congregation well. In 1992 I had spent a month with them as part of a ministerial exchange programme which brought their pastor, Dr Art Chartier, to Fitzroy. In the intervening years, Val and I had made three further visits – to conduct two weddings and a baptism for the Masson family, who had become our close friends. When Dr Chartier moved from Old Greenwich in 2001, Pastor Kermit Morris, a Southern Baptist Church Growth consultant, was employed temporarily to look after the congregation and help position it for growth. Bob and Ginnie Masson, with their daughter, Linda, and her husband, Matt, kindly opened their home to me.

My responsibility was to lead the Sunday morning Seeker Service for people with little or no church background, while Kermit would preach and address the questions they were asking. On Wednesday evenings we celebrated Holy Communion for those who were already professing Christians at which I taught a course on "Following Christ in the Modern World". At first I was nervous about working with a Southern Baptist pastor, but I need not have worried. He and his wife, Henrietta, were delightful company and so easy to cooperate with. His style of preaching was new to me: on Sunday mornings he would meander backwards and forwards across the choir area, speaking to the congregation like a wandering John the Baptist. He held us all in the palm of his hand – a brilliant communicator, especially to those not used to the language and thought-forms of the church.

Some of my Irish ministerial colleagues were surprised that my choice of study was centered on Church Growth rather than reconciliation. But both were strong passions within me: one directed towards the spiritual development of Fitzroy, the other towards the healing of division. It takes many skills to be a minister, just as it requires ten fingers to play a piano; while peacemaking was a one of my dominant fingers, it was never the only one. After my call to Fitzroy in 1976, it was Canon David Watson who first stirred my parallel interest in Church Growth. He had resurrected a dying congregation in York, turning it into a model of hope for churches everywhere. I had spent many years quietly planting in the soil of Fitzroy the key insights of his book *I Believe in the Church* (1978). The results were beneficial: every year new families were joining us; in a lean year, ten; in a good year, twenty. I had become convinced that God had not invested the life of his Son in the death of his church.

Two decades later, when the American Evangelical and Southern Baptist pastor, Rick Warren, published his best-selling book *The Purpose Driven Church* (1995), I pored over its contents with a passionate hunger to learn. He had founded Saddleback Church in 1980 and within 15 years it had grown to over 10,000 members. His book put fresh heart into a whole generation of ministers who were struggling with diminishing congregations in an increasingly secular environment and had begun to question their ability to halt the decline.

I was captivated by Warren's clear, simple and practical approach: "The issue," he insists, "is church health, not church growth! If your church is healthy, growth will occur naturally. Healthy, consistent growth is the result of balancing the five biblical purposes of the church." These he identified as Worship, Fellowship, Discipleship, Ministry and Mission; they were distilled from two core elements of the teaching of Christ: his Great Commandments that we should love God and love people (Matthew 22) and his Great Commission to go and make disciples (Matthew 28). The genius of Warren was to create an intentional people-building process at the centre of his church and to make it "stronger through worship, warmer through fellowship, deeper through discipleship, broader through ministry and larger through evangelism". He started me examining Fitzroy's weaknesses as well as affirming its strengths. Why PCOG proved such an attractive location for my sabbatical research was that it had bought into Warren's Church Growth principles and was attempting to put them into practice.

Before saying goodbye to Belfast there was one family matter that I was determined not to miss: Tim's wife, Siobhan, was getting very close to giving birth to their second child. On Sunday 24 June, Maya Siobhan Savage-Newell was duly born in Belfast's Royal Maternity Hospital and Val, Jennie and I joined the stream of family members and friends privileged to share the joyous occasion. We brought some baby clothes for Maya and a set of mini golf clubs for our grandson, Joseph. Holding Maya in my arms was another magical moment of wonder in the expansion of our family circle; I was amazed at how such a tiny bundle of life could arouse such proud and protective feelings within me. I did not want to hand her back to Siobhan as she lay in bed recovering from her ordeal; I would not see her for another three months. On 26 June 2001, I flew to New York and my friend Bob Masson, a former helicopter pilot with the US Navy, met me at JFK Airport.

The three months passed quickly in the warmth of the Masson household and in the friendships of PCOG. I developed a good rhythm of study and relaxation: mornings with the books, afternoons at the church office and evenings out enjoying the hospitality of the members of the congregation. Kermit was a good mentor. He made plenty of time to answer my questions about secular culture and to comment on the problems of transitioning from a traditional Presbyterian church ethos to a Church Growth model. But there was much more to my sabbatical than study and serious conversation. The highlight of my week was after the Sunday morning service, when the Massons would take me out sailing in their boat on Long Island Sound. Val flew over to join me for a month in the middle of July and, in late August, Jennie arrived for two weeks. In every way I felt fulfilled, relaxed and deeply refreshed.

### Strange Request

As my time in PCOG was drawing to a close, several members asked me to speak about my life as a minister in Belfast. In truth, Ireland had faded from my consciousness and I had revealed very little about the situation back home. They, however, had been following events in Northern Ireland on CNN. The coverage included night-long riots in north Belfast between nationalist protestors and the security forces on 12 July, and on loyalist demonstrators attempting to stop terrified Catholic children reaching Holy Cross Primary School in Ardoyne on 3 September. So, on my penultimate Sunday, 9 September, I told them my story — coming to Christ in my late teens, my early zeal for the Orange Order, how I had become a minister, married Val and moved to Indonesia. I described how, on our return to Belfast during the Troubles, I had got involved in the Peace Movement, which had led to my links with Clonard and dialogue with paramilitary leaders – some of whom, I explained, were now actively involved in the peace process. I finished by mentioning that, when Val and I now meet some of these characters at social events in Belfast, they shake our hands firmly, greet us with warmth in their eyes and, not infrequently, hug Val. "If we follow Christ with courageous hearts and open minds," I concluded, "then miracles of changed perspectives, lives and attitudes can occur."

I was taken completely by surprise when the congregation rose to their feet and started to clap. Afterwards, they swarmed around me to wish me well. In a strange way I felt more bonded to them than before, not just because our time together was almost over. There was something in the story of peacemaking in a situation renowned for conflict that struck a chord in their hearts. I did not realise just how timely our reflections on violence, conflict and peacemaking were to be. Something in the providence of God was working itself out in the background and would burst upon us all two days later. After the service, Jennie and I headed off by car to Albany, in upstate New York, to say goodbye to Val's brother, Billy, and his wife, Anita.

### Terror in the Sky

At 7.30 am on Tuesday morning, 11 September, we said our farewells to Billy and Anita and headed down Interstate Highway 87 towards New York. There wasn't a cloud in the sky – only the white, thin vapour-trails of planes etching their straight lines high above our heads. Jennie and I whiled away our time talking about going home and listening to an Elton John CD. I turned on the radio at 10.00 am to catch the news, and for a few seconds thought I had inadvertently tuned in to a science-fiction programme. In an alarmed voice, a newsreader was describing how hijackers had seized control of American Airlines Flight 11 after it had left Boston and crashed it into the World Trade Center's North Tower at 8.46 am. A similar situation had developed on board United Airlines Flight 175, which had struck the South Tower at 9.03 am. The heart of New York, she exclaimed, was a blazing inferno and a mass exodus from the city was underway by every available mode of transport. I was shocked when I realised that this was no sci-fi programme – it was happening at this very moment. I put my foot to the accelerator and headed for Old Greenwich, thinking about the members of the church who commuted into New York each day. I kept wondering whether any of the planes I had been noticing earlier were involved in the attacks. When we reached the sleepy little village of Old Greenwich two hours later, police cars with lights flashing and sirens wailing were clearing the beaches of sunbathers and power-walkers. Panic was everywhere.

**Gathering at PCOG**

By now, the full horror of what had been happening was becoming clearer. A third airliner, American Airlines Flight 77, had ploughed into the Pentagon at 9.37 am and a fourth, United Airlines Flight 93, intended for the White House, had crashed into a field in Pennsylvania at 10.03 am. All passengers on board the flights were killed, along with the al-Qaeda hijackers. Within two hours the Twin Towers had come crashing down in an avalanche of melting steel. Clouds of suffocating smoke billowed through the streets in huge waves, chasing the heels of the thousands scampering in every direction to find somewhere to breathe. The iconic monuments of America's commercial achievements lay smouldering in the rubble.

The four phones at the church office were ringing incessantly and it was difficult for Kermit and me to contact members of the congregation working in the city or close to the towers. As people gathered at the church to support each other, a crowd of us hunched around the small TV. Each breaking newsflash painted a grimmer picture as the death toll mounted. Anxiety intensified as most of our mobile phones went dead, gave a constant engaged tone or issued the usual "Leave a message and I'll get back to you." I knew Val and Tim would be worrying about Jennie and me, for we often took the early morning train into New York to go sightseeing. I was relieved, therefore, to get through to Val just as she was leaving Maghaberry Prison, where she worked as a teacher. I reached Tim at the BBC in Belfast. They were glad to know we were both safe and contacted our wider family circle to reassure them.

At PCOG, people kept coming and going all afternoon. Many were in tears. Some were walking up and down in the church grounds, talking with friends; others were huddled inside, linking hands in prayer. Kermit and I went around the people present, one by one, and sat down with those who were keen to talk. Occasionally some would rush out into the vestibule when their phones suddenly rang and burst into tears as a familiar voice was heard on the line. But most remained in a heightened state of fear. All commercial flights were cancelled and the skies over New York went silent except for fast-moving US Air Force planes detailed to take down any other aerial threats. Towards late afternoon we let it be known that a prayer service would be held at 7.00 pm. Over 70 of our members turned up. Some had received good news and came to give thanks, while others came just to sit with their friends who had heard nothing. We led prayers for the unfolding situation across the nation and also gave plenty of time for those who wanted to pray audibly about their concerns.

As evening wore on, police cars kept checking the Old Greenwich Railway Station car park. On most working days it would fill up early in the morning with the cars of commuters taking the train into New York; by 9.00 pm it would be empty. But on this occasion most of the cars had not been reclaimed by midnight and the police marked the rear bumpers with a chalked X. As the Xs were added to on each subsequent night, the full scale of the horror was becoming clear: 2,977 innocent lives had been claimed in the attacks. The whole world seemed to be in grief, for the victims of the World Trade Center attacks included people from over 90 different countries. In the Greenwich area, the toll of casualties reached 60. On Tuesday evening, 11 September, Americans went to bed traumatised and with heavy hearts. Few slept soundly; the repeated footage of the planes careering into the towers had seared itself into the mind of a nation.

Bob Masson and I usually began each day at 6.15 am with cycle ride around Greenwich Point, which commands a magnificent view across Long Island Sound to New York. On Wednesday morning, we got up and cycled our normal route in silence, until we came to a point where we were struck by what seemed like a scene from the Apocalypse: a huge pall of black smoke stretching for 25 miles downwind overshadowed the city. With eyes wide open to the horror unfolding across Long Island Sound, we prayed for those who had lost loved ones and for the heroic efforts being made by the New York Police and Fire Department teams still searching for survivors trapped under the smouldering rubble of the collapsed towers. Envisioning their plight and the plight of those who earlier had thrown themselves from the towering infernos was almost too much for the human mind to handle. Like most people, I was out of my depth and could not feel anything firm under my feet.

## Friday's National Day of Prayer

Overnight the Bush administration had worked with security chiefs to frame a national response to what had happened, and on Wednesday morning the president went public to declare that these attacks were more than acts of terror. They were "acts of war". He designated Friday, 14 September as a national day of prayer and remembrance. At 12.00 pm a three-minute silence was to be observed across America, followed by religious services to seek God's guidance for the nation and to comfort those who had lost loved ones. Given the turmoil in my own mind, I was glad to have something specific to focus on, but I wondered how we could mobilise the Old Greenwich community as a whole to respond to the president's request. Unfortunately, the churches in the immediate vicinity – Presbyterian, Congregational, Catholic and Episcopal – had little or no contact with each other, yet we needed to stand together, grieve together and support each other through the crisis. I discussed with Kermit and Walter Baker, PCOG's clerk of session, the idea of organising a united ecumenical service, and they encouraged me to pursue it. I was nervous approaching the local clergy, but each one thanked me for calling and was delighted to come along to PCOG the next morning to plan something appropriate.

On Thursday morning, Walter, Kermit and I were there to welcome them and introduce ourselves. I chaired the meeting and gave each of them time to talk through how their congregations had been affected. I explained that I was not the minister of PCOG but was just completing a three-month sabbatical and was soon to return to resume my ministry in Fitzroy and my reconciliation work in Belfast. Then we got down to business. We quickly agreed to act as one Christian community and Dr Thomas Stiers offered his large First Congregational church to host the service at 12.00 pm. Furthermore, as a mark of our unity in Christ, we would send representatives from each church to all four sister churches on Sunday morning to lead the prayers of intercession.

When we finally turned to considering who would preach, each declined one by one, citing pastoral exhaustion and shortage of time to prepare. As I waited for someone to have a change of heart, I noticed they were looking at me. At last, Dr Stiers spoke up: "Maybe, Ken, having lived through the Troubles in Northern Ireland, you might be able to speak into the trauma we are experiencing." I felt cornered and instantly replied that only a well-known and respected member of the Old Greenwich community could handle the situation with the requisite sensitivity. The rest now backed Dr Stiers's suggestion and urged me to reconsider. With great reluctance I agreed; in the back of my mind I instantly started wondering what on earth I would say.

## Sermon of a Shattered Man

I devoted Thursday evening to gathering my thoughts, but I was so tired that I kept falling asleep at my desk. Eventually I gave in and went to bed. I rose early on Friday morning, thinking that a fresh mind might be more receptive to the voice of God. But, as I sat in front of the blank pages, nothing came and I started to panic. At 9.00 am I turned on the TV to catch the latest news. Up flashed images of crowds in countries across the world observing a national day of mourning for the victims of the terror attacks. One of the locations shown was Belfast, with thousands gathered in front of the City Hall, observing the three-minute silence. I felt a sudden surge of pride flow through me and, when I returned to the task in hand, my mental logjam had eased and inspiration started to flow. By 11.00 am I had completed what I was going to say. I quickly changed into my clerical attire and then Jennie and I drove down to the First Congregational church on South Beach Avenue.

We parked our car and sat for a few moments, watching the crowds make their way into the church. Many were walking in silence, their spirits deeply crushed. Their subdued body language contrasted with the usual Sunday-morning buzz of excitement when friends meet friends. Inside the old grey-stoned meeting-house there was not a spare seat and, as the 400 worshippers rose to sing the first hymn, the clergy from all the churches processed up the central aisle. I had never been in such an emotionally charged environment, yet the atmosphere was dignified and calm. When the time came for me to enter the pulpit and I had to look directly into the faces of the people, I felt swamped by wave after wave of grief, rolling up towards me from the pews. On five or six occasions I choked with emotion and had to breathe deeply just to compose myself. Like everyone else, I was on the edge of tears.

This summary indicates the flow and content of my sermon, which I called "One Unforgettable Moment in the History of the USA":

I feel very inadequate to speak at this service, for I am from Belfast, a city that has known its own horrors, and I'm only here for three months as a guest of the Presbyterian Church of Old Greenwich. But I come among you as a friend of the United States and a follower of Jesus Christ who, more than anyone else, feels our pain. September the 11th has been like a crucifixion for America. But what is God saying to us through it? What can we learn? What should we do? The words of the Prophet Micah in the eighth century BC can point us to an answer: "What he requires of us is this: to do what is just, to show constant love, and to live in humble fellowship with our God."

1. Today is a time for weeping. A tidal wave of shock and grief has swept across this nation and many of you have been affected directly or know of neighbours and colleagues who have been affected. Perhaps you are waiting for news of someone still unaccounted for. We would need to have hearts of stone not to weep, but underneath our tough exteriors we are still people who value love. Our tears are part of the tribute we pay to those who are coping with loss.

2. Today is a time to let the world comfort America. Today, in thousands of locations, people have downed tools and come out of their workplaces and homes to stand beside America in this moment of her mourning. The leaders of Ireland's four main churches have written to President Bush, expressing their deepest sympathy. They say: "We grieve with our brothers and sisters in the USA and assure you that our people will be walking with you through this dark valley." Many of us see America as a loving and welcoming mother. When poverty and famine in Ireland wiped out a million of our people, another million sought refuge here and found a new beginning. We don't forget such kindness. But now it's the world's turn to comfort you.

3. Today is a time for honouring heroes and sheltering the vulnerable. As we watched the relief efforts in the wake of 9/11, it was humbling to see firefighters making their way up into the burning towers to rescue those trapped, aware that they may never come down again; New York police officers pulling out of

the rubble people trapped under concrete; emergency medical teams setting up makeshift tents to treat the injured; counsellors sitting with those haunted by sights that no human eye should see. What these heroic helpers have witnessed may scar many of them for life. When the present crisis is over, contact one of these agencies and offer a family a short break in one of your holiday homes in the mountains or by the sea.

But the tragedy we are living through has also exposed many vulnerable groups. In the last three days innocent Arab Americans, mostly of the Muslim faith, have been picked on in schools and on the streets by bigoted people looking for someone to blame. Many families are afraid to leave their homes. A Japanese friend told me yesterday that, when he was a child, the same thing happened to his family following Japan's air attack on Pearl Harbour in 1941. It is time to shelter vulnerable Americans from such hostility and to recognise their loyalty to the United States. Hundreds of their co-religionists also died when the Twin Towers collapsed.

4. Today is a time for careful thinking about your response to the attacks. Gut reactions can do more harm than good. That's why it is important to ponder the right approach to al-Qaeda, but to confront vigorously the threat it poses to your national security. America needs to protect her citizens with such a renewed sense of vigilance that acts of mass destruction such as those perpetrated last Tuesday cannot happen again. Gaping holes in America's defences were ruthlessly exploited. We know that complete security is rarely possible, but with active community support in terms of the flow of information to the police, the vast majority of planned attacks can be frustrated or intercepted by the work of the intelligence-gathering agencies.

But whatever steps America takes to hunt down her enemies, it needs to protect the innocent civilians among whom the terrorists move. They should not become victims of retaliatory violence. This would violate their God-given dignity and flood terrorist groups with an endless supply of volunteers out to avenge the killing of their loved ones. As with radiation therapy, we should target the malignant tumours but not harm healthy organs. A wise national response should be determined in its intentions but branded with an utter respect for human life.

In conclusion, 9/11 presents us not just with big national questions but also with extremely personal ones: "What am I going to do about the pain that surrounds me?" Jesus Christ challenges us to rise above a vision limited only to the pursuit of personal happiness; he insists, "There is more happiness in giving than in receiving" (Acts 20:35). In a world racked by poverty, crippled by corrupt regimes and angry at injustice, our mission involves more than commercial and military objectives; it is about those who live in the wealthiest country in the world lifting the most desperate communities into some of the blessings America herself enjoys. At the end of the day, the only safe world is a world of friends. The only peaceful world is a cared-for world.

Today America is enduring a kind of national crucifixion; but the truth that resonates through this service is that her resurrection will surely come, for Christ is here to redeem us from the depths of despair and usher us towards the light of a new dawn.

I was relieved to sit down again. When the service ended, each of the clergy was allocated a door at which to greet those who had come. As worshippers filed out, quite a few embraced me. I was used to hugs of affection at PCOG, but on this occasion people were leaning their weight on me – and, indeed, on all the clergy – a clue to the heaviness within. For the rest of Friday I was washed out and sought shelter in the company of my daughter, Jennie, and in the care of the Masson family. A large electronic road sign grabbed my attention: "Hug a loved one – today." Important values were being reclaimed.

## Farewell

My last Sunday conducting worship in PCOG witnessed a larger attendance than usual. Indeed, congregations across America reported that numbers attending church had increased by up to 60 per cent, most notably among 25- to 30-year-olds. I based my sermon, "Not Knowing Where the Future Might Take You", on the story of the Risen Christ cooking breakfast for his disciples by Lake Galilee and asking Peter some searching questions (John 21):

I'm sad to be leaving you tomorrow, but my soul has a label on it – "Made in Ireland". My suitcase may be full, but I'm carrying you all back home in my heart. You have been extraordinarily kind to me. I will never forget these last few painful days. But what can we learn from them about what it means to follow Christ into the future?

First of all, when Jesus calls us to follow him he reassures us that "I will be with you always, to the end of the age" (Matthew 28:20) – in other words, "You will not travel alone – I will accompany you." There is nothing coming towards us out of the future that we need to be afraid of, whether challenge or celebration, gain or loss, joy or pain. Our pathway will never take us beyond the boundaries of Christ's love. Secondly, Jesus assigns Peter a task: "Feed my sheep" – take care of my church. The Lord is saying to Peter: "Don't travel into the future as a tourist – I'm giving you a job to do." Following Christ banishes aimless living and, when we cross over into God's kingdom, the first thing we do is to apply for a work permit. Finally, the Lord advises Peter: "Don't buy a return ticket – there are no flights back to where you boarded." In a semi-veiled prophecy, Jesus then sketches Peter's destiny: "when you were young, you used to get ready and go anywhere you wanted to; but when you are old, you will stretch out your hands and someone else will tie you up and take you where you don't want to go." Christ hints that Peter's death will parallel his own. This was fulfilled after the Great Fire in Rome in AD 64, when the Emperor Nero put the blame on the Christian community and targetted its leaders for crucifixion. Peter, tradition recounts, asked to be crucified upside-down. He felt unworthy to die as the Lord had died.

Little did Peter realise when he left the beach after breakfast that morning that 34 years later his journey would take him 1,440 miles away to the heart of the Roman Empire and to a martyrdom that glorified his Lord. But, through dying like Christ, he also crossed over with Christ into the eternal light and everlasting embrace of his father, and into that communion with all of God's saints who set out on their journey of faith knowing there was no going back.

As we take our leave of each other this morning, let us renew our commitment to follow Christ into a future that he knows but we don't. Let every stride be taken in sync with him. We have everything to live for and a future beyond our wildest dreams.

With that I sat down and the representatives of our three sister churches led us in our prayers of intercession for the Greenwich community, the United States and the nations of the world. At the end of the prayers they invited us to stand, link hands across the sanctuary and join together in the words of the Lord's Prayer. We prayed with our eyes open, looking into each other's faces. This image of God's people united in Christ to care for each other in the critical months ahead was my final vivid memory of PCOG. I drove the short distance back home and, with Jennie, packed our cases for leaving the next day.

Early on Monday morning, Bob Masson took me to meet his boss, George F Landegger, chairman of Parsons and Whittemore of Port Chester, New York. Some weeks earlier he had invited me to join him and some friends on a boat trip around Long Island Sound. George was interested in the sermon I gave at Friday's memorial service and wanted me to address more fully the subject of America's foreign-policy response to 9/11 in the light of my experience of working in conflict resolution. He was planning to communicate his own perspectives and mine to some politicians in Washington. I promised him I would turn my mind to his request as soon as I got back to Belfast and had a clearer mind.

A few hours later, after saying our farewells to Ginnie, Linda and Matt, Bob drove Jennie and me into New York to pick up our flights. It was a surreal experience. The highway would normally be heaving with traffic and the journey would take two hours; but on this occasion few cars were travelling towards the eerily silent city and we covered the distance in 45 minutes. A handful of people were walking around the spacious airport halls. All flights had been cancelled following the attacks on Tuesday and, although restrictions were eased on Friday, 80 per cent of the passengers booked to travel stayed away. The fear was palpable; but Jennie had to get back to Glasgow and I needed to get home.

I realised how much fear I was suppressing when we joined the queue at the check-in desk. When we were handed our boarding passes, I turned around to look for a coffee shop and suddenly noticed, six places behind us, two bearded Pakistani men dressed in traditional clothing. They carried four large cases and several pieces of bulging hand luggage. I went as pale as a ghost and the hair went up on the back of my head. Prejudice leapt out of the cavernous recesses of my soul. However, once the half-empty plane was airborne, an uneasy peace settled on the passengers. When the wheels touched down on England's green and pleasant land, everyone broke into applause in appreciation of the captain, the flight crew and probably ourselves for having been among the first to take the risk of flying.

## Back on Terra Firma

By the time I got back to Belfast on Tuesday, I was on the edge of exhaustion, but it was great to be home again with Val and to spend time with Tim and Siobhan and play with our grandchildren, Joseph and newly born Maya. My 93-year-old mother's health had been poor for some time and a few days later she was rushed into hospital. My sister, Audrey, mobilised the whole family to make sure she was not left alone and a week later she had recovered sufficiently to be discharged back to a residential home in east Belfast. I was due to resume preaching in Fitzroy on Sunday, 16 September but our clerk of session, Denis Boyd, advised me to rest up for ten days. I appreciated his thoughtfulness.

## Fulfilling a Request

As my weariness began to recede, I turned my attention to George Landegger's request and sent him the following letter:

Wednesday 26th September, 2001

Dear George,

I apologise for not writing earlier with regard to the short conversation we had in your office on Monday 17 September, but my mother took seriously ill shortly after my return and is still in hospital. The question we discussed was "What should be the USA's response to the atrocities of 11 September?" I begin with a deeply held conviction that the only safe world is a befriended world; the only peaceful world is a world that feels cared for. I believe that should constitute the long-term goal of any American response to 9/11. Why?

Firstly, terrorism cannot be defeated by military means alone. After twenty years of intervention by the British Army in Northern Ireland, its military strategists publicly acknowledged that the IRA (at most about four hundred hard-core activists) could not be crushed. The IRA had also privately concluded that it could not win the war but needed help to wrap up the bloody confrontation. Some strident voices wanted to increase military engagement; however, they were not those directly involved in the dirty war, but those who feared change. The United States can damage terrorist organisations and take out their leading operators, but it can't eradicate the cause that drives them. A similar conclusion has long been reached by those dealing with ETA, Hamas and the PLO. You are dealing with an ideology of conflict deeply embedded in the hearts of Islamic fundamentalists the world over. It has been generated by decades of western political, military and economic decisions which are experienced as anti-Muslim. The present American response reinforces that belief-system and each so-called "heroic" terrorist death in war multiplies recruits for the cause, especially young people who want to honour their dead by fighting in the unfinished struggle. Furthermore, conflict compels terrorist organisations to become more sophisticated. They may take a hit, but they will regroup, tighten their internal security and develop more creative ways to be destructive.

Secondly, America's goal must include winning over those communities most alienated from her. Within the next few months al-Qaeda spokespersons will articulate the litany of anti-Islamic action taken by the USA. Some may claim not to be involved in violence, but that they understand the thinking of those who are. These spokespersons can become bridges of access to those behind the violence. In Belfast the bridges to the political wing of the IRA were Catholic priests who had pastoral connection with them. In 1990 they invited a small number of Protestant ministers, including me, to engage directly with Sinn Féin in a dialogue designed to bring the violence to an end. When we started talking our perspectives were miles apart, but as time passed our common humanity created a warmer connection; they listened with respect to our vision and we came to recognise the legitimacy of many of their grievances. Three years later the IRA announced a ceasefire. Since then peaceful political initiatives have replaced the sound of guns. Dialogue de-ices absolutist ideologies and awakens the desire for peace that lies deep within most of us.

Thirdly, the most advantageously placed people to open doors to dialogue are devout Muslim and Arab Americans. They share the fundamental faith-convictions of those involved in terrorist groups, but disagree with the methods they use. They also know those who are the most respected international teachers of Islam and can link them into dialogue with the thousands of mullahs in Afghanistan who interpret the Koran in a way that gives support to al-Qaeda. America needs to activate religious leaders to undertake this mission.

Finally, many of the underlying issues that feed the jihadist ideology are social. American and western businesses need to put more into the Arab countries from which they extract large profits. If even half of one per cent of their profits was set aside for investment in hospitals, health centres, schools, basic sanitation and leadership training centres, then some Islamic countries presently hostile to the US would start realising that friendship with America can be a good thing. A sustainable programme of social and economic development would give families hope that their children might access a decent standard of living rather than leave their impoverished homes to join terrorist organisations. As you know, the United Nations is drawing our attention to the plight of over one million Afghans presently living on the edge of starvation.

George, I had better stop. One thing that my experience in Belfast has taught me is that it is harder to make peace than to launch a war, but the benefits are greater and longer lasting. May you and I be instruments in God's hands to move towards the achievement of that goal.

Yours in Christ,
Ken Newell

## Thinking Things Through

When I resumed ministry in Fitzroy I found it hard to detach myself from 9/11. The decision of the USA, Britain and the other 17 European countries in membership of NATO to invade Afghanistan on 7 October 2001 forced me, like everyone else, to weigh up the morality of war. I reluctantly concluded that it was the lesser of two evils. I loathed the prospect of mounting civilian casualties caught up in a conflict not of their choosing. But the threats to America and the west were real. In his first interview after 9/11, Osama bin Laden, the founder of al-Qaeda, told a Pakistani journalist:

> If America used chemical and nuclear weapons against us, then we may retort with chemical and nuclear weapons. We have the weapons as a deterrent.

He went on to accuse the US and its allies of what he called the atrocities perpetrated against Muslims in Palestine, Chechnya, Kashmir and Iraq and said they had the right to attack America in reprisal. The crucial issue of the conflict, however, was Palestine, and al-Qaeda would continue to fight until "every last US Jewish soldier" left Palestine, the Arabian peninsula and all Muslim countries. Later in October he repeated the threats by means of video:

> The Twin Towers were legitimate targets … If avenging the killing of our people is terrorism, then history should be a witness that we are terrorists. Yes, we kill their innocents and this is legal religiously and logically.

To anyone who listened carefully to al-Qaeda spokesmen, it was evident that their anger was stoked by years of grievance, particularly against American foreign policy towards Israel and the Palestinians. I sensed that the voice of Islamic resentment was being toned down by the UK and US media and, as a result, many in the west felt they bore no responsibility for what might happen to Afghan civilians in their name. The problems, it was generally assumed, were being caused solely by "evil" Muslims. A self-righteous deafness prevailed, which I had encountered earlier in Northern Ireland, both in myself and in others.

To give expression to these developments I organised an inter-faith conference in Fitzroy, "Dying for Your Faith", on 19 October, along with representatives of the Muslim and Jewish communities in Belfast. Two contrasting interpretations of what was happening in the world in terms of the 9/11 attacks, the Arab-Israeli conflict, the radicalisation of young Muslims and the reasons given for the invasion of Afghanistan sparkled sharp exchanges between the Jewish and Muslim speakers. I attempted to offer a Christian perspective and took the line that the perpetrators of 9/11 were not martyrs but mass murderers. But I also insisted:

> We are called upon to go beyond condemnation of terrorism. Serious injustices have been inflicted on the Islamic world. There is now a gulf of misunderstanding between Islam and the west that we need to bridge so that we can start creating a world that is more just, more peaceful and thereby safer for everyone.

The conference had the effect of creating a spiritual space where sensitive world issues could be openly addressed and where the underlying distress burrowing away inside many of us could find a healthy outlet. It also brought greater clarity to the real motives behind the war in Afghanistan and the human and moral goals that must stretch beyond it.

## 9/11 One Year On

It was only slowly that I began to commend to Fitzroy some of the Church Growth principles that had been the reason for my sabbatical research in Old Greenwich. Part of that process was to think seriously about how we reconnect with that large section of the community that had severed all links with the church. It was exciting to turn our corporate mind to these new challenges and the months of teaching, discussion and practical reorientation of our approach flew by. Then the events of 9/11 began to loom large again as preparations got underway throughout Northern Ireland to mark its anniversary. The Clonard–Fitzroy Fellowship decided to mark the occasion with another public inter-faith conference in Fitzroy, this time under the title "September 11th and the Search for Peace". The Alexander Hall was again crowded with a remarkably mixed ethnic and religious audience who had come to listen to Felice Kiel, an American working in Belfast with the Northern Ireland Council for Ethnic Minorities, Omar Farouki, the Palestinian head of the Muslim Family Association, and Shoshanna Appleton, a Jerusalem-born leader of Belfast's synagogue. This time around, opinions were expressed with reasoned sharpness and considerable passion, but in more measured terms than the previous year. At the end of the evening I offered a personal response to how 9/11 had affected me:

1. It deepened my sense of being a patriot of the human race.

   On September 11th we all observed the gruesome spectacle of ordinary people dying very publicly. It stirred strange emotions in me as I watched husbands, wives, sons, daughters, fathers, mothers, sisters, brothers, grandparents and grandchildren dying, citizens of over 90 countries. I found myself grieving for them as if they were connected to me as members of a large extended family. While I may belong to one nation, I am first and foremost a citizen of humanity, a child in the family of Man created by our Father God. To be a patriot of your own country and its best values is important. But to empathise only with those you know and feel nothing for the sufferings of others reveals an underlying condition of chronic heart disease.

   As I looked down over Belfast today at 1.46 pm local time, a year after the moment the North Tower was struck, I paused to remember the victims of that sinister evil. But my thoughts were also travelling east to Afghanistan and to the even larger number of innocent civilians and children who have died as a result of the war. I wondered if anyone today was grieving for them and their devastated families. Were there any TV crews at hand to zoom in on their heartbreak?

2. It renewed my conversion from being a "passivist" to a peace activist.

   I don't mean a pacifist – someone conscientiously opposed to war – but a "passivist" – someone who watches tragedy but does nothing about it. Many of those I counselled in Old Greenwich couldn't sleep for days. The images of 9/11 kept playing over and over in their minds. I felt exactly the same, but also I found myself in the grip of a question: "What am I supposed to do?" It was the same question I asked 30 years earlier, in July 1972, when I was caught up in the Oxford Street Bus Station explosion in Belfast. That was the day I knew that Christ wanted me to do more than just pray, read the Bible and preach sermons. He was calling me to explore every avenue that would reduce violence and foster peace. Giving Christ the supreme say in our lives eliminates the option of doing nothing. In the face of tragedy we have two choices: become spectators of grief or players for peace, be "passivists" from whom nothing issues or become persons whose mindset is motivated by a love that shows up in our eyes, the tone of our voice and the tenderness of healing hands. 9/11 renewed my commitment to the latter course.

3. It made me ask God different questions.

Catastrophe normally triggers an avalanche of unanswerable questions. Almost every conversation I had with those who gathered in Old Greenwich brought up the "why" question: "Why would a God of love allow such barbarity?" "Why didn't he poke his finger out of the clouds and divert the planes to somewhere else?" "Why would people living as guests within the USA carry out such carnage without a qualm of conscience?" I was asking myself the same questions, but the answers I was coming up with sounded even to me hollow and unconvincing. Yet in my mind's eye I could see the figure of Christ at Ground Zero with the fire-fighters, the police and the army of heroic men and women who were risking their lives to save others. I visualised him, sweating and dust covered, searching frantically in the wreckage for survivors.

The "why" questions only led me into the shallow marshes of my own speculation, but the "what" question broke up what seemed like a prolonged divine silence. When I asked, "What, Lord, do you want me to do?" I became aware of a whisper: "When you get back to Belfast, bring together the Jewish, Islamic and Christian communities to talk through the issues that concern them most. All things are possible to those who believe."

This special conference today is the product of those whispers. I hope we'll all ask God the "what" question and wait for his internal reply: "Where you find hatred, sow love; where you encounter suffering, bring compassion; where you encounter oppression, champion justice; where you face conflict, become channels of my peace."

These were my thoughts today at 1.46 pm as I looked down over the city I love. September 11th may not have changed the world, but it has certainly changed me.

This address marked the culmination of my struggle to understand why God had permitted me to experience something of the impact of 9/11. The angst that lingered in me since returning from the USA in 2001 began to drain out of my system and this left more space to push on with the spiritual development of Fitzroy. Three years later, I gave a lecture in Belfast's synagogue on "Reconciliation between Christians and Jews" and, following my retirement in 2008, I was invited to be part of an international initiative on reconciliation in the Middle East.

My American interlude was originally intended to provide insights into Church Growth; instead, it turned out to be a steep learning curve. It redrew the boundaries of my ministry and clarified afresh the vocation to reconciliation that first sprang to life in me during the Oxford Street Bus Station bombing in 1972. It was a clarity I was to need in abundance quite soon.

# CHAPTER EIGHT

# Moderator in an Immoderate Time: 2004–05

Emotionally exhausted – that is how I felt on arriving home from New York following the 9/11 attacks on the Twin Towers. I was relieved to be back in the shelter of my family and was looking forward to planting in Fitzroy some of the Church Growth principles I had learned in Old Greenwich.

Slowly I renewed my contacts with republican and loyalist activists, but not much had changed. One initiative, however, did encourage me – in July 2002 the IRA issued an apology for its part in 650 civilian deaths. It was a course of action we had been commending to republicans for some time. We knew it would not dispel all the mistrust, but it might accelerate some movement towards normality. Any good that was achieved by this apology, however, was snuffed out two months later when an IRA spy operation was uncovered at the heart of the Northern Ireland Assembly at Stormont. For the fourth time our unstable political institutions were suspended and many now seriously doubted that they could survive in such a smoke-and-mirrors climate. However, more pressing and personal considerations were now commanding my attention.

### The Face in Which I First Glimpsed God

A dark cloud of impending loss was looming large over our extended family. My mother, now in her ninety-third year, was dying. Though she was well cared for in the nursing home, we wanted her to be surrounded by the people she loved. Fortunately, our daughter, Jennie, was working in the home for a year and was able on occasions to accompany her to the Ulster Hospital when she needed urgent blood transfusions. My sister, Audrey, and her husband, Ken, with their medical backgrounds, were a tower of strength and a source of wisdom. Working together as a team, the family circle devoted every spare moment we could find to being by her side, giving her sips of water, stroking her hair, praying with her and reminding her just how much we loved her.

In the long hours of sitting by her bedside, looking into that kind and strong face that formed my first impressions of the love of God, I paced through the gallery of my treasured memories: the summer bus trips we took as children to the beaches near Bangor; the overnight boat trips to visit her elderly mother in Lancashire; the music that filled our house as she took a break from cleaning to play her favourite hymns on the piano; the open house she kept for our childhood friends, who were always as hungry as locusts; the smiles that lit up her face when I would push her wheelchair to the end of Donaghadee Harbour to look out over the Irish Sea. Sometimes she thought she was a child again, back in County Mayo, sitting on the rocks, watching the wild Atlantic Ocean lashing the shoreline of Belmullet. Then there was the cold winter's day when the heavens opened and we both rushed into the Harbour Bar to seek refuge from the storm. When she asked for something to warm her up I ordered a small glass of whiskey and some Baileys Original Irish Cream, and advised her to sip it slowly. To my surprise, she downed it in one gulp, licked her lips and declared, "I think that helps my blood circulation." She then insisted on ordering another.

It was painful watching the woman who had been my first and finest evangelist drift towards death. But we knew that she was on her way back home to her heavenly Father and would soon cross over the threshold into the radiant light of the Risen Lord. She died peacefully on 20 October 2002.

Her funeral service was conducted in Seaview Presbyterian Church three days later by Rev John Dickinson, her friend, pastor and, on occasion, sparring partner in significant theological exchanges. Hundreds of our friends and acquaintances attended the service, including many from Seaview, Fitzroy and Clonard. She was laid to rest in Roselawn Cemetery alongside my father and my sister Margaret. Once again I was asked to compose an inscription for her headstone and what we agreed was: "Evelyn Margaret Newell – a river of faith, kindness and generosity". The loss of my mother made me examine even more closely the relationships I still enjoyed. I wrote in my journal: "Give yourself more fully to your family, to your circle of friends and to Fitzroy, especially the dying and the bereaved. Never forget kindness."

Early in January 2003 I received a phone call from Rev John Dunlop, asking if I would let my name go forward for moderator of the Presbyterian Church at the upcoming February election. "John," I laughed, "apologies for the language, but I wouldn't have a snowball's chance in hell!" I do not normally express myself so colourfully to the patriarchs of our church, but he had taken me by surprise, and I knew there was limited grass-roots support for the kind of ministry I had pursued in Fitzroy. He insisted, nonetheless, that I should let the church decide on whether I was suitable or not. I decided to talk everything over with Val and, three days later, called him back to thank him for his confidence in me and to give him permission to put my hat in the ring.

The vote for the new moderator of the General Assembly takes place annually on the first Tuesday of February, when the 21 presbyteries that represent our 560 congregations choose from a range of candidates. The person securing the majority of presbytery nominations is elected. Considerable public excitement surrounds the process because the Presbyterian Church, with 250,000 members, is the largest Protestant denomination in Northern Ireland. Many internal conversations take place about the suitability of the candidates, and featuring prominently is the attitude taken to the Catholic Church. February's meeting is often the best attended of the year.

As I sat in the meeting of the Presbytery of South Belfast on the evening of Tuesday, 4 February, I was anticipating that at most four presbyteries might select me, and it was an honour when my own presbytery supported my nomination and the result was phoned through to Church House. An hour later a return call confirmed the outcome: Rev Ivan McKay of Dundonald and I had each received seven votes. Another election would be required in March. I went silent with shock at the strength of support coming in my direction from across the church. When the March result was declared, Ivan received 11 votes and I got 10. I was humbled; never in my wildest dreams did I think I would come so close. If I had exited the moderatorial selection process at that point, I would have died a happy man, knowing that so many of my colleagues had affirmed my ministry.

Sometimes people outside our church wonder just how deep these expressions of support really go when the theological perspectives among ministers, for example, appear to diverge so markedly. In my experience they are genuine – for, on whatever wing of the church we position ourselves, we all carry a passionate commitment to Christ and his message. The biggest sin in Irish Presbyterianism is not to disagree with each other, but to do so in an uncharitable way.

Throughout 2003 strenuous attempts were made to reinstate the Stormont assembly, but securing a pledge from Sinn Féin to bring decommissioning to a convincing conclusion was eroding any of public confidence that remained. Attitudes on both sides were hardening. The November assembly elections witnessed the continuing decline of moderate unionism and nationalism as the chief combatants, Ian Paisley (DUP) and Gerry Adams (Sinn Féin), swept to power and now glared at each other across what many considered an unbridgeable chasm. A political chill accompanied the return of winter.

## Another Round of Voting

The start of 2004 catapulted me again into the church's search for a new moderator. I still did not believe that the church was yet ready to embrace someone so committed to cooperation with the Catholic Church and community as I had been since 1976. On 3 February the presbyteries again met to make their choice. This time round my friend from college days, Rev Harry Uprichard, was receiving strong backing, largely from the anti-ecumenical wing of the church, and the vote was again tied at 11 presbyteries each. A rerun was set for March.

The closeness of the vote for a second year in a row was scrutinised by the media for hints of underlying shifts in religious attitudes and corresponding political direction. Some noticed not just a traditional and progressive divide, but also a rural and urban one. My own analysis was that many still feared losing ground to Ulster's traditional enemy, while others were yearning for a new way forward. Was the tide for change in Ulster coming in or going out? Rumours reached me that a determined "Stop Ken" campaign was underway. Apparently some unexpected participants turned up at the February presbytery meetings in the form of very elderly ministers of various theological persuasions. They had been contacted, canvassed and driven considerable distances to cast their votes one way or the other.

On Tuesday, 2 March, the presbyteries again convened and I gathered as usual with my fellow elders and ministers in the Presbytery of South Belfast, which was meeting in May Street Presbyterian Church. When the result of the voting came through to our presbytery from Church House, Harry got nine votes and, to my great surprise, I received twelve. Next morning, 20 journalists and photographers gathered for the customary press conference in Church House and the questions came thick and fast.

"How do you feel?"

"I'm humbled beyond words."

"How would you define your churchmanship?"

"I'm proud of my evangelical background and at home in the wider ecumenical Christian family."

"How would you counter the sinister influence of the paramilitaries?"

"I'd love to assist them in moving from criminality and violence into activism for the social transformation of their communities."

"What role should churches play in reducing mistrust?"

"Construct bridges across the chasms around us. As a step in that direction," I added, "it is my intention to invite several of the church leaders to my installation in June."

I knew in myself that this would include the Anglican archbishop of Armagh, Dr Robin Eames, the Methodist president, Rev Jim Rea, and the Catholic archbishop, Dr Seán Brady, whom I had come to know through Fitzroy and the ICC. First I needed to seek permission from the committee that dealt with the moderator's guest list for the opening night of the General Assembly.

Before the start of the Sunday-morning service in Fitzroy our clerk of session, Denis Boyd, rose to express the congregation's congratulations to Val and me on the outcome of the election. He called us both forward and mentioned that I was the third of Fitzroy's six ministers since 1813 to be appointed to the position of moderator and they wished to assure us of their prayers during what would be an exciting, exacting and busy year. When he had finished, the congregation rose to their feet and started clapping. We were overwhelmed by the sense of love and affirmation flowing towards us, and felt deeply grateful for the people who had made such a courageous journey with us over 28 years.

My first concern for Fitzroy was to identify someone who could come in and pastor the congregation for the full year that Val and I would be serving the wider church. It was not a difficult decision to make. Within a few days I contacted Rev Dr Godfrey Brown, who had been moderator of the General Assembly in 1988 and minister of Ballycastle Presbyterian Church until his retirement in 2001. Since his ordination in Fitzroy in 1960 as assistant minister to my predecessor, Rev RE Alexander, he and his wife, Margaret, had maintained a close relationship with the congregation and Godfrey was from time to time a much-sought-after preacher. In 1992 he, along with the general secretary of the Presbyterian Church, Rev Dr Jack Weir, engaged in private discussions with both loyalists and republicans, including Sinn Féin's

Gerry Adams and Tom Hartley, at a time when even the Catholic hierarchy eschewed such contacts. Dr Brown was delighted to be asked to help Fitzroy as interim pastor and when I put his name before the Kirk Session for ratification there was instant and unanimous agreement.

## Targetted without, Rumblings within

The first hint of discord within the wider church came later in March, when I submitted to the Business Board my list of guests for the opening night of the General Assembly in June. It contained the names of family, friends and Christians leaders I had long respected – including Archbishop Brady. One person among the 20 committee members present voiced disapproval, but the custom that had prevailed since time immemorial was upheld: that the moderator-designate was free to invite whichever friends he wished, since they were his personal guests, not official guests of the General Assembly.

When the news filtered out, Ian Paisley launched a blistering attack on the Presbyterian Church for electing me: we were an apostate church riddled with heretics, hypocrites, liberals and evil schemers intent on undermining the pure Gospel of Ulster Protestantism. He called for evangelical ministers within the Presbyterian Church to protest, and for disillusioned members to separate themselves and join a "proper" church like his. He seemed to be anticipating a flood of converts.

I had never lost a night's sleep over the big man's demonising denunciations. I had first appeared on his radar in the 1970s, when I had supported our church's membership of the WCC. Then, in 1986, he had led a raucous protest outside Fitzroy against the presence of our moderator, Dr Robert Dickinson and Bishop Cahal Daly. My role in mobilising 250 Protestant ministers and elders in 1998 to support of the Good Friday Agreement may also have irked him. But why did the perpetual moderator of the Free Presbyterian Church and the undisputed leader of Ulster unionism launch such a sustained attack on an ordinary guy like me? I think he viewed the values I espoused as mirroring a growing stream of faith within the Protestant community that offered a real alternative to what he stood for. Over the years he had failed to crush it, and perhaps he feared that the voice of a new togetherness was clearing its throat. It was also motivated by pure opportunism. He hoped to gather into his flock hundreds of unsettled Presbyterians at a time when few were making that journey, in contrast to former years. Indeed, there was some evidence of a trickle heading in the opposite direction.

It has long been observed that, when Ian Paisley flexes his vocal cords, some in the PCI echo his sentiments. They shared much of his fundamentalist mindset, although not his abrasive manner. A handful of colleagues, some with Orange Order connections, went public with criticism of my actions. The pressure on me intensified when three presbyteries (Ballymena, Tyrone and Foyle) wrote to me privately about their disquiet. I offer a summary of my reply of 24 May:

> I am sorry for the hurt which this invitation has generated, but let me explain:
> 1. I have known Dr Brady for eight years and welcomed him to Fitzroy to speak at a reconciliation event with Dr John Dunlop in 1997; more recently I was involved with him at a conference on the *Dominus Iesus* document. My friendship allowed me to challenge some aspects of that document. My invitation is therefore based on our Christian friendship.
> 2. When I brought my request to the Business Board on 29 March they acknowledged the right of the moderator to invite as his guests whoever he chooses. He is my guest, therefore, not a guest of the assembly.
> 3. The invitation does not minimise in my mind the differences between our reformed faith and the Roman Catholic Church. For 12 years I helped to initiate discussion on every divisive issue between our churches, inspired by the Evangelical–Roman Catholic Dialogue on Mission (1977–84) in which John Stott played a prominent role.
> 4. There are differing views of the Catholic Church among us; they were present when I was ordained in 1968 and are still honestly espoused. We should therefore continue to respect each other's integrity and conscience.

The choices facing me as a result of the concern expressed by the presbyteries sharpened the decision I had to make. Should I withdraw the invitation to Dr Brady and live as a shadow of myself, or resign? I reasoned that if three presbyteries had voiced disapproval, eighteen had not, and that was significant. People with the Presbyterian Church had no illusions as to what I stood for and in varying degrees many were supportive. In the extensive media coverage of what was happening, public opinion was also weighing in behind my decision to be inclusive.

## Assembly Week: Facing the Free Presbyterians

The General Assembly opened on Monday, 7 June at 7.00 pm with public worship attended by 1,200 people. Because the moderator-designate is installed halfway through proceedings, I arrived at 7.15 pm at Church House with my chaplains, Ivan Hull, Cheryl Meban and Wilson Gordon. Dr Paisley and a 70-strong band of supporters swarmed around our car, waving placards denouncing me as Judas and Archbishop Brady as an agent of the Antichrist. In some ways it was amusing. One protester pressed his scowling face against the car window where I was sitting and, as I pushed my way out, he squared up to me. However, as I straightened up to my full 6 feet 3 inches, he backed away. The unregenerate rugby player in me was still alive and well.

As we robed up in preparation for entering the gathering of the General Assembly I began to tense up: the sense of occasion, the stirrings of self-doubt and the pressure of just ploughing through the thousand practical details just to get ready got to me. Then, as the 40 ex-moderators lined up in the concourse to escort me into the hall, I sensed the peace of God descending on my spirit and bringing me to a place of calm and joy.

As is customary, the outgoing moderator, Dr Ivan McKay, welcomed me and, after prayer, invited me to occupy the moderator's chair. A few moments later I was addressing the assembly and a live audience on Radio Ulster. The theme I had chosen for my year was "Living a Life of Love", words taken from Paul's Letter to the Ephesians (5:2). I explained how accepting Christ meant modelling our lives on his. He lived a life of love in Israel; we are called to live a similar life in the complexities and conflicts of Ireland. This would involve, I suggested, challenging the elements of sectarianism within ourselves, which most of us inhale and absorb from the atmosphere in which we grow up. I continued:

> A seasoned researcher into Ulster sectarianism explained to me how to identify traces of it when I examine my face in the mirror. Notice firstly, she said, the questioning look in your eyes: do you know who you really are? If so, you can grow to appreciate all kinds of people? The sectarian spirit distorts our personal identity so that we always see ourselves as "over and against" others. Secondly, do

Moderatorial Year 2004–2005: Ken and Val at the General Assembly of the Church of Scotland with the Rev Wilson Gordon and Mrs May Gordon (PCI) *(second and third left)* along side the Scottish Moderator Dr David Lacy, his wife *(second and third right)* and chaplains.

Representing PCI at the General Assembly of the Church of Scotland: *(l-r)* May Gordon, Phyllis and Denis Boyd, Val, Wilson Gordon and Ken.

2005: The launch of the book *Friendship towards Peace – The Journey of Ken Newell and Gerry Reynolds*, at Queen's University Belfast. *(l-r)* Fr Gerry, Philip Mateer, Val and Ken, Prof Ronald Wells (author) and Dr Barbara Wells.

2005: IRA Decommissioning Conference in Fitzroy with official witnesses Fr Alec Reid (in photo) and Rev Harold Good.

2005: The launch of journalist Brian Rowan's book 'Paisley and the Provos' at UTV Studios, *(l-r)* Ian Paisley Jnr, Val, Brian and Ken.

Fitzroy's Remembrance Sunday Service, November 2005: *(l-r)* Denis and Phyllis Boyd, Mr Herbert Kerrigan QC (Convener of the Church of Scotland's Chaplains to the Forces), Maureen and Chris Blake and Ken.

Fitzroy 2006: Ken and Gerry waiting on the arrival of the bridal limousine at the commencement of an Inter-Church wedding.

2006: Jennie, Val, Ken and Tim at Buckingham Palace for the presentation of the OBE.

2006 Political Dialogue evening at Fitzroy: *(l-r)* Ken, Caitriona Ruane (Sinn Féin), Fr Gerry, Jeffrey Donaldson (DUP) and Dr John Dunlop (Chairperson).

2006 25th Anniversary of Clonard–Fitzroy Fellowship: Morning Worship at Fitzroy with Presbyterian Moderator Dr David Clarke, his wife Hazel and Cardinal Seán Brady.

2007: Moderator, Dr David Clarke, guest speaker at the Clonard–Fitzroy Fellowship in Clonard Monastery.

2007: Ken at the Installation of the new Anglican Archbishop of Armagh, Rt Rev Alan Harper *(centre)* with other church leaders: *(l-r)* Ken, Archbishop Seán Brady, Dr John Neil (Anglican Archbishop of Dublin), Rev Ivan McIlhinney (Methodist President)

2007: Ken installed as the first Ecumenical Canon of St Patrick's Cathedral, Dublin: *(l-r)* Dr Denis Moloney, Ken and Val, Dean Robert MacCarthy, Phyllis Boyd, Archbishop Alan Harper and Denis Boyd.

2008: The elders of Fitzroy with Ken on the eve of his retirement, with Fr Gerry as a guest of the Kirk Session: *(top portraits, l-r)* Leslie Watson, Renee Pelan, Chris Blake, Patricia Drummond, Denis Gough; *(standing, l-r)* David McNeill, Desi Alexander, Michael Fitch, Stanley McDowell, George Mullan; *(back row seated, l-r)* Harold McCollum, Norman McConnell Albert Patterson, Jim Beers, Denis Boyd, Ken Newell, Gerry Reynolds, Ronnie Davidson, William McReynolds, Philip McElroy, Sloan Bell; *(front row seated, l-r)* Derek Boyd, Philip Mateer, Anne McMurray, June Pat Gamble, Alex MacPherson, Hunter Rutherford.

2008: Retirement Service for Ken and Val at Clonard with Fr Gerry presenting three volumes of daily prayer and meditation.

2008: Clonard celebration of Ken's retirement. The family gathers in the monastery garden: *(l-r)* Joseph, Siobhan, Val, Maya, Tim, Ken, Jennie and Gerry.

2008 Clonard Retirement Celebration: Ken and Val with Fitzroy's jazz band in the monastery garden.

2008: Ken and Val begin their retirement with a celebration dinner in their favourite restaurant, The Mill, Dunfanaghy.

2009: Help with the gardening. Ken with grandchildren Joseph and Maya on the lawnmower at their house in Dunfanaghy.

2009: The 500th Anniversary of the birth of John Calvin celebrated in First Lisburn Presbyterian Church using Calvin's original Communion Liturgy with the Rev John Brackenridge *(second left)* and Church elders.

2009: An evening of Theological Dialogue on Holy Communion in St Mary's College, Falls Road, Belfast. Ken and Gerry with *(l-r)* Dr Richard Clutterbuck (Principle of Edgehill College), Dr Con Casey (Redemptorist) and Professor Stephen Williams (Union Theological College).

2010 Overseas Peace Opportunities: Ken in Bosnia & Herzegovina with Palestinian and Israeli Bible Society directors and artists at Gazi Husrev-beg mosque, Sarajevo.

2011: The launch of the Calvin–Loyola Conference book at Union Theological College, Belfast, with the Moderator Dr Ivan Patterson *(centre)* and *(l-r)* Dr Tom Layden SJ, Fr Brendan McConvery (Editor), Prof Stephen Williams, Ken, Rev Patton Taylor (Principle) and Prof Drew Gibson.

2012: Ken and Val made 'Oblates' of Clonard in recognition of their long association with the Redemptorist Community. Fr Michael Murtagh (Rector) *(second left)* Fr Alec Reid *(fourth right)* and Bishop Noel Treanor *(third right)*.

2013: The screening of the BBC NI Documentary *14 Days* on the work of Fr Alec Reid in helping to break the deadly cycle of violence in Northern Ireland and open up political dialogue that led to the 1994 IRA ceasefire and the beginning of the Northern Ireland Peace Process: *(l-r)* Rev Steve Stockman (Fitzroy), Dermot Lavery (Director, DoubleBand Films), Fr Peter Burns (Clonard), Ken, Lord Mayor Mairtin O'Muilleoir, and Jonathan Golden (Producer, DoubleBand Films).

2014: Help with the gardening. Another grandchild, Toby, on the mower at our house in Dunfanaghy.

Saturday, 25 April 2015: Crusaders lift the Premiership Trophy, the Gibson Cup, at Seaview. Ken celebrates with Crusaders Colin Coates (Captain) *(above)* and Stephen Baxter (Manger) *(right)*.

May 2015 Overseas Peace Opportunities, Mozambique: Ricatla United Theological Seminary. Ken and Fr Michael Kelleher (Redemptorist) guest speakers to those preparing for ordination in various Protestant Churches with two women candidates and College administrator.

May 2015 Overseas Peace Opportunities: Beira, Mozambique. Ken with a leader of the Muslim community at the National Conference on Reconciliation and Peace bringing together the leaders of the Christian churches, the Islamic community and the three dominant political parties within the country.

2015 Quiet Peacemakers Art Exhibition in the City Hall: Fr Gerry and Ken with the artist Susan Hughes, Lord Mayor of Belfast Nicola Mallon, Derek Poole and Rev Dr Ruth Petterson.

November 2015: Corrymela 50th Anniversary Celebration Service in St Anne's Cathedral. Ken representing the Presbyterian Church in Ireland with (l-r) Rev Brian Anderson (President of the Methodist Church), guest preacher The Most Rev Justin Welby (Archbishop of Canterbury) and Archbishop Eamon Martin (Catholic Archbishop of Armagh).

you have a slightly upturned nose? If so, this would indicate that you assume that you possess the complete truth, which, in turn, stimulates the delusion that you are superior to those you consider benighted. Thirdly, note the presence of tight lips: you struggle to express appreciation of the faith or politics of those with whom you disagree. Finally, do you have tiny ears? This can reveal that you are not really interested in listening to the story and point of view of those with whom you disagree and consequently feel no empathy with them.

Finally, I proposed that "Living a Life of Love" should shape our vision for the future of Northern Ireland. I called to mind the example of the ministry of John Calvin, much beloved within Presbyterian circles: in sixteenth-century Geneva he laboured not just as a great preacher of the Scriptures, but also as a resolute force for social transformation. I concluded my sermon with these words:

> Today our people are wading through despair. The hopes raised by the Good Friday Agreement have been undermined by the failure of illegal groups to decommission their weapons. The political process has ground to a halt. But love can never give up. I believe that one day, gripped by Paul's words, we will embrace each other as brothers and sisters and work together as partners in creating a healthier community. Our long winter is over; there may be frosty nights ahead, but our summer is definitely coming. Amen.

After the formalities of the service the moderator's reception began. Family and friends mingled with church leaders and representatives of civic society, as Fitzroy's jazz band played in the background. Many assembly delegates made a point of shaking Dr Brady's hand. Next day, the front page of the *Belfast Telegraph* carried a photograph of the two archbishops sitting in the Assembly Hall, smiling. The headline was "Primate's Historic Date with Church".

The five packed days of the assembly passed quickly and delegates headed home on Friday afternoon. I was now free to counter Dr Paisley's allegations that I had slipped the archbishop in by the back door, and was a hypocrite to sign the Confession of Faith, which declares the Pope to be the Antichrist.

Both charges were easily answered. I explained to journalists the customary procedures regarding the guests of the moderator-designate, and the 1988 decision of our assembly that the Antichrist reference in the Confession of Faith was "not manifestly evident from Scripture" and therefore not binding on ministers or elders. In former years, Dr Paisley used to challenge opponents to a public debate; I was half hoping he would revive the custom.

Was the tension around the invitation worth it all? I believe it was. The church gave me space to be myself, for I was convinced by the inner voice of the Holy Spirit that Christ wanted me to invite Archbishop Brady. In addition, countless opportunities opened up for me to set before the general public the frequently evaded evangelical vocation to peacemaking. Furthermore, the clash of perspectives highlighted two contrasting attitudes towards the Catholic Church and community – perpetuating the antipathy of the past and cultivating a new respect; dogmatism from a distance and dialogue; exclusion and embrace.

Finally, having the courage to do what you believe is right emboldens others to step away from the paralysing fear that often holds them back from creative peace-building initiatives in their parishes and local communities. As a result, a toxic status quo prevails and rolls on down to the next generation. Controversy is alien to my nature, but I knew that if it came my way I was prepared to face it.

### Getting into My Stride

If getting through Assembly Week required the stamina to jog, managing the requests that flooded in afterwards required a capacity to sprint. June, July and August teemed with events: commissioning young people for short-term mission assignments, preaching in popular holiday resorts, visiting centenarians in care homes and attending garden parties at Hillsborough Castle and Buckingham Palace.

I also sought to make time to meet groups working in Belfast's loyalist communities, where many felt abandoned by politicians and churches. As one activist put it to me: "Nobody listens. Nobody cares. Nobody helps." Indeed, loyalists often look enviously at the social regeneration taking place in republican communities. An example of this is the annual West Belfast Festival, which asked me, through Fr Martin Magill of St Oliver Plunkett Church, Lenadoon, to speak in that church on Sunday, 8 August 2004 on the theme "Imagining Belfast – My Kind of City". Among those present were the Alliance Party lord mayor, Councillor Tom Ekin, and the MP for West Belfast, Gerry Adams.

I advocated various ways and means whereby we might transform Belfast into a city of friends. With regard to our annual St Patrick's Day Parade on 17 March, I suggested that Protestants would participate in it in much greater numbers if the event was flag free rather than awash with Irish tricolours. But the biggest step we could take would be resolving our dire political situation: "Though the clouds of mistrust are thick in the minds of many, I believe we are on the edge of the curtain coming down on physical-force republicanism. I would love to read again the hope-filled headline of 1994: 'It's over!', but with this addition: 'It's over for good.'" In a BBC interview at the end of the evening, Adams welcomed parts of my speech, but disagreed with other parts – largely, he said, because we look at the same city through different eyes. Afterwards we talked briefly together and wished each other well. I noticed that he did not react to my comment about "the curtain was coming down on physical-force republicanism". I sensed that something major was afoot.

### Tense Moments over Dinner

In September, Paul Murphy, the secretary of state for Northern Ireland, invited a small group of church leaders to dinner at Hillsborough Castle with Prince Charles, who was visiting the province. I had been to the castle before as one of a large gathering of guests, so I was surprised that the table was set for ten. Hugh Orde, the chief constable of the Police Service of Northern Ireland (PSNI), sat to the left of the secretary of state and I sat to his right. The prince and a few members of the royal entourage sat opposite us.

As the meal progressed, the conversation relaxed and, on occasions, became light hearted. I shared with Prince Charles my memory of him in 1967, cycling furiously through Cambridge on a cold winter's morning *en route* to the Archaeology Department, his undergraduate gown flapping in the wind behind him and his bodyguard gasping for breath.

In the course of the meal, Prince Charles turned the conversation to what we thought was happening at grass roots in our community. I mentioned that I had spent the morning in Sandy Row, a strongly loyalist area suffering from social and economic deprivation. When he questioned us as to how such complex situations could be reversed, I suggested that it would be a massive morale boost to the local people if a future visit of the Queen could include schools and community groups in similarly disadvantaged areas. An *aide-de-camp* interjected, "But there is a security issue involved."

"I know," I replied to the prince, "but loyalist communities are among the safest places for royal visits and many of the people have pictures of your mother hanging in their living rooms. They love her."

My recommendation created a distinct chill, and I realised I had crossed the invisible line of royal protocol. Shortly afterwards the aide suggested that it had been a long day and that the prince should retire. We stood and said our goodbyes. For me, a delightful evening had ended on an embarrassing note; I had innocently attempted to give an honest answer to an honest question.

## Pushing for a Breakthrough

Since October 2002 the Northern Ireland Assembly had been in suspension owing to allegations of IRA intelligence-gathering operations at the Northern Ireland Office. Nevertheless, the British and Irish governments, under Prime Minister Tony Blair and Taoiseach Bertie Ahern, had worked tirelessly to bring together the DUP and Sinn Féin for a three-day make-or-break summit arranged for September 2004 in Leeds Castle, Kent. As they prepared for these negotiations, the key issues were made clear: the DUP insisted that they would not share power with Sinn Féin as long as the IRA remained armed; republicans, for their part, refused to give in to these demands without guarantees that the DUP would form a power-sharing government. Hopes were high and well-placed sources informed me that on the table was an absolute commitment by the IRA to total decommissioning.

It therefore came as a shattering blow when the talks collapsed. A deal was not struck, but it had been tantalisingly close. The parties remained confident that further progress was possible. In media interviews, the four main church leaders spoke together to express the disappointment felt in the wider community. In light of the reputed IRA offer on the table, I was puzzled by the DUP response and pressed the DUP for further information in order to clarify why they had not jumped at this remarkable opportunity. Jeffrey Donaldson, one of the leading negotiators, called my comments "ill-informed and unhelpful", but gave no clarification and my question remained unanswered. A few days later I telephoned him and he told me that the DUP was more committed to doing a deal than many realised, but they wanted to copper-fasten it so that no party could renege on their commitments. It was encouraging to hear that.

## The Inauguration of Mary McAleese

In its preparation for the inauguration of Mary McAleese as president of Ireland for the second time, the Irish government decided to broaden the range of religious leaders taking part in the official ceremony in November. Along with the usual representatives of the mainstream Christian churches, they included the leaders of the Jewish and Muslim communities in Ireland. It was a wonderful occasion and I was glad to be participating as moderator of our church. I found it humbling that Ireland's faith communities were still allowed to play a prominent part in such an important national occasion, especially when secularists were increasingly raising their voices to have us excluded on the grounds that religion has had a largely negative influence on Irish society.

Two months after her inauguration, President McAleese found herself embroiled in a storm. In a speech marking the liberation of Jews from Auschwitz, she observed that Nazis "gave to their children an irrational hatred of Jews in the same way that people in Northern Ireland transmitted to their children an irrational hatred, for example, of Catholics". The unionist community was apoplectic with rage and numerous families let it be known that their relatives had died in the Second World War, fighting for freedom from the Nazis. She quickly apologised for her *faux pas*. When I was asked by the media to comment on her speech I began by urging unionists to accept her apology but not to dismiss the underlying issue to which she was drawing our attention – the transmission of prejudice within families from one generation to the next. I noted that prejudice is not the preserve of any one section of the community and I commended those parents who had deliberately chosen to inculcate anti-sectarian attitudes in their children and bring them up with a healthy respect for diversity.

## A Christmas like No Other

As the dust was settling over the failure of the Leeds Castle talks, press leaks confirmed that the IRA was indeed offering the total destruction of all their weapons and, in order to heighten confidence in the verification process, were willing to allow two clergymen to witness it. Now the debate shifted to the form that verification would take. While realising the significance of this offer, Ian Paisley and the DUP insisted there would be no deal without pictures, a demand to which the republican movement would never consent because it smacked not just of surrender but also of public humiliation. Unless flexibility was forthcoming from the DUP, the glittering prize of an agreed settlement would never be seized. We had reached an impasse.

I seriously doubted that the DUP's quest for certainty about the destruction of weapons would be substantially enhanced by pictures. At the end of the day, only the military thoroughness of General de Chastelain and the Independent International Commission on Decommissioning could establish the credibility and transparency of the destruction of the IRA's arsenal. In various media interviews I recommended that when we come to an impasse we should look for a bypass: "While photographs are desirable, they are not essential. Talking witnesses are better than silent photographs." Some within the DUP were angered by my interventions, but I believed that their passion for photographs would wane as the general public realised that it was becoming a dealbreaker. In my Christmas message, therefore, I urged politicians to grasp the prize of peace: "We are within touching distance of an historic, honest and fair deal that would see devolved government return to Northern Ireland." Then, suddenly, everything changed. Within a week the season of light was plunged into darkness by an act of brazen criminality.

### The Largest Heist in British History

In the biggest bank robbery in UK and Irish history, a gang stole £26.5 million in cash from the Northern Bank in the centre of Belfast on 20 December. Most people concluded that the only organisation capable of a crime of such daring proportions was the IRA. Within days the police confirmed what the public suspected, but republican leaders emphatically denied it. Few outside their coterie of comrades believed them.

Most of us were baffled as to why the IRA should carry out such an outrageous crime on the threshold of an historic deal. We had been led to believe that the IRA was preparing for decommissioning, and now a major felony had been authorised at the highest level of the Army Council. Trust had been decapitated and scepticism about republican motives turned to flint. I contacted some trusted journalists who confirmed my hunch that the robbery was designed by the IRA to provide a pension fund for its 350 active service members whose units had been put on hold since the Good Friday

Agreement. In media interviews I made no attempt to disguise my anger and disappointment. It felt as if the fragile hopes of the whole community had been plundered and those of us who had engaged with the leadership of Sinn Féin had been betrayed.

The General Board of the Presbyterian Church issued a hard-hitting statement in February 2005, declaring that "the robbery has destroyed trust in the commitment of Sinn Féin to seek peace". In turn, Sinn Féin rejected the charge and its spokesman Alex Maskey responded: "To date there have been no convictions and no evidence brought forward. All we have is innuendo and smear."

I had known Alex for several years through my links with Clonard and west Belfast. As a younger man, he had worked as a labourer in Belfast docks and was highly regarded as a successful amateur boxer who had lost only four out of seventy-five fights. He was a close ally of Gerry Adams and in 2002 became the first republican to serve as lord mayor of Belfast. In that capacity he attended the opening night of the General Assembly and, two months later, spearheaded an anti-violence rally in front of the City Hall. I had joined a crowd of several thousand who had responded to his call to demonstrate our disgust at a spate of recent murders across the province. Now, in a depressingly different atmosphere, the scene was set for a public clash. It came in February 2005, a few days after the PCI General Board statement, on a BBC political programme, *Hearts and Minds*. As we were taking our seats in the studio, just before going on air, I asked Alex and the presenter, Noel Thompson, if I could turn my chair to face Alex so that we could speak directly to each other. Both were happy with that.

It was a bruising encounter. I explained the intense anger felt within our church and throughout the community and was quite upfront in offering my own conclusion regarding the robbery. I did not claim to know more than the police, but I was 95-per-cent sure that the IRA was responsible. Alex hit back just as directly: he was 100-per-cent sure that it was not, because Sinn Féin had conducted an investigation with the IRA. From the murky world of a paramilitary organisation renowned for viciousness and sinister manoeuvrings, I was astonished that he could claim such absolute certainty. "If you have no element of doubt inside you, Alex," I replied, "then you must be some kind of extreme secular fundamentalist!" He felt affronted. When the programme ended, I looked to say goodbye to him, but he was gone.

The next day, on my way into the Royal Victoria Hospital, a Sinn Féin councillor crossed the main road to tell me that his party would never trust me again. His comments did not particularly concern me; I knew that there were times when we are called upon to express the true feelings of our community in a forthright and robust manner, and I had attempted to do that. It was never a personal clash, but something much bigger – a deeply wounded country yearning for healing and peace. Sometimes reconciliation requires a level of honesty that pulls no punches. To this day the robbery remains unsolved and if, in time, the views I expressed turn out to have been wrong, I will be ready to apologise.

In 2008 I was involved with Alex Maskey in events surrounding the death of the teenage son of a family of asylum seekers living in south Belfast. In preparation for his funeral in Fitzroy I asked Alex, as a member of the Northern Ireland Assembly for south Belfast, to read a Scripture lesson. He instantly agreed to do so.

### Victims' Groups and Orange Halls

One of the darkest moments of the Troubles was Saturday, 15 August 1998, when a car-bomb was detonated in Market Street, Omagh, by the Real IRA, a dissident republican group opposed to the Good Friday Agreement. It claimed the lives of 29 people – 6 children, 6 teenagers and 15 adults, including a woman pregnant with twins. Two hundred others sustained serious injuries.

Out of the carnage emerged the Omagh Support and Self Help Group, led by Michael Gallagher, whose 21-year-old son, Aidan, died in the blast. As part of their campaign to bring the perpetrators to justice, the group asked to meet me and the president of the Methodist Church, Rev Brian Fletcher. I travelled down to Omagh with Val on 19 January 2005. After sharing with us their stories of personal suffering and loss, they expressed continuing frustration at just how slow their campaign for justice was progressing. Despite words of sympathy, the UK and Irish governments had, over seven years, fobbed off their demands for a cross-border inquiry. Tony Blair had not even been prepared to meet the families and explain why the governments and police services were stalling. Brian and I assured the group that we would press home their concerns with any British and Irish politicians our respective churches would meet throughout the year.

From Omagh, Val and I drove 13 miles northwards to the village of

Ardstraw in County Tyrone, where the local Presbyterian minister, Rev David Reid, had gathered 20 senior Orangemen to meet us. I had requested the meeting because of an upsurge of dissident republican arson attacks on local Orange halls. For an hour we discussed the reasons behind the attacks and how the lodges were coping with the situation. Finally, when I asked if there was anything the wider church could do to support them, they replied, "Not really. Incidents like these just make us more determined than ever to press on with our own business, but we appreciate you both coming to be with us." I prayed for them as they bowed their heads with accustomed reverence and together we joined in the Lord's Prayer.

## Decommissioning: The End-Game

Peace processes can be notoriously slow moving, but when a breakthrough comes it restores faith in faith. Shortly after the IRA ceasefire of 1994, I had argued at a conference in Fitzroy attended by several leaders of paramilitary organisations that "the IRA should dispose of their weapons because a democratic resolution of conflict eroded the need for armed struggle". On that occasion, as I have explained earlier, my proposal was met with a stony silence. Yet, over the decade that followed, the IRA had moved from resistance to the idea of "Not a Bullet, Not an Ounce" to three events of partial decommissioning. But the question remained: "What do you intend to do with the rest of your weapons?"

No sooner had Val and I left Ireland on a moderatorial visit to communities in south-east India ravaged by the 2004 Boxing Day tsunami, than the heartening news broke on 6 April 2005 that Gerry Adams had called on the IRA to abandon its armed struggle and embrace exclusively peaceful politics. Everybody knew that the IRA Army Council must have already agreed to say yes; rumours were rife that conversations with the volunteers had already taken place at grass-roots level and a virtually unanimous decision had been taken to give Sinn Féin's peace strategy the green light. The Army Council now simply had to make its mind up to wind up and to say so publicly. Then on Thursday, 28 July came the dramatic announcement: "The leadership of *Óglaigh na hÉireann* has formally ordered an end to the armed campaign … All IRA units have been ordered to dump arms."

Within two months the whole issue of decommissioning, which had taken so long to resolve, had been signed, sealed and delivered. In September the final report of General de Chastelain confirmed that "the IRA has put all its weapons beyond use". Two Christian ministers, Fr Alec Reid of Clonard and Rev Harold Good of the Methodist Church, sat beside the general in front of the world's media. Their role as witnesses had been sanctioned by Sinn Féin and the British and Irish governments in order to add moral credibility to the final act of decommissioning. It had the desired effect. With more eloquence than photographs could ever have articulated, they recounted what they saw with their own eyes. "I will never forget that moment," Rev Good later revealed, "when Alec and I stood quietly and witnessed the very last moments of that decommissioning process, and Fr Alec said quietly into my ear, 'There goes the last gun out of Irish politics.'"

The new dawn that had taken so long to come was finally breaking over an astonished province and two simple Christian clerics of unquenchable faith were at the heart of it. They were unaccustomed to such international attention; in truth, they had dedicated three decades of their lives to working in the shadows, sustained only by the indomitable belief that, because Christ has risen, so can communities. I felt proud to know them and thankful that I had lived to see such a day.

## The Silence of Affection and Grief

The last public engagement of our moderatorial year was Sunday evening, 5 June, in Ballywatt Presbyterian Church. For generations most of the 150 families of the north-Antrim congregation had farmed the land and displayed a strong love for their church. Recent renovations had been completed and Rev Ivan Hunter had invited us to officiate at a service of thanksgiving at 7.00 pm. We arrived early, around 6.00 pm.

When Ivan and I went into the empty church to check out the sound system, I noticed a couple sitting in silence beside a plaque on the wall. Ivan explained that they were the parents of Tracy Doak, a 21-year-old RUC officer killed in a terrorist roadside bomb in 1985. Her parents often came early to church just to sit beside the plaque erected by the congregation in her memory. As I approached them we shook hands and I asked if I could join them for a few moments, just to remember Tracy with them. They invited me to sit down and for ten minutes we remained in silence until people started arriving. The thanksgiving service was a joyous occasion, but as we drove back to Belfast I could not stop thinking about a parental love that even after 20 years was as strong as ever. Truly its depth could not be fathomed.

**Handing Over to My Successor**

The following evening, mixed emotions were flowing through me as I presided at the opening service of the General Assembly on Monday, 6 June. There was a tinge of sadness that my time as moderator was now almost over, yet great joy at the many new experiences that had opened up for me and genuine relief that I had fulfilled all the responsibilities required of me to be best of my ability. I had no regrets. Val and I had worked well as a team and her wisdom and encouragement helped to get me through. My final address to the assembly encouraged our people to live with confidence in the Risen Christ and to reshape the future of our congregations and country by prioritising love, hope and a new evangelisation. I then asked the house to move to the appointment of my successor, Dr Harry Uprichard, my friend from student days in Assembly's College. After congratulating him, I led the assembled gathering in prayer for Harry and his wife, Maisie, and then invited him to take the moderator's chair.

# CHAPTER NINE

# The Flowering of a Vision

A year in Provence would have been desirable after the relentless schedule of being moderator, but only a fortnight exploring the French Pyrenees near Prades with Val was possible. By July we were back in Belfast. During our year-long absence, Fitzroy had been well looked after by Rev Dr Godfrey Brown. Slowly I resumed the familiar routines of preaching and visiting our members in hospital and at home.

## A Peaceful Garden

A belated request arrived in Church House asking me, as the past moderator, to dedicate a memorial gift in a public garden in Poyntzpass, County Armagh, in July along with Archbishop Brady. It came from the parents of Philip Allen (34) and Damien Trainor (25), who, despite being from Protestant and Catholic backgrounds, had been lifelong friends. In 1998 they had met up in the village's Railway Bar to discuss Philip's wedding, at which Damien had agreed to be best man. Two masked Loyalist Volunteer Force (LVF) gunmen had burst in and shot them dead in a hail of bullets as they crouched on the floor.

Thirty family members gathered with us in the sunshine for the short service in which we dedicated a memorial bench in honour of the iconic friendship between Philip and Damien. Seven years had passed since that fateful tragedy, but every day was a struggle for those left behind. We prayed that, in the days to come, all who entered the garden feeling burdened would find God's comfort and that, in a country where bitterness can run deep, these two friends would always be remembered for letting nothing destroy the bonds between them.

## "You May Say that I'm a Dreamer"

Two weeks later, on Sunday, 31 July 2005, I was involved again in the West Belfast Festival. My role this time was to introduce a public lecture in St Oliver Plunkett Catholic Church in Lenadoon, given by Dr Brady. It was entitled "What Freedom in Ireland Means to Me". Three days earlier, the IRA had declared an end to its armed struggle and the parish priest, Fr Martin Magill, asked me to sketch briefly my own vision for the way ahead. I indicated:

> A shared future will be healing centred, for we have caused each other pain. It will also champion cooperation because our country is like a bird with two wings and, if we work together, the bird can soar to new heights. I congratulate all of you who are demonstrating that our community can discover again what a wonderful thing it is to fly.

The archbishop's lecture was skilfully attuned to the immediate context:

> The statement by the IRA on Thursday was the most powerful and welcome move towards freedom in Ireland to have emerged from any paramilitary organisation since the beginning of the Troubles. By setting people free from the fear of violence, by confining the search for freedom to purely democratic and peaceful means, such actions open up the possibility of addressing the more urgent dimensions of human freedom. Part of the moral complexity of our past was the part played by the threat of violence from the unionist community in the decision to create Northern Ireland as a separate entity. That historic threat from the unionist tradition is also manifestly and verifiably removed from the debate about our shared future.

That evening I hummed to myself all the way home from west Belfast, thanking God for not letting my spirit succumb to the enticements and passivity of scepticism. Ending the armed struggle had been my dream from the moment I entered dialogue with Sinn Féin in 1990. While that would remove most of the violence, however, it could not by itself erode the lingering psychological and social alienation that kept our people divided. That would require the grace of reconciliation.

## A Perfect Storm

While unionist reaction to the IRA's decision was restrained, the British and Irish governments were convinced that the long war was over: army watchtowers on the hills of south Armagh began to be dismantled, soldiers retreated into their barracks and discussions began about troop reductions. On 26 September, General de Chastelain, along with fellow commissioners Brigadier Tauno Nieminen (Finland) and former US Foreign Service officer Andrew Sens, issued the *Report of the Independent International Commission on Decommissioning (IICD)*. It revealed:

> Over the past number of weeks we have engaged with the IRA representative [and] have observed and verified events to put beyond use very large quantities of arms which the representative has informed us includes all the arms in the IRA's possession ... A Protestant and a Catholic clergyman also witnessed these events: the Reverend Harold Good, former President of the Methodist Church in Ireland, and Father Alec Reid, a Redemptorist priest.

Despite this, Ian Paisley remained unconvinced. The decommissioning process had been completed without his demand for photographs being met or his request for an additional DUP-nominated church witness being granted. Nevertheless, the DUP wisely initiated in-depth conversations with the general and the two witnesses.

Fr Gerry and I felt the time was now right to create an open forum in Fitzroy to give the general public access to the testimony of our friends Alec Reid and Harold Good. With unionist suspicion continuing to be fuelled by many unanswered questions, we asked them to speak in Fitzroy on Thursday evening, 13 October. Their subject was widely publicised: "Decommissioning: What Did You See? What Does It Mean? Where Do We Go from Here?" Fr Gerry and I planned to co-chair the conference.

On the morning of the event I started getting phone calls from journalists, asking if they could attend. I was happy to give them permission, believing that wider coverage could only augment community confidence. But I was so busy getting the hall ready and making sure sufficient ushers would be on duty that I forgot to inform Fr Alec and Rev Harold. When they arrived in the Alexander Hall, extra seats were being brought in to cope with the crowd that had turned up, but they were surprised to notice TV cameras already focussed on the lectern from which they would be speaking. Nevertheless, the evening progressed well and the speakers presented a riveting insight into the clandestine nature of what they participated in, its professional execution and its historic significance. The audience was then given plenty of time to ask questions and offer comments. Some expressed doubts and were adamant that it was impossible to know for certain if all the weapons of the IRA had been destroyed. Most, however, were glad that decommissioning had been completed to the satisfaction of the professional overseers of the process and were prepared to trust its integrity and transparency.

Then, suddenly, the mood in the hall changed. A representative of a victims' group got to his feet and started rubbishing much of what Fr Alec had been saying. He dragged up from many years earlier a story about the British Army discovering weapons at Clonard Monastery, which the Redemptorists at Clonard had regarded as a violation of their property. He went on to imply that Fr Reid was an apologist for the IRA. Fr Alec was not accustomed to being challenged so forthrightly by loyalist victims of IRA violence and began to hit back, trading insult for insult. As tempers flared, I appealed to them both to sit down, give others a chance to speak and let order be restored. But they were so locked into verbal confrontation with each other that my pleas fell on deaf ears. Then it happened; Fr Alec lost control of himself and came out with the comment: "Unionists treated Catholics like the Nazis treated the Jews." Other loyalists, livid at this slur, rose to their feet, shouted back and stormed out.

For a few moments it was pure pandemonium, caught on camera for the whole world to see. The journalists hastily dismantled their equipment and headed out the doors for the newsrooms. There was no point in carrying on with our discussions. I apologised to the audience, closed the meeting and sought out a quiet corner of the hall to draft an apology, which I wanted Alec to release to the press along with the breaking news of his Nazi remarks. When I set it down in front of him to read, I could see that his mind was still spinning, but he was beginning to realise just how offensive his comments had been to the Protestants present. I pressed him to settle down, read through the apology slowly and, if it reflected his true thoughts, to sign it. We would take it down immediately to the BBC and UTV newsrooms. He did exactly as I requested. A minute later he lifted his pen and signed it with the sigh of a man who regretted his outburst.

It was now 9.00 pm. Fr Gerry, Rev Harold, Fr Alec I rushed down to the BBC and UTV to put the apology into the hands of the journalists working on the story. We urged them to include it in their reports. At 10.00 pm the story broke and by midnight it was circling the globe. I was distraught when I got home.

The next morning I was due to be on the Shankill Road with Rev Bill Campbell to present flowers to an elderly lady who was celebrating her birthday. As we walked up the road people recognised me and I immediately sensed their anger, for many of them carried memories of family members who fought against Hitler in the Second World War. I realised that my presence on the road was adding insult to injury and so I returned to my car and headed home, leaving Rev Campbell to deliver the flowers. A few days later, the fellowship conducted its own post-mortem and I acknowledged my mistake in not informing Alec and Harold of my decision to admit journalists to the event. The story ran and ran for weeks and it took me months to recover my composure. Despite the fiasco in Fitzroy, the IICD report continued to raise the level of public confidence in IRA decommissioning. The weapons issue was no longer an obstacle to the DUP and Sinn Féin doing "the deal of all deals" in the St Andrews Agreement. The impossible was now within touching distance.

**An Unexpected Honour**

I was still navigating my way through the nightmare in November when a letter arrived from Buckingham Palace, informing me that the Queen was considering awarding me an OBE (Order of the British Empire) for my contribution to community relations. If offered, it asked, would I be willing to accept? It took me by surprise because Christians involved in peacemaking often wonder if anybody pays the slightest attention to their endeavours, apart from a determined minority of zealous companions. For me, therefore, the letter proved to be a timely lift. But it was not primarily about me; it was the openness of Fitzroy and the courage of the fellowship. My immediate concern was to know if Fr Gerry had also received a royal letter. When I discussed it with him he was more than content just to be part of the corporate reconciliation ministry being honoured in this way. And so, on New Year's Day 2006, my name appeared on the Queen's Honours list.

The award ceremony was held in March at Buckingham Palace and Val,

Tim, Jennie and I travelled over to London to attend. It was humbling to be part of a huge crowd from all over the UK and the Commonwealth being honoured. Our only disappointment was that the Queen was out of the country. Prince Charles, however, deputised for her and I was delighted to meet him again. In the few seconds we had together, I simply smiled, expressed my thanks, received the medal, bowed my head and returned to my seat.

### RUC George Cross Service

Another official request came my way as past moderator – the fourth annual RUC George Cross Day Inter-Church Service, which was inaugurated two years after the RUC had become the PSNI in 2001. The purpose of the George Cross Service was "to mark the sacrifices and honour the achievements of the RUC". It is an extremely important and highly sensitive civic occasion: around 800 worshippers attend – mainly former RUC officers, their family members and public dignitaries. Feelings of loss mingle freely with memories of courageous commitment to duty – during the Troubles over 300 RUC members were killed and 9,000 injured. Each year all the main churches, Protestant and Catholic, send leading representatives to take part in readings and prayers, and one of the four main church leaders is invited in turn to preach.

My successor as moderator, Dr Uprichard, found himself in the eye of a media storm. He felt unable to accept an invitation to preach at the service on Sunday, 4 June 2006 in St Anne's Church of Ireland, Dungannon, because the local Catholic priest was taking part. He asked me to take his place and in my address I offered the following tribute:

> Many within all our churches have served in the RUC. We know from our own personal experience the sense of calling they brought to their careers, the pride with which they donned the uniform and the remarkable commitment they showed through days of darkness and destruction. Without their families sharing the stresses of their work, they could not have carried on. Entering into this service of worship with you is like entering a silent valley of sorrow: the painful memories, the damaged bodies, the fragile minds and the deep grief that so many carry reduce me to a silence filled with admiration.

An essential element in the social and political change of climate we have experienced in recent years has been the dedicated contribution made by the men and women of the RUC. They have helped to preserve a safe space in which hope can grow. But policing on its own cannot create the kind of society we desire. All people of good will need to work together and with the police to make our future very different from our past. It will not happen automatically, but only if we choose to devote our energies to turning that vision into a reality.

Following the media coverage of the service, I detected changes in the way some Protestants viewed the ecumenical nature of such events. Increasingly, most were glad to see the Catholic clergy involved, including the primate, Archbishop Brady. It was also evident that priests who took part could now do so without looking over their shoulders at parishioners who in the past viewed the RUC in a less favourable light. Spiritual boundaries were being redrawn with greater generosity and inclusiveness.

## High Point of My Journey

The best moment of the peacemaking ministry to which I committed myself when I came to Fitzroy in 1976 was on Sunday, 24 September 2006. It was the twenty-fifth anniversary of the Clonard–Fitzroy Fellowship. When it began to take its first hesitant steps in the tension-filled atmosphere of 1981, we felt isolated within a largely indifferent church and as vulnerable as a candle flickering on a battlefield. Now, in 2006, we stood at the centre of a network of friendships that emboldened us to invite the new Presbyterian moderator, Dr David Clarke, and Archbishop Seán Brady to preach together in Fitzroy. This time there were no placard-waving protesters outside or angry voices hurling abuse inside. Instead, local journalists were curious to probe the reasons why such an unlikely friendship between a Presbyterian church in south Belfast and a Catholic congregation in west Belfast had developed such staying power.

The theme we chose for our celebration was "Building Peace in a Divided Community – the Call and Challenge of Christ". The hymns were led by the combined choirs of Fitzroy and Clonard; Fr Gerry offered prayers, I conducted the service and the moderator and the archbishop preached. Dr Brady reminded us of the importance of what we were doing:

Political and legal processes can go a long distance but they are not in themselves adequate to the task of healing and reconciliation. Here Christians have certainly something to offer. The Good News is a story of the reconciliation of the human family with God and of people with each other. We thank God for the help which your fellowship has given in pointing us in that direction.

The moderator also encouraged us greatly:

To be peacemakers is not an idea to be discussed but a command of Christ to be obeyed. It is easy to be peace-loving, mouthing the "anything for a quiet life" philosophy, but we must seek peace in the same determined way that the Good Shepherd sought the lost sheep. Pioneers can always be recognised by the arrows in their backs, fired from their own side! We thank God for the pioneering courage the fellowship has demonstrated over the years.

The service concluded with the ancient biblical sign of peace, which triggered sturdy handshakes and heartfelt embraces all around the church. I was acutely aware that such mountaintop moments were rare, but every step of the climb to get there had been worthwhile: the birthing of the fellowship, the bonding of our congregations and now the leaders of our denominations preaching together. This side of heaven it does not get any better. Yet sadness also crept over my spirit for, realistically, local congregations still had a long way to go before they could witness to the healing grace of Christ with credibility. That was the unfinished task awaiting those who would come after us.

## One Small Giant Leap

A year had flown by since General de Chastelain had presented his report on IRA decommissioning and security sources were confirming that republican violence had declined to negligible proportions. This began to fuel speculation that the DUP and Sinn Féin might be up for a deal on power-sharing. In order to establish broad-based community support for such an initiative, the DUP undertook discussions with the main Protestant churches and other influential sectors of society. The stage was now set for the biggest step in Ian Paisley's religious journey – his first encounter with the hierarchy of the Catholic Church, for which he had, from his earliest days, reserved his most bitter invective. There were indications that it was not an easy decision for him to take; the fact that the meeting was arranged for 9 October, just two days before the all- party talks at St Andrews, gave the impression of nervousness. The timing, however, may have been strategically designed to ward off criticism from sections of the Free Presbyterian Church as well as party activists, panicking at the implied political trajectory that they had always considered anathema.

On Monday, 9 October, Ian Paisley crossed his Rubicon, like Caesar in 49 BC. With characteristic warmth he hosted an hour-long meeting at Stormont with Archbishop Brady and the Catholic Council for Social Affairs. The DUP delegation included Peter Robinson, Nigel Dodds, Gregory Campbell, Jeffrey Donaldson and Arlene Foster. They urged the hierarchy to encourage Sinn Féin to give its full backing to the PSNI, while the Catholic delegation sought a clear signal from the DUP of its intention to go into government with republicans and nationalists.

News coverage of the meeting was uniformly upbeat: "Today's meeting confirmed to me," declared Archbishop Brady, "that all of us have a part to play in creating a more stable and prosperous future. It is within our grasp if each one of us can find the courage to take account of the needs of the other and not just those of our own community." Dr Paisley was equally positive: "We touched on poverty, social need, building a strong local economy, achieving stable devolutionary arrangements and support for law and order. We look forward to further discussions with Archbishop Brady in the coming months."

Some journalists, however, latched on to the apparent contradictions in Paisley's action of meeting with the hierarchy. The *Sunday Times* claimed that "Paisley will be open to charges of double standards. As recently as 2004 he condemned Ken Newell for inviting Brady to attend the Presbyterian General Assembly as his guest."

This historic Paisley–Brady meeting was not just significant in itself. Its value lay in its potential to pave the way for a face-to-face meeting between the polar opposites of the DUP and Sinn Féin, and the two most powerful men in the politics of the province, Gerry Adams and Ian Paisley. I had always hoped that, in some small way, my invitation to Dr Brady in 2004 might have cleared away some of the debris within the church and community to allow healthier developments to take place. The pictures of Rev Ian and Archbishop

Seán smiling at each other across the conference table at Stormont started me wondering whether "the Doc" was changing. He was crossing bridges he had never before attempted; his attitudes were becoming more inclusive; his language was becoming more conciliatory; and his vision was now more about "healing" than "smashing". My admiration for his courage began to grow, but so did my fears for his future.

## Era of the Troubles Draws to a Close

Two days after the Paisley–Brady meeting, from 11–13 October, the major parties in Northern Ireland gathered in St Andrews in Fife, Scotland, for talks arranged by the British and Irish governments. Would Sinn Féin back the PSNI? Would the DUP commit to power-sharing with republicans? A timetable was accepted: if an agreement was reached, the parties would be given until 10 November to confirm their acceptance. If the response was positive, the first and deputy first ministers would be appointed on 24 November, a general election held on 7 March 2007, and a new ministerial executive installed in Stormont by 26 March. To the relief of an expectant community, all sides rose to the challenge. Adams cautioned that the core elements of the deal now needed now to be digested by the parties involved, but "restoring the political institutions was an enormous prize". In buoyant mood, Paisley claimed that "unionists can have confidence that their interests are being advanced". Hopes were high, but we had all been there before.

A week before the 10 November deadline for the parties to respond to the draft agreement, the fellowship organised a public discussion in Fitzroy entitled "Vision-Casting: What Kind of a Country Do You Want to Live in?' Two influential figures in the negotiations at St Andrews agreed to speak – Caitríona Ruane of Sinn Féin and the DUP's Jeffrey Donaldson. While exchanges between them were measured and respectful, they gave nothing away about the direction in which the consultation process within their parties was going. The audience, however, was far from reticent about the kind of leadership they were expecting our politicians to demonstrate. They needed to reach out to each other in generosity, do the deal, shake hands and start moving the country forward. One person asked Jeffrey Donaldson: "When are the leaders of the DUP going to shake hands with Sinn Féin in public?" Up to that point, no senior DUP figure had attempted to do so.

But all was not well within Sinn Féin. Major hesitations remained over giving unequivocal backing to the PSNI. In response to this, the DUP made it absolutely clear that it could not commit to power-sharing in those circumstances. Deadlines once again lapsed and community confidence sagged. In contrast, the party leaders assured us they were inching closer to the mother of all deals. But how long would it take? Christmas 2006 came as a welcome escape from the intensity of public expectation that surrounded the political process. As the new year opened, the unexpected death of a friend reduced the inches to millimetres.

## A Funeral Few Will Forget

On 6 January 2007, David Ervine, the leader of the loyalist PUP, suffered a heart attack and died at the age of 53. His passing removed from us a refreshingly spin-free politician whose accommodating unionism won him friends and allies across the community. He was an unlikely advocate for reconciliation. Born in 1953, he grew up in a staunchly Protestant working-class area of east Belfast. As he later acknowledged: "You were never frightened of the Catholic you knew, but of the Catholic you didn't know. My da's argument was, 'We're all just people.'" I first met David in the early nineties and instantly liked him. His bushy moustache, razor-sharp intellect and visionary cast of mind convinced me he would become an attitude-changer. When we got into conversation we discovered to our surprise that the Oxford Street Bus Station bombing in July 1972 had changed both of our lives in very different ways: I had committed myself to peacemaking, while he had pledged his future to the paramilitary UVF. Two years later, he had been arrested driving a car-bomb into west Belfast and sentenced to 11 years in the Maze Prison. There he had come under the influence of Gusty Spence, the UVF commander who had renounced violence and was using his position to urge UVF inmates to see the future in terms of an exclusively peaceful political struggle. The questions he posed had forced David to rethink his beliefs. Eventually, he had come to the view that only an inclusive political agreement could guarantee the security of the union and reverse the economic and educational disintegration ravaging loyalist communities.

After his release from prison in 1980, David Ervine entered full-time politics with the PUP and in 1998 was elected to the Northern Ireland Assembly, where he championed the Good Friday Agreement. His attitude to Sinn Féin contrasted with that of a begrudging unionism: he was the only unionist to vote against a DUP motion to condemn the display of lilies at

Stormont commemorating the 1916 Easter Rising. Significantly, he sat next to Martin McGuinness at the funeral service of the legendary Manchester United and Northern Ireland footballer, George Best, held at Stormont in 2005.

In 2002 Fr Gerry and I invited him to a fellowship initiative in Clonard with Alex Maskey, the first republican lord mayor of Belfast. The combination guaranteed a capacity crowd. Their speeches dovetailed around the desire to conserve a fragile peace, promote partnership and lift their respective communities to new levels of social and educational opportunity. Nobody wanted to go home. At the end, dozens of west Belfast Catholics queued to shake his hand. As we were leaving, he asked me for a lift back across town to his local pub and, on arrival, said: "Ken, would you like to come in and meet some friends of mine?" The opportunity of meeting east-Belfast paramilitaries in a more relaxed environment proved appealing to me, but it was already 11.00 pm and I reluctantly declined: "It's a bit past my bedtime, David. Can we do it again sometime – a wee bit earlier?"

When news of his death came through, I phoned his wife, Jeanette, to express my shock and to let her and the family know how much I appreciated him. She invited me to recount some of my impressions of David at his funeral on Friday, 12 January in East Belfast Methodist Church. As Val, Fr Gerry and I were making our way into the church, I caught my first glimpse of the extraordinary events that were unfolding outside. Forty of David's UVF colleagues had formed up outside as a guard of honour – not only to marshal the crowds who would follow the service by loudspeaker, but also to protect the space in front of the church for guests arriving by car. They had been briefed that Gerry Adams and Alex Maskey would be attending, their first public visit to the loyalist heartland of east Belfast. When their car pulled up in front of the church, no one in the large crowd or the guard of honour moved to confront them. The UVF acted with impeccable dignity. When Adams was asked why he had come, he answered that it was out of respect for David's family, and to express his sympathies to the paramilitaries "who have lost their most articulate leader".

A microcosm of those carrying Ulster's dreams and difficulties was gathered inside the church: British and Irish government officials sat side by side; police chiefs exchanged nods across the aisles with seasoned paramilitaries; Catholic priests chatted freely with their Protestant counterparts; and rival politicians, squeezed into the same pews, were soon singing from the same hymn-sheet. Gerry Adams sat just behind Peter Robinson. Everyone knew the score; in the background the deal between DUP and Sinn Féin was balanced on a knife-edge.

It was a service like no other I have ever attended. Streams of tears mingled freely with peals of laughter. Speaker after speaker recounted David's fondness for lengthy and obscure words rarely heard in the pubs of east Belfast, and hush descended as we listened to stories of lives turned around by the impact of his friendship. In all, 12 speakers were given a few moments each to highlight aspects of his character as well as to draw out the nature of the political convictions that motivated him. The most moving tribute came from his brother, Brian:

> He had the guts to climb out of the trenches, meet the enemy in no-man's land and play ball with him. With all the sincerity of my heart I welcome to this service today so many people that, ten years ago, we would have classed as our traditional enemies.

The congregation erupted into sustained applause, which was taken up by the crowds listening outside. You could hear it rippling its way right up the Newtownards Road.

I was the tenth speaker and I had made up my mind to direct my tribute to the politicians sitting right in front of us:

> The dream that came to possess David's heart and mind was of a future of peace for all our people, built on reconciliation and cooperation. Your greatest tribute to him, therefore, is not simply to come here today and commemorate his death, but to celebrate his life by valuing what he stood for. This means going out and doing the deal he advocated so passionately and for which our community has waited so patiently.

When a final hymn brought the service to an end, mourners filed out slowly, each one taking a few seconds at the front door of the church to express their condolences to Jeanette and the other members of the family. When Adams came face to face with Jeanette, those outside looked on as if in slow motion; the two opened their arms and embraced each other.

Val, Gerry and I made our way down the steps of the church and joined the huge procession of mourners following David's coffin as it was carried up the road by his family and friends. Hundreds streamed out of the shops, offices and pubs to line the pavements in his honour. It all brought a lump to my throat. For me it was an Easter moment: Christ was walking with us, not on Jerusalem's Emmaus Road, but on Belfast's Newtownards Road. David's death created an intense sense of communal bonding at a time when our politicians were struggling to close a deal that could open up a future for which he had long campaigned.

## Irrepressible Smiles

Two months after David's funeral, events moved quickly. Northern Ireland went to the polls on 7 March 2007, and the result was an overwhelming endorsement of the policies pursued by DUP and Sinn Féin. On 25 March, Peter Hain signed the order to restore the assembly, and the following day Paisley and Adams led their respective delegations for the first time into a meeting at Stormont to demonstrate that agreement had been secured. Sinn Féin had pledged its support for the PSNI, while the DUP would share power with them from early May. The image of Paisley and Adams sitting, relaxed, at the same table, almost side by side, stunned many. But the biggest eye-catcher was the size of Paisley's smile — the brand-image of a new reality.

When the assembly convened in the debating chamber at Stormont on 8 May, it elected Ian Paisley and Martin McGuinness as first minister and deputy first minister. After they were sworn into office, they walked together down the marble steps of the Great Hall to be greeted enthusiastically by the assembled guests. Journalists from around the world were there to capture a moment of national and international significance. It was hard to concentrate on their speeches; most people were transfixed by their smiles. The St Andrews Agreement brought to an end the era known as the Troubles and ushered in what many were calling "the miracle of Belfast". The summer of 2007 was one of the most relaxed and congenial in living memory.

But not everyone felt comfortable with the warmth of smiling faces. Leadership in Northern Ireland comes at a price, and the speed with which some of Paisley's former allies exacted it shocked many. The widespread euphoria, however, was not to be denied its day. The BBC hastily invited Fitzroy to celebrate the achievement on Sunday, 13 May with an act of worship and thanksgiving which would bring Catholics and Presbyterians in Belfast together.

## Don't Just Pocket Miracles, Reproduce Them

Fr Gerry and I, along with our music director, Chris Blake, compiled a service of joy to give some of the members of our congregation the opportunity to offer their interpretation of what had been happening. Chris O'Neill, a bus driver from Clonard, told his story:

> One day, when I was eleven and on my way to school, a shot rang out as I was passing a British foot patrol. A young soldier lay dead eight metres away. We live and work here together in this land and need to be one, as Jesus prayed. Each day I do my own little bit of reaching out as I drive through the city I love. Today is a good day for Catholic and Protestant, British and Irish.

Fr Gerry then presented a challenge:

> We now have the opportunity to showcase to the world God's vision of peace. The people of Ireland and Britain have been through immense pain during the years of conflict. In the end the wounded live with their wounds, but the burden of pain must not inhibit our capacity for generosity. That would be to betray God, who in Christ is reconciling the world to himself. He longs to see the walls dividing us levelled to the ground.

I decided that my sermon should reflect the mix of excitement and sadness coursing through the community:

> Waves of amazement surged through me when Ian Paisley and Martin McGuinness pledged to share power and sat side by side, smiling. The transformation happening among us is not due to the cold hand of history, but to the strong hands of a loving God. But my joy is tinged with sorrow; I'm thinking of those who every day carry a burden of injury; I'm recalling some of our peacemakers who died before they saw the sunrise they assured us would come. Jesus Christ spells out clearly how we should relate to each other: "Love the Lord your God with all your heart" and "Love your neighbour as you love yourself." In Northern Ireland we have 2,000 churches, often in places where our people maintain a distance

from each other. Imagine the changes that could sweep across our land if Christians embraced the agenda of Jesus and turned their churches into welcome-spaces for the whole community. Don't just pocket the miracle of Belfast; reproduce it where you live.

## Paisley Steps Down as Moderator of His Church

In Ulster's fractured terrain, breaking new ground can be costly. Ian Paisley himself had long set his face against those with progressive ideals and the words "No!" and "Never!" overpopulated his speeches. When he chose to sit beside Gerry Adams, therefore, for their first press conference at Stormont on 26 March 2007 and announced to the world that a new power-sharing government would be formed in May, I instinctively knew that this would spark opposition within his own church. A few days before the press conference, he was visited by a group of disgruntled Free Presbyterians, who threatened action against him if he went ahead with power-sharing. To his credit, he continued on course, assuming he could ride out the storm. After all, he had been moderator of the Free Presbyterian Church for over half a century.

Fundamentalism is a creed that brooks no deviation from its principles, and any whiff of change can result in an avalanche of suspicion. It characteristically expresses itself in an antagonistic worldview of eternal opposites: truth v falsehood, light v darkness, Christ v Antichrist and God v the Devil. Adherents see this cosmic battle being fought out locally. Though quick to demonise opponents, a more intense wrath is reserved for those "Judases" from within their own ranks who start to question its inflexible mindset. Where issues are not resolved, schism looms large. The Free Presbyterian Church in Ulster had grown rapidly during the 1970s and, though not officially linked with the DUP, was the dominant religious influence in it. When the DUP became the largest unionist party in 2003, increasing numbers of mainline Protestants flowed into its ranks, bringing with them less dogmatic and more pragmatic views, open to doing the right thing in the right circumstances. When Ian Paisley, therefore, assumed the mantle of first minister of Northern Ireland on 8 May, he intended to complete his four-year tenure of office. However, just four months later, he was forced to step down as moderator of his own church. At the pinnacle of his political power, he may have forgotten that he had positioned himself at the summit of an active volcano whose fault-lines had been visible for centuries.

It was a humiliating experience for the 81-year-old. He knew he was in for a rough ride when he arrived at the annual meeting of the Presbytery of the Free Presbyterian Church of Ulster in Martyrs Memorial Church, Belfast, on Friday evening, 7 September 2007. Over 200 elders and ministers had assembled to elect their new moderator for the incoming year, among other things. This was a position to which Paisley had been routinely re-elected for 57 years running. This time he found himself the target of, outside the church, a hostile crowd of jeering pickets and, inside it, fierce criticism from some ministers who had been his closest allies from the earliest days of the church's formation in 1951. Daggers were hidden in their criticisms of his dual role as moderator of the church and first minister. In his opponents' eyes, Paisley had entered a Faustian pact with Sinn Féin/IRA and had sold his soul to the devil for political gain.

After five hours, those present voted by 112 to 96 to re-elect him for another year, but the presbytery was so bitterly divided and the vote so close that the spectre of a split was hanging over the 10,000-strong denomination. A decision was taken to adjourn the meeting and reassemble in January on the understanding that Paisley would step down and be replaced by a more unifying candidate. The octogenarian put a brave face on it, but it was surely a bitter pill to swallow.

Yet, despite the tensions within his own church, he was increasingly seen by the majority of people in Northern Ireland as a courageous leader who sacrificed a lot to create an inclusive future. The changed atmosphere in the province and the growing stability of the political institutions were evidence of this. But one question lingered after the meeting in Martyrs Memorial: having been toppled from the leadership of his church, would he now lose his grip on the party?

## The Witness of Completed Lives

On 22 December 2007, one of Ulster's greatest peacemakers quietly passed away. William Rutherford died after a long and influential life. Born in 1921, he grew up in Warrenpoint, where his father was the Presbyterian minister. After graduating in medicine from Trinity College, Dublin, he became a missionary doctor in Anand Hospital, India, and took up his duties in 1947, a few months before the partition of India and Pakistan. He vividly recalled the chaos into which he had stepped: 1,000,000 Hindus and Muslims dead and over 12,000,000 forced to flee their homes. The rawness of that violence instilled in him a passion for peace.

In 1966 he and his wife, Ethne, returned to Belfast where he was appointed to the Casualty Department of the Royal Victoria Hospital on the Falls Road. Shortly afterwards, the Troubles erupted and his department was inundated with the victims of the conflict. He and Ethne joined the Fitzroy congregation in 1982 and shortly afterwards he was co-opted onto our Kirk Session as an elder. In the spring of 1994 Sinn Féin established a peace commission to enable their supporters to discuss the future direction of the party. Behind the scenes, the continuation of the armed struggle was under serious review. I was asked to make a presentation to the commission in Conway Mill in March, but I had other commitments and asked William to take my place.

The argumentative atmosphere of the meeting settled down when the tall and quietly spoken Presbyterian medic rose to his feet. His face looked familiar. When he informed them that he was the consultant in charge of the Accident and Emergency Department of the Royal Victoria Hospital, the penny dropped. He had treated some of them and their friends over the years. They listened even more intently when he revealed that he had no difficulty in seeing himself as Irish. Finally, he told the story of how their president, Gerry Adams, had been shot in a UFF assassination attack in 1984 and rushed to hospital. William had been on duty and, with his team of surgeons, had removed three bullets and saved Adams's life. The time had now come, he concluded, for all of us to join forces in saving the life of a traumatised and wounded community and the best way to do this was by supporting the peace process now being contemplated by the leadership of Sinn Féin.

There was no applause when he sat down, just a silence, coaxing into life a connection with each other that had been buried under decades of anger. Press reports of the event seized on William's speech and one journalist wrote that those present "had seen a portent of what the new Northern Ireland might be like if peace and reconciliation would follow from such acts of grace". Six months later the IRA announced a "complete cessation of military operations".

William's funeral service was held in Dunmurry Presbyterian Church, whose congregation he had decided to join in his later years. People from all walks of life gathered to pay their respects and Fr Gerry and I were invited to pay tribute to one of our greatest friends. He had slipped away just as the country whose wounds he had tended was finding its feet.

## Paisley Bows Out as First Minister

The storm of opposition that engulfed Ian Paisley in September 2007 from within his own church and swept him out of the office of moderator was bound to have a knock-on effect in his party. Though only 5 per cent of the DUP's electoral support now came from his denomination, Free Presbyterians dominated the party's representation on local councils, at Stormont and at Westminster, occupying somewhere between 50 and 70 per cent of the seats. The party's increased mandate, delivered at the ballot box in March 2007, strengthened Paisley's leadership and he looked secure when he confidently assumed the mantle of first minister for the four-year term. It came as a shock, therefore, when he announced just ten months later that he was relinquishing his roles as first minister and DUP leader. Everyone was asking why.

At the time, a veil of secrecy cloaked the real reasons for his swift departure, but some things were not difficult to discern. The DUP had a problem with his leadership image. The pictures of him sitting in the Great Hall of Stormont side by side with Martin McGuinness, his deputy first minister, were difficult for unionists to swallow, even if they had been half-prepared for them. Even his brilliant speech that day, 8 May 2007, with its eirenical tone, presented few problems: "I have sensed a great sigh of relief amongst all our people who want the hostility to be replaced with neighbourliness." What rubbed salt into wounds of the DUP was the sustained stream of heartfelt smiles, the exuberant sense of bonhomie and the many occasions of laughter that were captured up close by the world's media. Quickly and dismissively, Paisley and McGuinness were dubbed "the Chuckle Brothers". Given three decades of IRA violence in which McGuinness had played a leading role, unionists felt stung by Paisley's apparent insensitivity. Some lifelong party members started to jump ship and transfer their loyalty to the independent member of the European Parliament, Jim Allister, who had broken ranks with the DUP over power-sharing. Allister had begun to awaken fears that the real winners at Stormont were not law-abiding unionists but terrorist-inspired republicans.

What many conjectured also began to be confirmed – the smiles were not a publicity stunt but evidence of a good chemistry between the two leaders. Paisley revealed that on his first official meeting with McGuinness he explained to him: "We can work this new relationship between us in two ways: fight about everything or decide now to seek as much practical agreement as possible in a spirit of goodwill and for the benefit of all our people." They adopted the latter course, a pattern of generous and cooperative leadership between unionist and republican never witnessed before in the history of the province.

Another major reason for Paisley's demise was that, although the DUP had garnered support for the St Andrews Agreement from the top echelons of Northern Irish civic society, they had not invested sufficient effort in winning over their traditional heartlands. Many were not prepared for power-sharing and it was questionable whether they ever would be. In particular, they were reservations about Paisley himself, who had spent 30 years denouncing power-sharing as well as promising to "smash Sinn Féin". So why now was he doing a U-turn? They were never given a satisfactory explanation. To add insult to injury, Paisley and those around him argued that nothing had changed, but that the charade of some kind of political continuity smacked of the deception with which Paisley had so often charged others. His supporters sensed that a different Paisley was emerging, one intoxicated by the lure of power. As trust haemorrhaged daily from the party, some insiders concluded that the only remedy lay in the leader's removal.

In striking contrast to this internal tension, the community at large was increasingly appreciative of the united leadership of Paisley and McGuinness. On the completion of their first 100 days in office, an Ipsos MORI poll revealed that most republican voters believed Paisley was doing a good job, while 48 per cent of unionists felt the same about McGuinness. Many welcomed what they termed "the conversion of Ian Paisley".

An additional cause of his collapse only surfaced as the new assembly got down to business. As chair of the Northern Ireland Executive he was expected to master a huge volume of detail on a host of issues, and keeping on top of it all began to prove too much for the 82-year-old. Many around the table wondered if he was out of his depth. The electorate would judge the success of the new assembly on its ability to deliver real change for everyone. If there was to be a new leader, it would have to be one with a talent for organisation; and replacing a legend would not be easy.

Only after the passage of several years was the dramatic process behind Paisley's removal revealed in an interview that he himself gave to the media. Early in 2008 the DUP conducted a strictly confidential Stormont Assembly Group attitude survey, asking their MLAs, among other things, how the party had fared over the previous 12 months, how Dr Paisley had performed, and how future leadership change might be handled. When Paisley was presented with the findings in February, he was shocked and realised quickly the direction in which it as pointing. Aware from the survey of the strength of opposition to his leadership, the seasoned campaigner knew that he had no option but to bow out graciously. It was another hammer blow that he did not see coming, but his actions saved the party and stabilised the government.

Paisley announced in March that he was standing down as DUP leader after almost 40 years, and as first minister of the new assembly. In May, those roles were transferred to the party's deputy leader, Peter Robinson. The relationship between Robinson and McGuinness was managed with much greater public reserve and never reached the level of personal warmth characteristic of the earlier pairing. In fact, it was often to appear workmanlike and cold. The pivotal role Ian Paisley played in creating the stage for a new era of political partnership in Northern Ireland was rightly recognised in 2010 when he was elevated to the House of Lords at Westminster.

In June 2008 the *Presbyterian Herald*, the magazine of our church, invited me to assess Paisley's contribution to Northern Ireland. At first, I was inclined to draw upon the reservoir of negative impressions that many in our denomination – including me – held of him; yet privately I knew that I had long admired his energy and often wished he could have harnessed it to more constructive ends. Never in my wildest dreams did I or anyone else I knew think that he would undergo such a radical change in outlook and demeanour as we had witnessed over the previous two years. This welcome reality led me to pen a much more positive evaluation:

> The First Minister has emerged today as a leader whose inclusive vision and concern for the well-being of the whole community has taken us all into a better place than most of us ever dreamt was possible. Our children and grandchildren will grow up to lead normal lives in a new and healthier atmosphere generated by the decisiveness of Ian Paisley. While other courageous political leaders played a major part in preparing us for these initiatives, he opened doors to co-operation in our institutions of government, doors rusted for centuries by mistrust and bitterness and sectarianism. We owe him thanks. What the Gospel teaches us is that Jesus Christ is more interested in who we become than who we have been! This is the grace of God, and Ian Paisley should be seen in that light.

## Resignation and Celebration

Retiring from Fitzroy in September 2008 required the permission of our Kirk Session and so I submitted the following letter in February:

> When I was installed in Fitzroy in 1976 some people commented that I was only the sixth minister in 156 years and that the average ministry lasted 31 years. I remember thinking to myself that ministries of such length were a noble feature of the past and couldn't possibly be continued by me. How wrong can you be? Now, as I enter my thirty-third year, I realise what a special place Fitzroy has been and continues to be.
>
> You are a church where people's faith-gifts and soul-passions have been moulded by the hands of the Master-Potter into something unique that witnesses to his grace. We have seen many changes since 1976 and the years ahead will bring more. We should be unafraid of change; embedded in it is Christ's challenge to walk with Him, learn from Him, and embrace afresh His mission of transforming lives through the Gospel. I therefore request the permission of my fellow elders to retire on Sunday, 21 September 2008.

As Denis Boyd read out the letter to our elders, I struggled to rein in my emotions, but I had one final request: a photograph of the whole Kirk Session to hang in my new home. I asked if we could invite Fr Gerry to sit as guest of session in one of the photographs, and they agreed. It is one of my most treasured possessions: we sit at the Lord's Table, with the elders around us, with the Scriptures open and the Communion chalice on display; we sit as brothers and sisters in Christ, enlightened by his word of truth and nurtured by the sacrament of his sheer grace. It also speaks of a journey of grace that few of us would ever have anticipated, but that none of us will ever forget.

It was decided to mark my retirement with a dual celebration, firstly in Clonard in June and then in Fitzroy in September. And so it was that on Sunday evening, 8 June, Val and I gathered with our family and a host of friends from Fitzroy for a service in the majestic setting of Clonard. I entitled my farewell homily "A Journey of Joy: the Person I Was, the Places I've Been, the People I've Met and the God I Love". During the worship, with its choirs, prayers, readings and praise, I felt like the man whom the apostle

Paul described in his Second Epistle to the Corinthians (12:2) as "snatched up to the highest heaven". My spirit was bursting with gratitude. If signs and wonders are still happening, I thought to myself, surely this must be one – a service of thanksgiving in a Catholic Church for a Presbyterian congregation and its minister! At the end Fr Gerry presented Val and me with the three volumes of the Divine Office; then Val presented him with a photograph of us both in clerical attire, standing at the door of Fitzroy, ready to conduct a wedding. The photograph carried this inscription: "In grateful thanks for a remarkable journey with the Risen Christ and with each other on a path of discovery, grace, love, joy, friendship and peace from 1981 to 2008".

Following the service, the congregation made its way into the sun-drenched monastery garden for refreshments. The Fitzroy jazz band played in the background. Children rushed around, playing games on the grass; elderly members found seats on which to strike up conversation with old friends; and some more nimble feet started to dance as the sun went down over the city. In 1984 Fr Gerry and I had been on our own when we had first walked in this garden. Twenty-four years later it was crowded with those who had joined us on a journey with the great Redeemer.

**Party with a Twist**

As is the custom in Presbyterian circles when a minister retires, a party was planned whose contents were shrouded in mystery. All we knew was that Friday evening, 5 September 2008, would be full of fun and surprises and shared with the 250 friends we had put on our guest list: our extended family, Val's colleagues from Maghaberry Prison, local Anglican, Charismatic, Congregational and Catholic ministers, our moderator, Dr Donald Patton, and a posse of Presbyterian colleagues who had always encouraged me. Val and I had discussed inviting a small number of republican and loyalist friends, but some members of Fitzroy had suffered at the hands of paramilitaries and we felt it would be insensitive to have them sitting in the same building. We decided not to invite them.

The weather was wild. High winds and driving rain greeted those who parked around Fitzroy and sprinted to get inside the church. When we arrived we were humbled to be greeted by a sea of familiar faces and slipped into the front pew beside our family and our grandchildren, Joseph and Maya. When the clerk of session, Denis Boyd, welcomed everyone with his usual mischievous asides, we knew that we would soon be rocking with laughter.

But before that, we were all invited to participate in a time of rousing praise led by the choir and orchestra.

Several speeches of a more serious nature broke up the flow of fun. Fr Gerry spoke of how we both helped each other to walk with God and then confided in us how much he felt at home within Fitzroy, a congregation he had grown to love. Belfast's lord mayor, Tom Hartley, the first Sinn Féin politician I had ever engaged with, mentioned how our views had often clashed, but a legacy of friendship remained. Roy Garland of the UUP recalled our first tense and public engagement with republicans at Conway Mill in 1995, at a time when unionists refused to talk with them. Now, he quipped, everybody is talking to Sinn Féin – even in Presbyterian churches!

The biggest surprise came towards the end of evening, when Denis Boyd calmly and slowly announced: "I now invite to speak someone who has known Ken for some years, the Right Honourable Mr Gerry Adams, member of parliament for West Belfast." I thought he was cracking another of his jokes until I heard footsteps behind me in the aisle of someone walking towards the lectern. Suddenly he was there, about to speak. I kept wondering how he had got an invitation. In a whisper I asked Val if she had got in touch with him privately; she had not. Later I discovered that the organisers of the party who knew of my contacts with republicans since 1990 had decided to ask him to come along. Despite being locked in a meeting in Dublin late into the afternoon and expected at another one after Fitzroy, he made it to the church, stayed longer than anticipated and enjoyed an experience that was unique for him – and for us.

He spoke about the strength of the convictions we had both brought into the Clonard dialogue in 1990, and how this had produced an unexpected connection between us as well as a greater sensitivity to the hurts and aspirations of our respective communities. These conversations had played a part, he added, in the development of a peace process that was transforming the environment in which we all now lived. He paid tribute to the supportive role that Val had played over the years in keeping our life at home on an even keel when social tensions were running high. Finally, he urged everyone present, as people of Christian conviction, to release the energy of their faith into reshaping the country. He asked them to pray that both communities would build something out of the present God-given opportunities, something that everyone could own and take pride in – a future that was inclusive, harmonious and prosperous.

I was nervous as to how the congregation was responding to his words but, as he turned to us for a final time to wish us well in our retirement, we returned his good wishes. When he stepped down from the lectern, his speech was greeted with sustained applause; then some of our elders and ushers escorted him to the waiting car.

I wondered, however, whether some had found his speech difficult to sit through. A few confided in me that some painful memories did surface, but that they were also jostling with aspirations for peace. Overall, I detected in the applause a liberality of spirit that was willing to acknowledge the pain we had caused each other as well as to reach out towards mutual forgiveness and in good faith embrace the new era that was opening up for us all. This was a moment of healing in which we were moving well beyond "them" and "us".

As is customary, the last speech was left for me and I struggled to put 32 years of memories into 10 minutes. I began by thanking God for my parents and sisters, the church of my childhood that had pointed me to Jesus Christ and the unfailing love with which Val and my family had surrounded me. Looking back, I now knew without a shadow of a doubt that God had called me into the Christian ministry, guided me to Fitzroy and there gifted me with so many friends who had helped to bring the best out of me. And what about special people like Fr Gerry, who had come into my life when I was enclosed in the box of my own certainties? The Swiss psychologist Carl Jung once noted that "the meeting of two personalities is like the contact of two chemical substances: if there is any reaction, both are transformed".

The evening then drew to a close with more heartfelt praise, just as it had begun. I pronounced the Benediction, supper was served and, at the end of it, Val and I headed to the church doors to say our farewells to those who had come. It took ages to hug everyone, share memories of days gone by and express those moments of tender affection displayed when friends say a significant goodbye.

### "I Hope You Dance"

In the run up to our final Sunday in Fitzroy, Val and I were surprised to find ourselves caught up in various media interviews. In a news release, Stephen Lynas, PCI press officer, captured Val's thoughts well:

> When Ken and I leave Fitzroy it will be a sad occasion, but we are also thankful because we have felt so supported over the years.

Fitzroy is a proactive congregation, full of drive and vision for God's work. We look forward to seeing what is next for them, as well as for ourselves.

Our last service in Fitzroy was held on Sunday, 21 September 2008. We deliberately designed it to be a family service so that the whole congregation could be there. I chose the theme "Like a Candle Flame", for it reminded us that Christ's light always shines in an outward direction. We asked our young people who had just returned from summer mission assignments overseas to tell us about their experiences, and we commissioned the leaders of our Youth and Children's Ministry as the new season of service was starting up again. Just before the last hymn I informed the congregation that refreshments were awaiting us all upstairs in the Alexander Hall; then I asked Val to join me at the Communion table. I wanted both of us to be able to look into the faces of our friends for one last time as we sang the final hymn. Then, as everyone remained standing, I raised my hands in blessing over the congregation for one last time, as I had done for 32 years, and pronounced over them the beautiful words of Aaronic Blessing (Numbers 6:24–6):

> May the Lord bless you and take care of you;
> May the Lord be kind and gracious to you;
> May the Lord look on you with favour and give you peace.

With that, our ministry in Fitzroy was over – almost!

As we were stepping away from the Communion table, the orchestra suddenly struck up the rousing gospel folk song that had almost become Fitzroy's anthem, "This Little Light of Mine". I whispered to Val, "Fancy a dance? Come on, let's do it." With that, we gave ourselves over completely over to the music. We just could not stop ourselves from dancing; we had been privileged to witness a congregation blossoming in the love of the Risen Christ and to watch the Holy Spirit turning around intractable situations in the province on the way to reconfiguring the universe. As the Anglo-American poet WH Auden put it: "If there when Grace dances, I should dance." Huge smiles of amusement and laughter broke out across the congregation and some people started to clap their hands and to sway freely to the rhythm of the music. I imagined the angels dancing, and with them some of my grace-filled friends who had graduated into God's eternal light.

I pictured them all, caught up in a swirl of excitement at a time when two unexpected political partners were attempting their first steps in a waltz of peace.

My private reverie reminded me of the American country singer Lee Ann Womack's song "I Hope You Dance". It is a parent's dream for her children, but it also reflects my prayer for Fitzroy at the parting of our ways, and my hope for all the churches and people of Ireland:

> I hope you never lose your sense of wonder;
> You get your fill to eat but always keep that hunger.
> May you never take one single breath for granted;
> God forbid love ever leave you empty handed.
>
> I hope you still feel small when you stand beside the ocean;
> Whenever one door closes, I hope one more opens.
> Promise me that you'll give faith a fighting chance,
> And when you get the choice to sit it out or dance,
>
> I hope you dance,
> I hope you dance.

# CHAPTER TEN

# Retirement: A Continued Vocation

T he end of active working life, and then retirement, comes to those of us who have been blessed, as I was, with the right job for me and with good health. I realise that is not true for all, I am very grateful.

Readers of this book will appreciate that there were some ups and downs as I made the transition from a very active working life to what it meant for me to be retired. But, despite that, a deep conviction emerged that my true life's vocation would not change. As my friend Archbishop Cahal Daly advised, "The best way to happiness in retirement is to keep active in the service of the Lord, but in ways different from those one trod in pastoral ministry." The feeling was very clear that the overarching story of my life, both in active work and in retirement, was that I was called to a life of extending God's kingdom. For me, that meant – and continues to mean – engagement with issues of reconciliation among all the people of Northern Ireland.

As detailed in previous chapters, my engagement was formed in the context of the Troubles. To be sure, my first responsibility was to the people of Fitzroy Presbyterian Church. But, along with my faithful friend and partner, Fr Gerry Reynolds, my eye was always on the ways in which I and my church might bring an end to violence and promote peace between unionist and nationalist communities. In recent years my calling to work for reconciliation has taken me into new and different issues and to unexpected places of service.

## Migrants, Asylum Seekers and Xenophobia

The ceasefires of 1994 which had brought peace to Northern Ireland had also turned the province into an attractive proposition for migrants coming, for example, from countries in central and eastern Europe where wages were low. Article 45 of the Lisbon Treaty guaranteed EU citizens free movement to other member countries to seek employment without requiring a work permit, and access to all social and tax advantages. On the international front, the flow of economic migrants and asylum seekers into the EU soared to 2,000,000 a year, driven by the poverty of Africa, the conflict in Syria and the "global war on terror" which had devastated Iraq and Afghanistan.

I had always, perhaps naïvely, assumed that our new neighbours would, here in Ulster, meet with the same welcoming attitudes we had received as a young family in Indonesia in 1972. However, the 2006 report from the Northern Ireland Council for Ethnic Minorities detailed the experiences of 162 victims of verbal abuse, arson attacks and physical assaults. Some UK newspapers branded Ulster as "The Race-Hate Capital of Europe" because racially motivated crimes were running at levels higher than in England and Wales. The new immigrants usually moved into working-class areas close to the city centre, where property was cheaper and where schools, hospitals and work opportunities were within walking distance. Many of these areas were proudly loyalist, but had been struggling for decades with economic decline as well as the ever-present shadow of paramilitary criminality. They felt politically neglected by unionism and culturally demonised by the middle classes for their intense loyalty to the British crown. Patience and tolerance were not in abundant supply. Similar examples of xenophobia were also surfacing within the Catholic community and, alarmingly, the virus was spreading beyond Belfast.

Towards the end of my ministry, several racially motivated attacks took place within a stone's throw of Fitzroy's front door. Through incidents like this I met Anna Lo, the chairperson of the Chinese Welfare Association (NI). At a meeting convened by the police, social services and representatives of political parties and churches, she shared with us a personal experience:

> I was walking into Belfast one evening about 5.30 pm when suddenly out of the crowds four young men walked directly towards me and started shouting abuse at me. I manoeuvred myself to the other side of the pavement to get past them, but within seconds one of them came up behind me and kicked me on the back of the legs. I stood there, stunned and shaken. There were lots of people around but nobody came over to ask me how I was. The young men ran across to the other side of the road and continued to hurl abuse

and laugh. Not a soul said anything to them. The general public just walked on by; they didn't even bat an eyelid.

On Sunday night, 14 June 2009, 113 Roma migrants living near Queen's University were expelled from their homes close to the trendy bars and restaurants of the "Golden Mile". A gang of 30 young loyalists from the Donegall Road descended on their houses, taunting them with Nazi salutes and screaming that the foreign "gypsy scum" should pack up and go. The following evening they returned, armed with bottles and rocks, and proceeded to smash windows. Only after the police were called did the mob disperse and the frightened families emerge, clutching old suitcases and blankets. Thankfully they were given overnight shelter in nearby City Church, where they received emotional support as well as toiletries, food, clothing and blankets. Eventually they were transported to a leisure centre, where they were offered 24-hour police protection as they waited to be flown back to Romania.

The shadowy group behind these attacks was a micro-cell of the neo-Nazi organisation known as Combat 18, which first surfaced within the UK in 1992 and later spread across Europe. The "18" is derived from the initials of Adolf Hitler, A and H being the first and eighth letters of the alphabet. Indeed, the group turned their threats into rhyme and emailed them to other loyalist groups, hoping to spark similar attacks:

> Romanian gypsies beware, beware,
> Loyalist C18 are coming to beat you like a baiting bear.
> Stay out of south Belfast and stay out of sight
> and then youse will be alright.
> Get the boat and don't come back,
> there is no black in the Union Jack.

This was the background against which Rev Wilfred Orr, as moderator of the Presbytery of South Belfast, asked me to preach in Fitzroy on Sunday evening, 21 June 2009, at a service bringing together the Protestant and Catholic churches to make a united stand against racism. The theme was taken from the words of Christ: "I Was a Stranger and You Received Me in Your Homes" (Matthew 25:35), and the Scripture lessons were read by the lord mayor, Councillor Naomi Long, and Valentina Covaci, one of the

Roma teenagers attending Fitzroy's youth group. I found myself sitting in a front pew between the deputy first minister, Martin McGuinness (Sinn Féin) and the MP for South Belfast, Alasdair McDonnell (SDLP). On his way into Fitzroy, Martin McGuinness was asked by the press why he had chosen to be present. He said:

> It is wonderful to see the churches in south Belfast come together to make clear that we deplore what has happened. We are here in solidarity with the Romanians who were so badly abused last week and we passionately hope that as many of them as possible will stay.

I based my sermon on the great Gospel truth that "In Christ's eyes, everyone is someone special". Here is some of what I said:

> When the police in Northern Ireland first began to record racially motivated crimes in 1996, there were 41 incidents; last year there were over 1,000. The Troubles have bequeathed to us a culture of intolerance that often manifests itself in distaste towards people who are of a different faith, skin colour or ethnic background. The spleen vented on the Romanian community has also been felt by those from Africa, the Philippines, East Timor, the Middle East, Asia, Lithuania, Slovakia and Poland. We are here tonight to declare that as Ulster people we are determined to build an inclusive society where everyone is respected and now is the time for us to trumpet out the message that "in Christ's eyes everyone in this province is special". But what does this mean for us?

I made three main pleas for Christian action in this context:

> Firstly, we've got to be much more visible and vocal. If we have been invisible in promoting our convictions or silent in voicing them, now is the time to change. For every racist sentiment expressed, let there be hundreds of voices raised to challenge it. For every racist attack on a person or family near us, let there be dozens of us on their doorstep with food or flowers to say, "You are welcome here. This is where I live and here is my phone number."

Secondly, we've got to live an inclusive lifestyle. The Gospel is crystal-clear: I cannot confess Christ as my Redeemer and be a racist, or acknowledge him as my Saviour and be sectarian. His example of Christ commits us to living an inclusive lifestyle in Ulster just as he did in Palestine. After graduating from university, Barack Obama worked in a community-development programme on Chicago's gang-ridden South Side. From it he learnt, "If you want to change communities, move towards the centre of people's lives." It is a gleaming witness in a fractured society when others see us mixing freely with those who are racially, ethnically and religiously different from us. It also gradually kills off all known xenophobic germs.

Thirdly, turn your church into a welcome centre. In Northern Ireland there are 83 police stations whose purpose is to fight crime and provide security, and over 1,400 churches whose purpose is to touch our country with Christ's transforming love. We should be the first point of welcome for those wanting to settle among us, offering friendship, support, language classes and opportunities to explore each other's cultures. During my rugby-playing days it was drilled into us that a strong scrum was the key to success. So let us reach out our arms over each other's backs, bind tightly together and push with passionate determination to drive back every force that makes people feel small and unwelcome.

In 2015 the rate of race-hate crimes continue to soar, while an alarming 2007 survey concluded that 44 per cent of people "did not want someone from at least one of the following five groups living next door to them: homosexuals; immigrants or foreign workers; Muslims; Jews; or someone from another race". Reshaping the soul of Ulster in this regard is a very large but vital undertaking for the future of all our churches and peoples.

## Royal Grace and Homespun Favour

The first time I ever heard Mary McAleese deliver a speech was in 1997 at her inauguration as Ireland's eighth president in Dublin Castle. Now, with six months left before her final term as president expired in November 2011, she delivered her finest contribution to reconciliation – a four-day state visit to Ireland by Queen Elizabeth II in late May. The Queen had, of course, visited

Northern Ireland many times, but she had never visited the Republic of Ireland; indeed, the last British monarch to do so was her grandfather, King George V, just before the Irish Home Rule crisis over a century ago.

For years the Queen had privately longed to visit Ireland, which she felt was "like a door that's been locked against her for a long time". With the Good Friday Agreement of 1998, several visits to Buckingham Palace by President McAleese and years of delicate diplomacy, it finally became a distinct possibility. These two influential women were determined that the ghosts of a turbulent past would be laid to rest forever. When the visit was announced on 4 March 2011, reactions in Ireland were mixed. Peter Robinson, Northern Ireland's first minister, welcomed it as "a sign of normalisation", while Gerry Adams of Sinn Féin commented, "I don't think this is the right time for the English queen to come here." His colleague, Martin McGuinness, Northern Ireland's deputy first minister, refused to participate in the visit. Some smaller republican groups threatened to oppose it, despite the fact that opinion polls indicated that 77 per cent of the Irish people welcomed the idea. Dissident republicans even threatened to kill the Queen and, on the day before her arrival, a pipe-bomb was found on a Dublin-bound bus.

The security operation around the Queen was the largest in the history of the Irish Republic. Nevertheless, as the monarch's jet touched down at an air base outside Dublin at noon on Tuesday, 17 May, Ireland watched with bated breath. Dressed in an emerald-green coat, the 85-year old sovereign descended the aircraft stairs with Prince Philip and stepped on Irish soil for the first time, in one of the most dramatic reconciliation initiatives of her 59-year-long reign. Like everyone else, I was riveted to the live television coverage.

For me, the three stand-out moments of the visit were: first, the joint wreath-laying ceremony on Tuesday afternoon at the Garden of Remembrance. The Queen, in white, stood side by side with President McAleese, in black, as "God Save the Queen" was played by the military band. She then stepped forward and laid a green laurel wreath in front of the war memorial, stepped back and bowed her head in respect for "all those who gave their lives in the cause of Irish freedom". The memorial commemorates those who fought for freedom from Britain in the six rebellions stretching from the United Irishmen (1798) to the Irish War of Independence (1919–21). That dignified bow of the monarch's head was a tacit acknowledgement of the legitimacy of the Irish struggle and an expression of sorrow for the pain our two nations had caused each other.

Second, the counter-balancing moment came on Wednesday afternoon at the Irish War Memorial Garden in Islandbridge, dedicated "to the memory of the 49,400 Irish soldiers who gave their lives in the Great War (1914–18)". Once again, it involved a joint wreath-laying ceremony by President McAleese and the Queen, but this time it offered an unprecedented opportunity for Ireland to honour the 300,000 Irishmen who had fought in Irish regiments of the British Army during the Great War. Their sacrifice had been virtually airbrushed out of Irish history in the face of an unsympathetic public. The action of the two heads of state in the presence of 500 representatives of veteran organisations, the churches and the unionist and nationalist traditions signalled the long-overdue righting of a wrong.

My third moment of note was the Queen's speech given on Wednesday evening at the state dinner hosted by President McAleese in Dublin Castle. Among the guests were Prime Minister David Cameron, Taoiseach Enda Kenny, First Minister Peter Robinson and the Nobel laureate Seamus Heaney. The Queen, in a glamorous white dress, opened her address with five words in Gaelic – "A uachtaráin agus a chairde" ("President and friends"). It drew a triple "Wow!" from President McAleese and sparked a spontaneous round of applause. Her carefully nuanced speech reminded us of "the ties between our people, the shared values and the economic, business and cultural links that make us so much more than just neighbours, that make us firm friends and equal partners". Then came a moment of heartfelt emotion when she hinted at the loss she felt at the IRA murder in 1979 of her cousin Lord Louis Mountbatten in a seaside village in County Sligo:

> It is a sad and regrettable reality that through history our islands have experienced more than their fair share of heartache, turbulence and loss. These events have touched us all, many of us personally ... To all those who have suffered as a consequence of our troubled past I extend my sincere thoughts and deep sympathy ... No one who looked to the future over the past centuries could have imagined the strength of the bonds that are now in place between the governments and people of our two nations ... A knot of history [has been] painstakingly loosened by the British and Irish governments, together with the strength, vision and determination of the political parties in Northern Ireland.

Everyone in St Patrick's Hall gave her a rapturous ovation, shared by a TV viewing audience of 30 million. On Thursday morning she woke to find herself an unlikely star in the Irish Republic. That evening she attended a gala concert at the Dublin Conference Centre featuring the boy-band Westlife. At the end, when she went on stage to thank the performers, the 2,000-strong audience cheered and whistled as she waved back to them. Gay Byrne, the TV personality who compered the event, told the crowd: "I never dreamed I would live to see this day. You were present at an historic occasion. Remember it." The Queen's visit was a game-changer for Anglo-Irish relations – but how would it play out, I wondered, in the more entrenched environment of Northern Ireland?

**Legacy**

I realised that what gave the Queen's visit such benign energy was the pure honesty of intention flowing from the Queen and President McAleese. This, I believed, would also be its continuing legacy. The first indication of that came a year later with the Queen's diamond-jubilee visit to Northern Ireland in June 2012. She chose Enniskillen as the prelude to her two-day tour, a town devastated by an IRA bomb on Remembrance Sunday 1987. On Tuesday morning, thousands lined the road to St Macartin's Anglican Cathedral as the motorcade made its way to the gates. The Queen and Prince Philip were welcomed by Dean Kenny Hall, who escorted them inside to join a congregation of 750 for a thanksgiving service to mark 60 years of duty, devotion and service. The first minister, Peter Robinson, read the Scriptures and the prayers of intercession were led by the four main church leaders. In his sermon, Rev Michael Harper, the Anglican archbishop of Armagh, acknowledged that:

> Your Majesty's state visit ... to the Republic of Ireland ... was for many of us an occasion of profound significance and deep emotion. It felt like the completion of an assent ... to a process announcing a new day ... that sets us free to build, perhaps for the first time ever in the recorded history of this island an authentic Pax Hibernica ... [C]onsolidating the Pax ... shall require more enduring foundations ... than those that proved so inadequate in the past. We must build on the rock of a shared future, not the sand of divide and rule.

As the service ended, there followed another of those unanticipated breakthrough moments that prise our minds open to new possibilities. Guided by the dean, the Queen, Prince Philip and a long line of dignitaries walked down the steps of the cathedral, across Church Street and straight through the open doors of St Michael's Catholic Church. There to welcome her was the parish priest, Canon Peter O'Reilly, a close friend of Dean Hall. In the church the Queen admired the magnificent floral displays adorning the building, and many children from the local Catholic and Protestant schools welcomed her with beaming smiles. Among the first she stopped to speak with were seven survivors of the bombing. Since her first visit to Ulster in 1953, the Queen had never ventured into a Catholic place of worship, primarily because of nationalist ambivalence towards the British monarchy and the inevitable security concerns. However, since the 1994 ceasefires, the province had moved forward and the Queen was determined to encourage that trend. For some unionists brought up to believe that no self-respecting Protestant should set foot in a Catholic church, this royal example laid to rest a long and restrictive taboo. What few observers realised was that this remarkable initiative had been commended to and accepted by the organisers of the royal visit because of the strength of friendship between Dean Hall and Canon O'Reilly. "It was an expression of the unity there is in this place," declared the Canon, "a Fermanagh welcome, a gracious Queen, a lovely lady."

Another surprise followed the next day. The Queen and the former IRA commander Martin McGuinness, the deputy first minister of Northern Ireland, shook hands for the first time in public at a charity event in the Lyric Theatre, Belfast. John Simpson, the BBC's world-affairs editor, commented: "In 1972 it would have seemed the most absurd fantasy that the Queen would ever shake hands with a leading figure from the Provisional IRA."

But in the months leading up to the visit, a fierce internal debate within republicanism cast doubt on its possibility. McGuinness was warned by the police that the Continuity IRA was out to kill him. Aware of the risks he was facing, I contacted him via a mutual friend and encouraged him, as I had done a few times before, to push ahead. I was delighted when the Sinn Féin leadership gave him the go-ahead. The Queen's presence in Ireland had produced a thaw in republican thinking and they were moved by her intention to be a reconciliatory force. But they also realised that boycotting such occasions would not win them the new political support they needed to broaden their electoral base south and north.

A month later, Dean Hall phoned to invite me to speak at the Community Harvest Thanksgiving Service in St Macartin's on Sunday evening, 14 October. The local churches that were represented at the Queen's jubilee service wanted to celebrate harvest thanksgiving together for the first time in Enniskillen. Along with Canon O'Reilly, Rev David Cupples (Presbyterian) and Rev Sam McGuffin (Methodist), I processed into the well-filled church. In my address, entitled "The Day I Glimpsed God's New Reality", I spoke about the effect the Queen's visit had on me:

> Tuesday, 26 June 2012 will always be remembered as a luminous moment for a country crawling towards a brighter future. For me, it was like a rocket of hope exploding in the night sky into shards of colourful light and dropping into a thousand lives. When God gives us such glimpses of the future, he always promises to guide us along the route to it; "grace-nav" is the Gospel's equivalent to sat-nav. Tonight we ask ourselves the question: "Lord Jesus, where do you want to take me, my church and my community here in Enniskillen?" This is what I hear him saying to us in response:
>
> 1. Carry my new prayer in your heart: "Father! May [my disciples] be in us, just as you are in me and I am in you." (John 17: 20–3). I see Jesus slipping into the back of each of our congregations and quietly praying: "Father, make them one so that Enniskillen may see that you have sent your Son."
>
> 2. Embody my new commandment in your life: "If you have love for one another, then everyone will know that you are my disciples" (John 13:35). Live an inclusive life in Enniskillen and look for the best in each other.
>
> 3. Embrace my new vision for your town: "I assure you that many will come from the east and the west and sit down with Abraham, Isaac and Jacob at the feast in the Kingdom of heaven" (Matthew 8:11). This vision of universal reconciliation motivated the mission of Jesus; it lies at the heart of his cross and is the goal of his risen life among us. Let it energise us to weed out every vestige of estrangement among our people and in its place plant seeds of trust and harmony. Then let us wait patiently for the abundant harvest of the God whose goodness we glimpsed on Tuesday, 26 June 2012.

The first hints of this harvest manifested themselves as Christmas drew near. The dean and the other clergy decided to hold a joint community carol service on Sunday evening, 9 December, which would follow the historic footsteps of the Queen. Worshippers would start the service in St Macartin's and then process across the street and complete it in St Michael's. Nobody was sure how this new venture would be received, but in the event they were all taken by surprise: "We were planning for about 80 people to turn up," said a delighted Dean Hall, "and over 400 arrived."

As I later reflected on the Queen's visit to Enniskillen, two observations clarified themselves in my mind. Firstly, even in the most desolate of community circumstances, opportunities present themselves for sensitive initiatives of healing. Despite some initial resistance, the key to unlocking such actions is often the friendship among the local faith-leaders who know each other well, trust each other implicitly and relate well to their own people. Secondly, the influence of those in positions of authority, like the Queen, can be a catalyst for real change. It can bring together a hitherto divided community and put forward the dream of a better future.

### Flag Fury

When Val and I danced out of Fitzroy on our final Sunday morning in 2008, there was still a lingering hope that the encouraging example of Ian Paisley and Martin McGuinness might percolate down to the grass roots. But, with Paisley's removal in May 2008, those promising initiatives gave way to a more restrained relationship between the new first minister, Peter Robinson, and the deputy first minister. Nevertheless, they steered the assembly through to its finest achievement, staying together for a full term (2007–11). Looking back over his time as presiding officer of the house, the DUP speaker, William Hay, commented: "Some of our politicians had never ever spoken to one another on any issue. I'm now pleased to see them all in the one room and not standing at the door shouting in."

Over the next three years (2010–12) there were some significant shifts in our political landscape: in 2010 the DUP and Sinn Féin finally reached agreement on the devolution of policing and justice powers; in the Westminster election, Peter Robinson surprisingly lost his East Belfast seat to Naomi Long (Alliance Party). Then, in 2011, Gerry Adams moved his political attention southwards and successfully stood for election in the Irish Republic.

However, the success of the Queen's Jubilee visit in the summer of 2012 was almost totally eclipsed by the flag protests in Belfast six months later. On Monday evening, 3 December, 1,000 loyalists bedecked with Union Jacks streamed towards the City Hall to remonstrate against a proposal being debated in the council chamber to fly the UK national flag over that building on several designated days only. Sinn Féin's motion to the council called for the complete removal of the flag, arguing that this would create a more neutral and equal environment. Unionists, on the other hand, warned that tampering with the 107-year-old custom of flying of the flag every day was an attack on their British identity and would unleash massive loyalist anger. In the weeks prior to the vote, DUP and UUP activists in east Belfast, desperate to win back the parliamentary seat back from Naomi Long, had distributed 40,000 misleading leaflets depicting the City Hall without a flag and blaming the Alliance Party if this happened. In fact, Alliance, which held the balance of power in the council, was advocating a compromise motion – to fly the Union Flag on 18 designated days, in line with the practice at Stormont and government buildings in the UK.

The issue was always going to touch a raw nerve in Northern Ireland because flags are the visible and public expression of deeply held political and cultural identities. They are also used to mark out territory where one section of the community is dominant and the other tends to keep its head down; and, at times of public confrontation, flags are waved in the faces of opponents in a highly provocative manner.

As soon as the news filtered out that the councillors had voted by 29 to 21 to accept the compromise motion, all hell broke loose. Many of the protestors covered their faces with masks, broke through police cordons and stormed into back courtyard of the City Hall. As frightened families scurried to get out of the city centre, rioters hijacked a bus, hurled bottles at a Catholic church and launched into a running battle with the police, leaving 15 officers injured. Such disorder had not been seen on the streets of Belfast for two decades. The flag decision had driven many loyalists mad. At 7.00 am the following day, council staff lowered the flag.

As the days passed, nightly confrontations became the norm as mobs attacked the police with bricks, fireworks, petrol bombs, hatchets and sledge hammers. Within a fortnight, 80 solidarity protests were held across the province and loyalist communities were festooned with tens of thousands of Union Jacks, fluttering from every available lamp-post and every sympathetic household. It soon became evident that loyalist paramilitaries were involved in orchestrating the violence. In the days before Christmas, tidal waves of marchers from north, south, west and east Belfast streamed into the crowded city centre with Ulster flags, Union Jacks and large banners declaring, "Ulster is British, Then, Now and Forever. No Surrender." Cheers went up whenever some youths set fire to the Irish tricolour. Some Alliance Party councillors and assembly members received bullets through the post; others had the windows of their homes smashed and their offices fire-bombed. The MP Naomi Long received a death threat and was advised to leave her home.

After a lull for Christmas the protests started up again in January 2013; roads were blocked and rioting became so widespread in Belfast that almost all bus services were suspended. Then, slowly, the tide began to turn. An alternative social force showed its face when 1,000 citizens of the city gathered at the City Hall for a peace rally on Sunday, 13 January. At the same time, unionist leaders came under pressure to respond to the ferocity of the rioting, the economic loss sustained by Belfast traders, the cost of policing the protests, which had now risen to £20 million, and the injuries suffered by 66 police officers. They convened at Stormont the multi-strand Unionist Forum to address unionist concerns and direct loyalist anger into peaceful political channels. Though launched with a fanfare, the forum's capacity to achieve anything substantial was disabled by infighting. By March the massive weekly flag protests on Saturdays at the front of the City Hall had dwindled to around 150 devotees arriving in a few half-empty buses. By the time of the second anniversary of the movement in 2014, only 200 turned up to affirm their Britishness. Their resentment, however, remained, and its energy had relocated to another issue – the decision by the Parades Commission to ban Orangemen in north Belfast from parading through the nationalist area of Ardoyne on their way home from the Twelfth of July commemorations. Resolving these volatile issues remains a political priority in a country that longs to move forward.

For me, the big question posed by the flags issue is "What does it reveal about Belfast and our future together in Northern Ireland?" First, Belfast is a changing city. In the affections of its people it is as much Irish as it is British. In the 2011 local-government elections Sinn Féin became, for the first time, the largest party on the 51-member city council, and nationalist councillors outnumbered unionist councillors by 24 to 20. That abrupt reality shift has been hard for unionists to accept after years of feeling secure in being the majority and frequently referring to nationalists as the minority. This new reality of an Irish-British capital city is something that both sides of the community have got to get used to and, if possible, they should see the challenge in it rather than the threat. Churches, schools, colleges, businesses, sports organisations and political institutions have a responsibility to redefine the character of the city so that it thrives for the benefit of all. If they are content to change nothing, then nothing will change.

Second, Northern Ireland is similarly in transition. The 2011 census revealed that our population of 1.8 million largely identifies itself as Protestant (41.6%) and Catholic (40.8%). As a result of the older Protestant community declining slowly and the younger Catholic community growing marginally, it seems likely that by 2021 Protestants could find themselves for the first time as a religious minority. This does not mean that a united Ireland is imminent, since 40 per cent of the population classify themselves as British only, while only 25 per cent claim to be Irish only. A new phenomenon has thrown the normally simple calculations of sectarian demographics into confusion: 21 per cent declare themselves to be Northern Irish only. They allege that they have more in common with each other by virtue of their birth in the province than those who espouse a British-only or Irish-only identity. As a country we are now into a critical era of transition and no one can predict what the outcome will be. As a Calvinist, I often ask myself the purpose question: "Why has God from all eternity destined Protestant and Catholic, unionist and nationalist in this small country to be joined at the hip? We have been conjoined anatomically and historically since the Plantation of Ulster 400 years ago, and one thing is certain – we'll still be around each other in 2416. This is our destiny."

Nevertheless, we need a mindset that takes us beyond the redundant and cheap national pride of "winners" and "losers" and into a faith that values each other as brothers and sisters, not enemies; as friends, not strangers; and as partners, not rivals. The seemingly undiscovered and certainly unlived teaching of Jesus Christ remains, in my opinion, the single most powerful ingredient in such a vision of hope. Its practical exhortations to treat others as you would like them to treat you, to seek first God's kingdom and his justice and to love your neighbour as yourself could unite our people in a single aspiration and restore respect and tolerance to our streets.

## Overseas Opportunities

Since retiring I have had the privilege of spending time in Mozambique, Bosnia and Herzegovina, Palestine and Israel as a theological advisor and peace activist. In this last section I detail some of those activities.

I received a request from Cristian Romocea, the international advocacy officer of the Bible Society, to be part of a theological and arts-based team which would attempt to work towards a reconciliation initiative that might be encouraged in Israel and Palestine. Our ten-member team would assemble for a week in September 2010 in Sarajevo, the capital of Bosnia and Herzegovina, where Bosniak Muslims (49 per cent of the population), Serbian Orthodox (33 per cent) and Catholic Croats (15 per cent) were still emerging from a vicious war (1992–6).

My responsibility was to speak about "Following Christ in a Divided Society" in the light of 14 biblical passages that recur in peacemaking literature: "The Dignity of Every Human Being" (Genesis 1:26–7), "Cain's Murder of Abel" (Genesis 4), "The Inclusive Lifestyle of Christ" (John 4), "Christ's Two Great Commandments" (Mark 12:28–34), "Love of Enemy" (Matthew 5:43–8), "Reconciliation as the Heart of Worship" (Matthew 5:23–4), "The Gospel's Power to Reduce Prejudice" (Matthew 7:1–5), "The Good Samaritan" (Luke 10:25–37), "The Prodigal Son and His Elder Brother" (Luke 15:11–32), "Christ's Vision of Universal Reconciliation" (Matthew 8:11; Luke 13:29), "The Peacemaking Mission of the Messiah" (Zechariah 9:9–10; Isaiah 2:1–5), "The Destructive and Creative Cross" (Ephesians 2:13–18), "One Lord, One Church" (Ephesians 4:3–6), and "Love Is the Greatest" (1 Corinthians 13). Further on in the programme, we discussed how to commend an artistic expression of these peace and reconciliation themes to sympathetic members of Israel's Knesset and the Palestinian Authority. In May 2011 our group reconvened in Israel and met up in Beit Jala, a Christian town on the Palestinian West Bank.

### Beit Jala

From the moment of its birth in 1948, the state of Israel has been at odds with its Arab neighbours and periodic conflicts have erupted following its occupation of the Palestinian West Bank, the Gaza Strip and east Jerusalem. At our conference centre we were welcomed by the directors of the Palestinian Bible Society, the Arab-Israeli Bible Society and the Bible Society in Israel. These courageous leaders not only serve their distinctive communities, but also endeavour to undertake joint initiatives designed to heal the fractured relationships among Christians and foster a common witness to their unity in Christ. They had assembled representatives from a diverse range of Christian congregations to meet with us and to bring us, through their experiences, into the spiritual, social and political realities within which they live out their daily lives.

It quickly became apparent how complex and difficult it is to work for peace in a social environment ladened with anger, where ordinary people feel so much on edge with each other. The Jewish community craves security and freedom from fear, while Palestinians yearn for justice and liberation. Many of those present in our meetings voiced despair at a deteriorating situation that offered few reasons to be hopeful that a peaceful and just political settlement might emerge in a land of such extreme perspectives. Indeed, some believed that Israel's control of Palestinians was becoming progressively more restrictive, with its system of permits, roadblocks and checkpoints. The most glaring sign of this was, they suggested, the Israeli Separation Wall, which continued to snake further and further around occupied east Jerusalem.

Nevertheless, some courageous initiatives have taken root. Dr Salim Munayer, the founder of the Musalaha Organisation (Arabic for "reconciliation"), explained that for 20 years they had worked to bring Israeli and Palestinian believers in Jesus together as a first step in drawing together the larger Jewish, Muslim and Christian communities: "The common moral values shared by all three monotheistic religions serve as a starting point for our discussions, and we seek to emulate Christ's model of forgiveness, mercy and love."

Musalaha promotes "desert encounters" for young adults, who travel into the Sinai Desert by camel to learn survival skills, a process that fosters more open communication and lifelong friendships. It also organises inter-faith conferences, where Muslim, Jewish and Christian theologians and leaders can grow in appreciation of each other and at times of tension function as conflict mediators.

I repeated my Sarajevo presentation on the key biblical passages relating to "Following Christ in a Divided Society", and then gave our discussion groups an assignment: to select in order of priority the five most relevant texts to their church and community. Their choices were:

1. "The Inclusive Lifestyle of Christ"
2. "Christ's Two Great Commandments"

3. "Love Is the Greatest"
4. "The Destructive and Creative Cross"
5. "The Good Samaritan"

All were aware of the long road ahead. The Jewish people longed for security and peace, while their Arab and Palestinian neighbours yearned for freedom, justice and peace. Only when they find a way to affirm each other's dignity and rights will the elusive "shalom" come within reach.

In June 2013, Katharine Dowson, one of our artists, unveiled a window inside the Christian Cultural Centre in Bethlehem in the presence of the town's mayor. Her work was entitled "The Transforming Light through a Veil of Tears". She explained, "I was inspired by the healing and cleansing qualities of water, and paired this with the tears of Mary's pain in childbirth and at the suffering of her son's death. Through tears can come the relief of pain and the possibility of moving forwards to live, forgive and heal."

### Mozambique

Just as the request to join the Bible Society team visiting Bosnia and Herzegovina and Israel took me by surprise, so also did an invitation from another source, Eric Morier-Genoud, professor of African History at Queen's University. He was involved in Mozambique's Religious Network for Reconciliation and Peace, which was launched in 2014 by leaders of the Christian (representing 56 per cent of the population), Muslim (representing 18 per cent) and other faith communities. It arose just after the signing of *Armed Hostilities Cessation Agreement* in September 2014 by the president of Mozambique, Armando Guebuza (of the FRELIMO Party), and the opposition leader, Afonso Dhlakama (of RENAMO). The network was planning a national conference in May and wondered if Fr Gerry and I would be willing to participate. As it turned out, Fr Gerry was not free to attend, but I was delighted when Fr Michael Kelleher, a former provincial of the Irish Redemptorists and a fluent Portuguese speaker, agreed to join me.

Eric had lined up for us speaking engagements at the United Seminary of Ricatla, where 35 ministerial students, male and female, from Methodist, Presbyterian, Congregational and Lutheran backgrounds, were studying for ordination. On Sunday morning, 24 May, we preached at North Katanga United Methodist Church in Maputo as part of its John Wesley Day celebrations. It was exceptionally warm and crowded. While my sermon was simultaneously translated, Fr Michael spoke directly in Portuguese, with such humour and challenge that the sense of connection with the congregation was electric and the reception they gave us was immensely enthusiastic. When it came to the Offering, worshippers danced forward in rhythmic lines up to the Communion table, where they placed their gifts. When it came our turn, Michael and I could not resist the pulse of the praise, and we too fell in line and danced to the front. The service lasted three hours, but no one seemed to mind.

On Monday, 25 May, we flew 1,200 kilometres up the coast to Beira, Mozambique's second largest city and a stronghold of RENAMO. The following morning, our conference got underway in the Rainbow Hotel under the direction of Rev Anastacio Chemeze, one of the five national mediators in the negotiations between the FRELIMO government and RENAMO. Most of the 100 delegates were representatives of the Christian denominations, the Muslim community, minority faith groups and the international non-governmental organisations working in the country. Significantly, senior political figures from FRELIMO, RENAMO and the new Mozambique Democratic Movement were also in attendance. The theme of our time together was "The Mozambique We Want – Truly Reconciled and in Peace". With the failure of FRELIMO and RENAMO to live up to their obligations under the *Armed Hostilities Cessation Agreement* in September 2014, particularly regarding the demilitarisation of the armed wing of RENAMO, there was a fear that violence could erupt once again.

In his keynote address, "The Role of Different Actors of Society in Reconciliation: Action, Challenges and Opportunities", Tomas Vieira Mario, a respected journalist, gave an overview of Mozambique's situation in the light of the turmoil experienced in the previous three years. That afternoon I shared my experience of working for reconciliation but opened up those central tenets of our faith that can motivate people in political, social and religious spheres to dedicate themselves to peacemaking. I was not sure how my presentation was being received until a simple remark sparked a sustained round of applause:

> The resurrection of Christ took three days; in Northern Ireland our resurrection took thirty years. I don't know how long the resurrection of Mozambique will take, but of this I'm convinced – if we trust in God and work together, it will definitely come.

The following day, Fr Michael told the story of the peace vocation pursued by his friend and fellow Redemptorist Fr Alec Reid. As he showed pictures of Fr Alec praying over the bodies of two British soldiers shot by the IRA, a hush descended over the delegates. Most of them had experienced their own tragedies. In Mozambique it was a privilege for me to meet with so many people of wisdom and experience who are battling for peace and reconciliation in situations teetering on the brink of chaos and conflict. While the story we share with them is one of hope, we desire more than anything else to listen to them and encourage them to believe that, despite the knocks we take in life, the best things come to those who persist in moving forward even when it is easier just to lie down and give up.

**Final Thoughts**

I am grateful for the opportunities that came my way to travel in the last five years, to Bosnia and Herzegovina, Israel and Palestine and Mozambique. It has opened my eyes to the world's chronic need for peace, justice and reconciliation. I am more convinced than ever that, to attain such blessings, people of faith, benevolence and compassion need to unite in the vision of turning such hopes into reality. It has been humbling to meet with so many heroic people who are doing remarkable things in difficult circumstances. Their faces often flash across my mind, as well as the places where they serve their people with dedication and love. I hear again the tone of their voices, smile at their humour and cherish the generous friendship they have extended to me.

But the place I most frequently resort to in memory is the gravelly beach at Tabgha on the north-west shore of the Sea of Galilee, which Val and I visited in 2011. It is the spot where, at sunrise, a stranger appeared on the shoreline and called out to seven weary and frustrated friends who were returning in their boat after a night of fruitless fishing (John 21:1–14). The stranger asked, "Young men, haven't you caught anything?"

"Not a thing," they replied.

"Then throw your net out on the right-hand side of the boat, and you will catch some."

So, for one last time, they threw out the net and discovered that they could not pull it back in, because they had caught so many fish. At that moment, in the dim morning light, the apostle John realised it was the Lord; the Risen Christ had come once again to be with them.

When the haul of fish had been drawn up onto to the beach, Jesus cooked breakfast for them as they all sat around the fire, warmed themselves and chatted. After a searching and reaffirming conversation with Peter, Jesus said to him, "Follow me," just as simply as he had three years earlier when they had first met, 20 minutes further up the beach.

When I stood for the first time at the Sea of Galilee at Tabgha, that early morning encounter with Christ kept playing in my imagination with the same joy I used to feel when retelling the story at Fitzroy almost every Easter. As I peered across the lake, now well into my retirement, I was astonished how the spirit of the Risen Christ, who had conversed so personally with Peter on this beach 2,000 years earlier, had somehow made its way across the world to Belfast in May 1943, when I took my first breath, and started drawing me also into his life. My life is one of gratitude for grace received.

# Index